DAYS AND CUSTOMS OF ALL FAITHS

DAYS AND CUSTOMS

OF ALL FAITHS

The Reverend Howard V. Harper, D.D.

FLEET PUBLISHING CORPORATION

NEW YORK

Why were the saints, saints? Because they were cheerful when it was difficult to be cheerful, patient when it was difficult to be patient; and because they pushed on when they wanted to stand still, and kept silent when they wanted to talk, and were agreeable when they wanted to be disagreeable. That was all.

It was quite simple and always will be.

Anonymous

Foreword

>>>->>>->>>->>>->>>->>>->>>->>>->>>->>> · <<<-<<<-<<<-<<<-<<<-<<<-<<<-<<<-<<<-<<<

In these days of high tensions, both international and personal, the need for better understanding among peoples of all countries, all races, and all creeds is greater than ever before in the history of the world. An increased spirit of brotherhood, predicated on a clearer concept of the religious beliefs of others could well result in a new appreciation of their tenets, thereby creating an attitude of respect which is frequently lacking today both in business and in political contacts.

Over the years, as I have read Doctor Harper's columns, which appear regularly in a long list of newspapers throughout the country, I have discovered a wealth of interesting and informative facts about the religious beliefs of others and learned many things about my own Church which I might otherwise never have known. I have been impressed by Doctor Harper's revelations of the sources of certain customs, ceremonies, and rites of the various religions which he has presented so succinctly and so lucidly in his columns.

I, for one, am grateful to Doctor Harper for the long hours he has spent in the meticulous research necessary to uncover these fascinating facts, and for his work in assembling in this convenient, concentrated form the fruits of his labors.

HARVEY S. FIRESTONE, JR.

Introduction

➤➤➤-➤➤➤-➤➤➤-➤➤➤-➤➤➤-➤➤➤-➤➤➤-➤➤➤-➤➤➤-➤➤➤-➤➤➤ · ◄◄◄-◄◄◄-◄◄◄-◄◄◄-◄◄◄-◄◄◄-◄◄◄-◄◄◄-◄◄◄-◄◄◄-◄◄◄

As every clergyman soon finds out, there are many facets to his ministry. There is a pastoral ministry, a preaching ministry, and a sacramental ministry, as well as several other kinds. This book attempts to deal with some small segment of the teaching ministry. It cannot be claimed that this is the most important aspect of the clergyman's various functions. No one is ever brought to the depths of any faith by information or history or explanations. But it is nevertheless true that people like to "get things straightened out" in their minds with regard to their own religion and the religion of others. And it is also true that by doing so they benefit considerably.

The value of what might be called "sidelights" on religion first began to engage my active interest one day some years ago when I was having lunch at one of those clubs where everyone sits at a big round table. A man a few seats away from me asked me the meaning of "Maundy

Thursday." All conversation at the table stopped while I gave the answer. It was something everyone wanted to know. After that, I made a point of keeping a notebook and recording the questions people asked me about such matters. I was surprised to see how quickly the notebook was filled.

The questions were of three types. People asked about personalities, both Biblical and ecclesiastical, about special days in the calendar, and about customs and traditions. The results of my efforts to provide the answers were first, a syndicated weekly newspaper column, and now, this book. There is no doubt in my mind that this kind of information-service has been a valid part of my ministry, and, incidentally, a very rewarding part.

In digging up the facts and legends required by this somewhat extracurricular activity, I suppose I have profited far more than have my readers. My own life has been enriched by a familiarity with persons and customs and times that I would not otherwise have taken the trouble to know much about. I have discovered, of course, a great deal more than I have had space or ability to communicate, and so have built up a surplus, a sort of overflow, that has become a mental climate in which I live, among pleasures other men might miss.

But best of all, I have learned these things that *can* be passed on to others: that all faiths, once one's own wall of ignorance and misunderstanding is penetrated, have high truths to tell him that can save his soul; that the saints of all faiths, once the encrustation of legend and fancy are scraped away, are seen to be people much like one's self, except that they were better at letting God direct their lives; and that the customs of all faiths, once one gets past the provincial notion that whatever is strange must therefore be absurd, are meaningful, intelligent, and natural.

It is very much like what happens to the man who travels in what he has been accustomed to call foreign countries. He finds that they are not foreign at all except geographically. The people he meets turn out to be essentially the same as his neighbors down the hall, or down the block. Language, clothes, habits may be different, but men and women are pretty much the same. He wouldn't have known that, though, if he hadn't gone to see them where they live.

This is important in these times when we are worried about international conflict. The more one knows about the citizens of another nation the less he is likely to think of them as impersonal units to be shot at. You and your neighbor may disagree, but you don't have a war. You work it out together.

It is the same when we travel into the foreign land of other faiths. We find out that it isn't really foreign after all. The more we know about one another, and about one another's ideas and ways, the better it will be for all of us.

HOWARD HARPER

New York City, July, 1957

Contents

-»»-»»-»»-»»-»»-»»-»»-»»-»»-»» · «««-«««-«««-«««-«««-«««-«««-«««-«««-«««

Chapter

PART ONE

Days

CHAPTER I

‑»»»‑»»»‑»»»‑»»»‑»»»‑»»»‑»»»‑»»»‑»»»‑»»»‑»»» · «««‑«««‑«««‑«««‑«««‑«««‑«««‑«««‑«««‑«««‑«««

January

‑»»»‑»»»‑»»»‑»»»‑»»»‑»»»‑»»»‑»»»‑»»»‑»»»‑»»» · «««‑«««‑«««‑«««‑«««‑«««‑«««‑«««‑«««‑«««‑«««

The Circumcision of Jesus
JANUARY 1ST

January 1st has not always been New Year's Day. Under the old Julian calendar, the year began on March 25th. This seems strange to us for we always expect things to begin at carefully marked-off points. March 25th does not sound like the beginning of anything. But to the people who were familiar with the old calendar it was every bit as normal as the twenty-first of June is to us as the beginning of summer, or the day after Labor Day as the beginning of the school term. It is more than likely that this idea of New Year's Day was a carry-over from the Jewish custom of starting the year at the time of the full moon after the spring equinox.

When the Gregorian calendar came into use, New Year's Day was moved up to its present date. That was in the sixteenth century in Roman Catholic countries, France for example. But England, and, of course, her colonies, held out against the change until 1752. Consequently there were one hundred fifty years in the life of this continent in which March 25th was New Year's Day.

The first of January has had a two-fold significance for Christianity since the fourth century, quite aside from the question of when the year began. For one thing, it was the end of the Christmas "octave." (An octave, in Church language, is the eight-day period including and following a great festival. In addition, it was the day set apart as the anniversary of the Christ's circumcision. Both these festivals, Christmas and the Circumcision, were only then beginning to be celebrated, and their observance was at first by no means universal.

In Genesis, chapter 17, verses 9 to 14, it is recorded that God gave a command to Abraham and his descendants that every male child should be circumcised on the eighth day after his birth, as a "token of the covenant between me and thee." This custom, still followed by Jews and Mohammedans, has been replaced in the Christian Church by the sacrament of Baptism, but St. Luke, chapter 2, verse 21, tells that the parents of Jesus, good Jews that they were, conformed to the ancient practice. There may be some extra significance in the fact that they took this special Child to the Temple at Jerusalem for the rite, even though it could have been performed as well at home. The festival of the Circumcision was first celebrated in the eastern part of the Church. The west did not even begin to adopt it until well into the sixth century.

Martyrs for the Holy Scriptures

JANUARY 2ND

In the year 303 the cantankerous Roman Emperor Diocletian, who hated everything about Christianity, decided that every copy of any New Testament book that could be found anywhere in the Empire should be seized and burned. It was not an easy order for Diocletian's men to carry out. This was, of course, long before printing had been invented, but many Christians possessed handwritten copies of one book or another, and hundreds of these devout people thought more of the sacred writings than they did of their lives. In great numbers they were willing to die rather than to let the soldiers get their profane hands on these holy treasures.

Of all communities, Lichfield, a town in England, was perhaps the hardest hit by this imperial order. *Lich* means "corpse"—Lichfield means a field strewn with corpses. The name of this town is said to go back to the day of January 2, 303, when almost the entire population was slaughtered for its refusal to give in to Diocletian's demand that the sacred books be surrendered. The fields all around were covered with martyrs for the Scriptures. January 2nd has been set apart in the Roman Catholic calendar in honor of those who did so die—Martyrs for the Holy Scriptures.

He Spent His Life Atop a Pillar

JANUARY 5TH

The sophisticated modern world makes fun of St. Simon Stylites, calling him a holy flag-pole sitter and using his name as a symbol of religious fanaticism. But Simon-of-the-pillar (*stulos* is the Greek word for "pillar") was a great and influential man who wanted nothing but privacy. He may have been eccentric, but he was no fanatic. As a boy living near Antioch, Simon heard the Beatitudes read in church one day, and as he heard the promises of blessings made to those who mourn and weep and hunger and thirst, he made up his mind that eternal happiness comes only to those who suffer. He thereupon chose a life of self-inflicted suffering. He went out into the country to live as a hermit, but his reputation for holiness soon spread over the whole Roman Empire, and people would not let him alone.

In order to get away from the people he set up a pillar and climbed to the top of it. Once he was up there he liked it so well that he decided to stay. Wild Arabs, Ethiopians, desert bandits, and perfumed noblemen milled together around the base of Simon's pillar. Occasionally he would preach to them from his strange pulpit. It is said that he converted thousands and that it was out of respect for him that the wild people of the desert stopped their persecutions of Christians. Simon died in 459 on top of his pillar, at the age of sixty-nine.

The Epiphany

January 6th

This day, observed by all Catholics and a growing number of Protestants, commemorates the moment when Jesus was first glimpsed to be not only the Messiah of the Jews but the Saviour of all mankind. The symbol of this widening of the horizon is the visit of the Three Wise Men to the Babe in His crib at Bethlehem, for the Wise Men were Gentiles, heathen from outside the pale, and their recognition of the Babe's divinity took the ancient racial limitations off what had until then been an exclusively Jewish expectation. The word *Epiphany* means "manifestation" or "showing." Less literally, it means "a moment of recognition." Ordinarily everyone associates the Wise Men with Christmas, but this is an error. Their festival, the feast of their visit, is Epiphany, which comes on this first day after "the twelve days of Christmas" are over.

If we confined ourselves to what the New Testament tells us of these three important strangers, we would have to omit most of the material we have come to cherish about them. It is legend that has given them their great appeal. The Bible does not say they were kings, or even that there were three of them. Man's imagination has supplied the details, giving them names and personalities, and even locating and naming their kingdoms.

Gaspar is said to have been king of Tarsus, land of myrrh; Melchior was king of Arabia, land of gold; and Balthasar came from Saba, where frankincense flows from the trees. And each king brought to the Babe the chief product of his own country. "And when they had opened their treasures, they presented unto him gifts; gold, and frankincense, and myrrh." (Matthew, chapter 2, verse 11.) There was a special symbolic meaning in each of these gifts. Gold was given to show that the Infant was Himself a king; frankincense to show that He was divine; and myrrh, a burial spice, to show that as a man He was doomed, as all men are, to die. According to one legend, Jesus returned to the kings even greater gifts than they gave Him. For their gold He gave them spiritual riches; for their incense, faith; and for their myrrh, truth and meekness.

Another term by which these famous visitors are often called is *magi*, which, in both Latin and Greek, means "wise." It is the same stem from which we get our word "magistrate."

Also a Season

The name Epiphany is applied not only to the festival observed on January 6th, but also to the Church season that follows this day. The season varies in length because it terminates when Pre-Lent begins, and that depends on Easter. On the average, Epiphany as a season lasts about four weeks. Because Epiphany commemorates the extension of Christianity to the whole world, the National Council of Churches appropriately devotes the season to special emphasis on the Church's worldwide missionary goal. They call it "The Season of the Evangel."

St. Distaff's Day

JANUARY 7TH

January 7th is St. Distaff's Day—or used to be, many years ago. But there never was any St. Distaff. The name is a joke, a piece of medieval humor. A *distaff* is a part of a spinning wheel; the short pole or staff around which the wool or flax is wound. Women, of course, were the spinning wheel operators in the household, and it became customary to call women the "distaff" side of the family. January 7th in old times was the day on which the housewife returned to normal routine after the Christmas holidays, which were observed from Christmas to Epiphany. So because it was the day on which the distaffs started twirling again, some medieval wit named it St. Distaff's Day.

A Slandered Saint

JANUARY 9TH

Some words start out with one meaning and end up with quite another. *Hospitality*, for example, originally had to do with keeping a hospital, providing refuge for the sick and the poor. St. Julian and his good wife Basilissa, who lived in Egypt at the turn of the fourth century, opened their commodious home to all comers and devoted their time and income to the care of any who needed them. It was for this reason that Julian was called the patron saint of hospitality.

Over the centuries the word hospitality evolved into something almost entirely different. It began to mean showing your guests a high old time, on terms that were usually pretty pagan. And as the word changed, so did the idea of what St. Julian's patronage means. By the Middle Ages, poor, kind, simple Julian was thought of as "the epicure of saints"—a party-giving, luxury-loving playboy. When Chaucer, in his *Canterbury Tales*, calls his dissolute Frankleyn "a St. Julian in his own country," it shows how far the mistake had replaced the truth. Actually, it amounts to slander of the pious Julian, whose hospitality was a deep Christian concern about those in need of help.

St. Julian died a martyr in 313. It is probable that his death occurred on January 6th, but because that is the great feast of the Epiphany his commemorative day was moved to January 9th.

The First Hermit

JANUARY 15TH

One of the strangest movements in all Christian history occurred in the fourth century around the southeastern corner of the Mediterranean. Everybody wanted to be a hermit. Thousands of people, both men and women, left home and flocked into the desert to live in solitude and contemplation. In the year 394 a traveller in Egypt and

Palestine observed that there were as many people living in the desert caves in that part of the world as there were living in the towns.

Although St. Anthony of Egypt is generally credited with having started the movement, the first hermit was really St. Paul of Thebes, who is remembered in the church calendar on January 15th. He was out in the desert alone, fifty years before St. Anthony arrived. It all happened quite naturally in Paul's life. He was a Christian, twenty-three years old in the year 224, when one of the worst of the Christian persecutions was raging. To escape the danger he went to the desert to hide, and was lucky enough to find a cave which opened at one end into a fertile hidden oasis. Paul liked the place so well that when the persecutions were over he didn't want to leave. So there he stayed, praying and meditating, for ninety more years, during which time he never uttered a word. He died in 314 at the age of one hundred thirteen.

During the Middle Ages, orders of hermits were organized in Hungary, Portugal, and France, with St. Paul as their patron. These orders, though still in existence, have given up solitude and have become normal monastic congregations.

Pope's First Throne

JANUARY 18TH

January 18th is celebrated in the Roman Catholic Church under the somewhat unusual name of "St. Peter's Chair at Rome." In ancient times it was the custom in many dioceses (geographical areas) to keep an annual festival on the anniversary of the date when the diocese first received a bishop. This particular festival is perhaps the only remaining observance. It commemorates the oc-

casion when St. Peter ascended the throne as Bishop of
Rome and first Pope. An ancient wooden seat, said to be
Peter's first throne, is still preserved at the Vatican. The
present celebration takes place in St. Peter's Church in
Rome.

Until fairly recent times the Pope, wearing his triple
crown and vestments of gold cloth, was carried in his
chair of state on this day, while beside him bearers carried
a huge fan of ostrich feathers into which had been set
the eye-like parts of peacock feathers. The eyes symbolized the vigilance of the Bishop of Rome and his universal supervision.

On January 18th the Roman Catholic Church begins its
"Church Unity Octave," which is an eight-day period of
prayer for the reunion of Christendom. The Octave runs
from the Feast of St. Peter's Chair to the Feast of the
Conversion of St. Paul (January 25th) and is observed
throughout the Roman Church.

His Left Hand Gave Off Light

JANUARY 19TH

You don't hear much about St. Fillan any more. He has
become so obscure that there is now only one church
named for him even in his native Scotland. But there was
a time when the wonders of this seventh century abbot
were known far and wide. Fillan had so much holiness in
him that he just couldn't help performing miracles—
without even seeming to notice that they were miracles,
or that he was performing them. For example, when the
oil in his lamp went dry one night he simply went on
reading and writing by the light given off by his left
hand, and thought nothing of it.

He had a great reputation as a healer of the insane.

This, too, was accomplished with no effort on the part of Fillan. People brought the insane to his cell, tied them on his bed for the night, and in the morning they were normal. Stories of this sort always mean that the real saint has been buried somewhere under the folklore and peasant superstition, but never forget that such stories are not told about average men. And when it is said that Fillan unconsciously worked wonders with the mentally disturbed, one thing you can count on is that all men felt a peace and serenity when they were near this godly abbot.

Seven centuries after his death, Fillan's shrine was still so popular that the great warrior Robert Bruce went there to spend the night in prayer before the battle of Bannockburn. What happened to Bruce's English foe next day on the battlefield is a matter of record.

Fillan's name is still attached to a holy well at a place in Scotland called, in his honor, Strath-Fillan. The waters are reputed to be particularly soothing to the insane.

For New, Better Hymns

JANUARY 19TH

On January 19, 1922 there came into existence the Hymn Society of America, an interdenominational group dedicated to the improvement of both the music and the poetry of Protestant hymns. One important function of the Society is to encourage the writing of new hymns related to contemporary life. For example, five new hymns on modern city life have been produced under the Society's auspices. A concise statement of the Society's goal might be: "up to high standards and up to date."

When the Revised Standard Version of the Bible appeared in 1952, the Society brought out ten new hymns

on the Holy Scriptures. For the meeting of the World
Council of Churches in 1954 at Evanston, Illinois, they
published eleven new ecumenical hymns, that is, hymns
dealing with the unity of Christendom. Many of these
hymns find their way into the official hymnals of various
denominations. Although the Society does not have official status in the National Council of Churches, the cor-
dial unofficial relationship is indicated by the fact the
Society's offices are in The National Council's headquarters.

Patron of Archers

JANUARY 20TH

If you see a picture of a young man whose whole body
is bristling with arrows, that will be St. Sebastian, the
third century saint who, for obvious reasons, has become
the patron of archers. There was nothing especially remarkable about Sebastian except his complete disregard
of personal security. He needn't have faced martyrdom
even once, but having miraculously escaped it once he
walked right into it a second time.

It was in the days of the terrible Emperor Diocletian,
the most vigorous of all persecutors of the Christians.
When Sebastian's two brothers were imprisoned on suspicion of being Christians, Sebastian could have stayed
away from them. But he went to the prison, persuaded
his brothers to stand by their faith, and converted many
of the other prisoners and their visitors. Naturally, this
put him in the same trouble his brothers were in, and all
were condemned to die—Sebastian by being shot with
arrows. The sentence was carried out and Sebastian,
pierced by many arrows, was left for dead. A Christian
woman who came to claim the body for burial, however,

found that he was still alive. She took him home with her and nursed him back to health.

Certainly no one could have blamed Sebastian if he had stopped at that point. But he was made of stern stuff. As soon as he was well enough, he confronted Diocletian again, rebuking him for his treatment of the Christians and demanding that he behave properly toward them. The Emperor, more enraged than ever, sentenced the saint to be beaten to death, and this time personally saw to it that the job was really finished.

Arrows have from ancient times been the symbol of pestilence. Sebastian, because he recovered from the worst the arrows could do, is invoked against pestilential disease.

Dreams of Future Husbands

JANUARY 21ST

Any girl who wants a preview of her future husband might try going to bed without any supper on St. Agnes' Eve. The old legend said that if a girl fulfilled this fasting requirement, she would dream of the man she was to marry. Some said she would even learn his name in the dream. You can read about one lady who tried it with unexpected results in John Keats' poem, "The Eve of St. Agnes."

Agnes herself did not want a husband, and it is strange that this kind of tradition should grow up around her memory. She was rich, young, and beautiful. She lived in the glamorous city of Rome, late in the third century, and it was a great surprise to everyone when she turned down an excellent match arranged by her wealthy father.

It finally became known that Agnes had secretly become a Christian, and although she had nothing against

either the young man or marriage, she did have strong
views about devoting her life to the Lord. Those were
the days of the persecution of Christians, and when it
was revealed that Agnes was one, she was ordered to be
burned. The fire, however, refused to harm her. She stood
unhurt in the midst of the flame—a flame so intense that
it destroyed two soldiers who were standing guard beside
the pyre. Other soldiers then put Agnes to death with
swords, and she joined "the noble army of martyrs."

There is an ancient and lovely custom connected with
St. Agnes Day which comes from the fact that *Agnes* is
the Latin word for "lamb." Each year in Rome two lambs
are blessed on this day and then taken away to the convent by the nuns of St. Agnes. When shearing time comes
the lambs' wool is taken and woven into an article of
apparel known as the *pallium*. The pallium is a small
band of white wool in which are embroidered four purple crosses. It is received by archbishops direct from the
Pope and is worn by them on solemn occasions as the
badge of their high office.

The First Archbishop

JANUARY 24TH

St. Timothy was the most beloved of all of St. Paul's
friends and followers. Paul called him "my son in the
Lord," and in a very real sense their relationship was that
of father and son. The 16th chapter of Acts tells how St.
Paul, on a visit to Lystra, baptized young Timothy and
then took him as his special protégé and assistant. The
lad traveled with St. Paul for two years or more, and was
so apt a pupil that he was soon able to substitute for his
teacher if the occasion arose. When Paul sent him to
Corinth he told the Corinthians that having Timothy with

them was the same as having Paul. They were of one mind.

All through the Acts and in many of the Epistles there are references to Timothy that show the happy relationship between the Apostle and his favorite disciple. After Timothy had been sent out on his own, Paul wrote him two letters which are included in the New Testament, and in these letters the old man did not hesitate to scold the youngster for his temper, his timidity, and sometimes his laziness, but these scoldings were mild and sound like the admonitions of a father to a beloved son.

Timothy outlived St. Paul by thirty years, most of which time he spent as Bishop of Ephesus. In those early days of the Church a bishop ordinarily was responsible for only one town or community. Timothy, however, apparently had jurisdiction over several neighboring districts, which has led to his being called the first archbishop. Timothy's life was a long one, but it finally ended tragically. Every year the people of Ephesus held a great celebration in honor of their goddess Diana of the Ephesians. Timothy was beaten to death by pagan revelers while he was trying to restrain his own Christian people from taking part in this festival. He was eighty years old. For some forgotten reason, St. Timothy is the patron saint of those who suffer from stomach trouble.

The Conversion of St. Paul

JANUARY 25TH

January 25th commemorates one of the most dramatic and important events in Christian history: the sudden change of Saul of Tarsus, blasphemer and persecutor of Christianity, into Paul the Apostle, one of God's principal instruments in the conversion of the world. A Jew of the tribe of Benjamin, pupil of the great rabbi Gamaliel, Saul was a Pharisee, a learned rabbi, and a scrupulous observer of the Mosaic Law. The new Christian faith was to him an abomination, and he personally took on the responsibility of exterminating it. In his fury he went to the High Priest and got an order that permitted him to go to Damascus, arrest every Christian he could find there, and bring them all in chains to Jerusalem.

About noon on the last day of the journey, Saul and his companions were suddenly surrounded by a brilliant light. Saul, knocked down by the impact, heard the voice of Jesus. His response, "Lord, what wilt Thou have me to do?" was the key that let loose the greatest missionary power Christianity has ever seen. His new zeal for the faith was even stronger than his old hatred of it had been. His great missionary journeys from then on took him to every part of the known world, "in weariness and painfulness, in watchings often, in hunger and thirst, in fastings often, in cold and nakedness." (II Corinthians, chapter 11, verse 27.) He was finally beheaded at Rome.

His original name, Saul, he changed to Paul in honor of Sergius Paulus, whom he converted to Christianity (Acts, chapter 13, verses 6 to 12). St. Paul is the patron of preachers, for obvious reasons, and of tentmakers because throughout his career he preferred to finance his ministry by practicing the tentmaker's trade rather than depending on the contributions of the faithful.

St. Paul's Day Tells of Weather

"If St. Paul's Day be fair and clear, it does betide a happy year," says an old English folksong. Something about this halfway mark in the winter season has always made weather prophets out of people. Candlemas (February

2nd) for example, which we know more familiarly as Groundhog Day, is supposed to tell what the next six weeks will be like. But St. Paul's Day does much better than that—it gives advance information not just about a season but about the whole year to come. And not only about the weather. The rest of the song referred to states that by the conditions of rain, clouds, and wind it is possible to foretell what will be the price of grain, the health of livestock, and the prospects of war. The song was already old when it was translated into English from the Latin. All of western Europe had believed it for many centuries.

St. Paul's Chapel, New York

In the city of New York there is a quaint custom connected with St. Paul's Day. St. Paul's Chapel, an Episcopal Church in the Wall Street district, has an iron-fenced churchyard (burial ground) through which many thousands of people walk because it provides them with a short-cut between streets. The Chapel authorities have no objection to this use of their land, but they are at the same time mindful of a law which says that the owner loses control of any property that is used without interruption as a public right-of-way. Therefore each year the gates of St. Paul's churchyard are closed for forty-eight hours before St. Paul's Day, and the hurrying office workers are forced to go around the long way.

When the hour arrives for reopening the gates, the rector, in full vestments, appears at one of the gates and reads four verses of Psalm 68 and all of Psalm 91. He then says, "Open the gates that the people may enter," and the path through the churchyard becomes a public thoroughfare for another year—minus forty-eight hours.

St. Ananias of Damascus
JANUARY 25TH

A very important man in the early history of Christianity
was St. Ananias of Damascus, who is honored on January
25th. It was he who brought St. Paul into the Church. It
is appropriate that Ananias should be commemorated on
January 25th, the day that also celebrates the conversion
of St. Paul. The story is told in the 9th chapter of the
Acts of the Apostles.

Saul of Tarsus, having been struck down, blinded, and
converted on his way to Damascus, proceeded, still blind,
to that city. In Damascus a faithful Christian named
Ananias was also visited by a vision, in which the Lord
told him to go to "the street called Straight" and restore
Saul's sight. But Ananias had heard of Saul's persecution
of the Church and he protested strongly against this assignment. Nevertheless, he obeyed, went to Saul, restored
his sight, baptized him, and fed him. So it was that Ananias was the intermediary in what might be considered
the most important event in the early Church: the recruit-
ing of the greatest Christian missionary of all time.

This Ananias is not to be confused with the infamous
Ananias whose story of deception is told in the 5th chapter of Acts, and whose name has for centuries been a
synonym for "liar." St. Ananias is believed to have become bishop of Damascus and to have been stoned to
death.

St. Polycarp
JANUARY 26TH

St. Polycarp must have been just a boy when he became
a Christian. The records, which do not show his age, say

that he was converted in the year 80, became Bishop of Smyrna in 96, and was martyred in 167. Any man who is a Christian for eighty-seven years starts very young and ends very old. The most important thing about Polycarp, though, is not his age nor or the length of his Christian service. Rather it is the fact that the custom of celebrating saints' days first started in connection with him.

In the year 167 a great persecution of Christians was ordered by the Roman Emperor, Marcus Aurelius. Those were the days when a Roman's idea of great fun was to spend the afternoon watching Christians fight with lions and wild bulls. In the midst of this persecution Polycarp, the old bishop, was burned at the stake. After Polycarp's death the Christians of Smyrna met to consider how they might best carry on the memory of their great friend and bishop. And what they decided was the beginning of one of Christianity's richest traditions—they agreed to make a special day each year of the anniversary of Polycarp's death. Thus began the custom of keeping saints' days.

College Boys' "Saint"
JANUARY 28TH

January 28th is St. Charlemagne's Day, but Charlemagne was actually not a saint at all. He was an emperor, and a great one. *Charlemagne* means Charles the Great. The idea of calling him a saint comes from French college students, to whom he has always been a hero because of his intense interest in education. Tradition says he was the founder of the University of Paris, a rather surprising act for a man who himself was never able even to learn to read and write.

Beginning as Emperor of the Franks, Charlemagne finally rose to be the first ruler of the Holy Roman Empire.

He was crowned on Christmas Day in the year 800, by Pope Leo III. Despite the emperor's own illiteracy, his reign was marked by a tremendous cultural revival, with scholarship, literature, and philosophy making great advances.

Throughout France, St. Charlemagne's Day is still celebrated by college students with a great breakfast, at which the champagne flows freely, and professors and top students show off their learning with poems and erudite speeches.

Anglicanism's Own Saint

JANUARY 30TH

In the early days of Christianity great heroes of the faith became saints simply by popular acclaim. People, at least locally, knew about them, respected them, and honored their memory by spontaneous general agreement. Later on, the Church felt that it was necessary to have some official action behind the statement that an individual was worthy of sainthood, and the present elaborate "canonization" procedure of the Roman Catholic Church was developed. But after the Reformation, when many churches were no longer in union with Rome, there was no longer any machinery by which the reformed groups could canonize a saint. Only the Church of England claimed to have retained the necessary authority, and this church has used its power only once: in the case of King Charles I, who was beheaded by Puritans in 1649.

There has been a great amount of disagreement even among Anglicans about whether Charles should be considered a saint, but there is no doubt that the proper authorities, in 1661, did the following things:

1. They stated that he was a martyr for the Church.
2. They established the day of his death as a special day in the Church calendar. (January 30th).
3. They sanctioned a prayer in which he was called a saint.

It seems obvious that they intended to canonize him.

Charles Stuart was the King of England from 1625 to 1649. In 1645 Oliver Cromwell and the Puritan party took over the English government. Much of the struggle between them and the King was over the organization of the Church of England. Many people say that if Charles had been willing to give in to the Puritans, which would have meant giving up bishops and the Church's link with ancient Christianity, he would not have been executed. He was, however, tried for treason on January 27, 1649, and beheaded three days later.

In 1859, by Act of Parliament, the service in commemoration of King Charles the Martyr was removed from the English Prayer Book, after having been included for one hundred and ninety-eight years. Churchmen claim, however, that Parliament has no power to "uncanonize" a saint, and many parishes in England and Episcopal parishes in America continue to celebrate January 30th as St. Charles' Day.

VARIABLE HOLIDAYS AND OBSERVANCES

Universal Week of Prayer

Borrowed perhaps from the Jews, who start each new year with ten days of solemn penitence, the idea of a Week of Prayer has become a universal one. Acting on what everyone instinctively believes, that the new year is a time of new beginnings in every man's life, the World

Evangelical Alliance of London, England, away back in
1846, inaugurated the Universal Week of Prayer. The
thought behind this century-old observance is that religious values should be the foundation of each person's
approach to whatever the coming year may hold for him.

The London group set the first full week in January as
the time for this serious dedication of life, and their idea
found an immediate response. Within a few years the
Universal Week of Prayer was being observed by Protestant groups in almost every Christian land. Now, more
than one hundred years later, the London society still
sponsors the Week of Prayer and sends appropriate literature to all parts of the world, but in the United States the
promotion has been taken over by the National Council
of Churches, which believes that it can produce material
more suited to the special needs and problems of American life.

The Week extends for eight days, beginning on the
first Sunday in January. For this eight-day period the
National Council each year produces a booklet containing
a prayer, a Bible reading, and a meditation for each day,
intended for private, individual use at home rather than
for public services. The Week is also the occasion for
union church services in many American communities.
These services, mostly in the evenings, move from one
church to another throughout the week and are interdenominational.

The Sunday After Epiphany

Every year in the Roman Catholic Church the Sunday
after Epiphany honors the Holy Family. Although each
of the three members of the sacred household at Nazareth has always been venerated as an individual, there

also has always been a special regard in men's hearts for the family life they must have lived there. Artists and poets have found it one of their favorite subjects over the centuries. The home life of Jesus, Mary, and Joseph is thought of as the perfect pattern of what family relationship should be. It was only natural that a Feast of the Holy Family should find its way into the Christian calendar.

It was not until the seventeenth century that the veneration of the Holy Family as a family began to appear, and the feast itself was not officially instituted until 1921. But the growth of the idea in popularity has been worldwide within the Roman Church. There are now several orders of sisters under the patronage of the Holy Family, besides an organization known as The Confraternity of the Holy Family in which membership is open to any Roman Catholic—man, woman, or child.

Plow Monday

The Monday after Epiphany is called "Plow Monday." The day itself has little or no connection with religion, but it is associated with and dependent upon two other days of definitely religious character: Epiphany and Plow Sunday. The women in medieval times went back to their spinning on "St. Distaff's Day," January 7th, but the men managed to stall a little longer, until the Monday after Epiphany. This was the day on which they were supposed to get on with their plowing. The preceding day was called Plow Sunday because all the churches on this Sunday held a colorful ceremony of blessing the plows that were to be put into operation next day.

But the men found a way of putting their work off for one more day: They made a big holiday of Plow Monday.

Dragging a beribboned plow, they went in large groups
about the countryside, playing a game much like the
"tricks or treats" of Halloween. Stopping at a farmhouse
they would shout "God speed the plow," which was the
householder's cue to come out and put some money in a
box carried by the plowmen. If they did not get a contribution, they plowed up the man's front yard. When the
money box was full enough, the procession ended at the
nearest tavern. Plow Monday is still celebrated in some
parts of England and Scotland.

Church and Economic Life Week

One of the clearest and most important trends in modern
American life is the growing concern about how to apply
religious principles to men's daily business lives. Big cor-
porations are providing chapels for employes in offices
and factories. Prayer services are held daily in many
shops. People are buying more and more books about
religion as it relates to the problem of making a living. It
has become popular for men of one profession or trade to
meet together to discuss the implications of their religious
faith in their work: what, for example, is a *Christian* lawyer, or carpenter, or manufacturer?

What it all means is that Christians are worried about
how to be Christians in a competitive, materialistic society. Our culture is built frankly on principles of self-
interest. Men are asking where Christian ethics fit into
such a culture. Every year in mid-January the National
Council of Churches proclaims Church and Economic
Life Week to promote discussion and study of this per-
plexing question. The point certainly is not any attempt
to condemn the American system. The Council is inter-

ested rather in helping the individual Christian to see his work as a daily opportunity to serve God and man.

"The New Year of the Trees"

Trees always have been an important symbol in Jewish religious thought, signifying what is good and noble and steadfast in life. A religious man, the ancient rabbis said, is like a tree planted by a river. Now in the new country of Israel the tree has taken on an additional meaning. As a part of the agricultural development of that arid land, trees are needed for practical as well as symbolic reasons: to provide fruit and shade, and to hold the thin soil in place. The tree, therefore, has come to stand also for the revival of Israel as a nation.

Each year on the 15th day of the Jewish month of Shebat, the children parade through the streets carrying spades, hoes, and watering cans. After speeches by local dignitaries there are planting ceremonies much like those of our American Arbor Day. Because trees cost money to buy and still more to import, the people of Israel need financial help in this program. It has become customary, therefore, for Jews of other countries to send money for "tree memorials" for relatives and friends. Cities and districts of Israel are in this way gradually being filled up not only with useful parks, orchards, and woods, but also with the beauty of many "living green monuments," as the memorial trees are called.

National Youth Week

National Youth Week, first observed in 1944, is a week set aside each year by the National Council of Churches, during which young people are helped to consider the

Christian values involved in the choice of a career. All work, says Christian theology, is to be dedicated to God. A profession or trade is to be selected only secondarily as a way of making a living. The first consideration is whether or not this particular kind of work offers the workman his best opportunity for creative use of his God-given talents.

Some denominations devote this week to the specific matter of careers within the organization of the church. While not minimizing the Christian significance of all work, they nevertheless concentrate on holding before the young people a call to commit their lives to the ordained ministry or to laymen's opportunities in missions and teaching.

CHAPTER II

February

"A Little Child"

FEBRUARY 1ST

In the first six verses of his 18th chapter, St. Matthew tells the charming story of how Jesus, when His disciples asked Him who is the greatest in the Kingdom of Heaven, "called a little child and set him in the midst of them." According to tradition St. Ignatius of Antioch, who is remembered on February 1st in the Christian calendar, was that child. In the story the Lord was using the boy as an example of the humility that is the basis of the Christian's attitude, and it must have made a permanent impression on the lad. Intimate friend of two apostles (Peter and John) and Bishop of the important diocese of Antioch, Ignatius did indeed rise to greatness in the Kingdom. But humility remained his chief characteristic, even to the day when, as he was thrown to the lions in the Roman arena, he said, "I am the wheat of Christ; I must be ground by the teeth of the lions."

For being a Christian Ignatius was condemned to death in Antioch and taken to Rome to be executed. All along the way other bishops came out to greet him, and in gratitude for their good wishes he wrote them letters which are now famous as the "Seven Epistles." These letters are among the earliest of Christian writings now available, and are of tremendous value for the clear picture they give of the Church of that time—the beginning of the second century. At Rome many of Ignatius' Christian friends wanted to arrange for him to escape martyrdom, but he would not hear of it. He told them, "I fear that your charity may harm me. Never will so fine an opportunity be given me to go to God." He was killed before 80,000 spectators on the last day of the great winter season of public games. This was in the year 107, which means that if Ignatius really was the boy in St. Matthew's story he must have been very old when he died. Assuming that he was four or five years old at the time of his encounter with Jesus, which would have happened sometime just before 30 A.D., he would have been well over eighty in 107.

"The Wonder Worker"
FEBRUARY 1ST

No saint could ever really share St. Patrick's place in the hearts of Irishmen, but there is one that comes close to it. That saint is St. Bridget, or Bride, for whom many Irish colleens are named. Born in the early part of the fifth century, Bridget grew up in the times when the great Patrick was taking over Ireland for the Christian Church. Her father was of royal blood, but it didn't really count as far as Bridget was concerned. Her mother was not a wife but a bondmaid, so Bridget did not have royal status. She became associated with one of Patrick's followers, a bishop named Mel, under whose authority she became a nun and founded the famous convent at Kildare, which grew so rapidly that the community was forced to divide itself and spread throughout the land.

Bridget was called "the wonder worker." One miracle story the Irish love to tell about her is that she sat with a blind nun one afternoon as the sun was going down, and the sunset was so beautiful that Bridget, moved with pity because her companion could not enjoy it, touched the blind one's eyes and restored her sight. The surprise in the story is that the nun was not pleased. She asked Bridget to make her blind again. "For," she said, "when the world is so visible to the eyes, God is less clear to the soul."

Irish lore is full of such tales about the holy, beloved woman, most of them quite incredible. But the fact that they could not be true does not spoil their value. In the first place, they attest to the imagination and lyrical enthusiasm of the Irish people who made them up. When the Irish have a great saint, they do not bother with prosaic facts. Only the most extravagant legends would be worthy of the dignity of a Bridget—or a Patrick. And in the second place, these legends have in them that basic truth that is beyond facts and which is found more in poetry than in historic documents. They tell something about Bridget that couldn't have been reduced to chronicled details. Taken all together, they say in effect that there was once in Ireland a woman whose life was filled with such beauty, such charity, and such a love of God and man that only the fantastically impossible can come close to giving you an idea of what she was really like. And this is true, even if the stories, one by one, are not.

The Purification of the Blessed Virgin Mary
FEBRUARY 2ND

Here is another of those occasions on which a Jewish custom is behind a Christian holy day. Every Jewish mother in olden times was required to go to the Temple forty days after her first male child was born to "present him to the Lord." The forty days between the birth and this presentation were considered a time of purification for the mother. Being a good Jewess, Mary made the trip to the Temple forty days after Christmas, and February 2nd is known as the Purification of the Blessed Virgin Mary.

When Mary brought her Baby to the Temple, an old man named Simeon took the little Lord in his arms and said the now famous "Lord, now lettest thou thy servant depart in peace." (See St. Luke, chapter 2, verses 25-32.) One thing Simeon said about this Child was that He would be "a light to lighten the Gentiles." The day therefore came to have an association in people's minds with the idea of light, and it began to be the custom to bless the year's supply of candles for the church on the Feast of the Purification. For this reason the day acquired a secondary name, Candlemas.

Groundhog Day
FEBRUARY 2ND

To most Americans, February 2nd is known as "Groundhog Day." There is a story about that, too, but it hasn't much to do with religion. In medieval times there was a superstition that all hibernating animals—not only ground-hogs—awakened for a while on Candlemas and came out of their caves and dens to see if it were still winter. If they could see their shadows, that is if they found clear and sunny weather, they assumed that it was simply a crisp midwinter day, and went back into their holes and slept for forty more days. The peasants believed that the winter would continue until the animals came out again. So everyone wanted Candlemas to be a cloudy day.

In this country the German immigrants whom we call the Pennsylvania Dutch attached this superstition to the hibernating animal that was most plentiful in those parts, the groundhog, and that is why it is Groundhog Day to us.

Blessing of Throats

FEBRUARY 3RD

On February 3rd, millions of Roman Catholics go to special services for the blessing of their throats. St. Blasius (or Blaze, or Blaise, or Blas) on whose day this ceremony is performed was Bishop of Sebaste, a place in Asia Minor, sometime around the beginning of the fourth century. Not much is known about Blasius, but legend says he was a physician before he was a bishop, and that he achieved local fame for unusual healing skill not only with people but with animals. Certainly, something of the sort must have been true. People would not be invoking his aid in healing sixteen centuries after his death, if there had not been some pretty solid foundation for his reputation as a healer. His special connection with the cure of throat ailments seems to have resulted from a contemporary story about his having saved the life of a boy who was choking on a fishbone.

Baptist Vs. Puritans
FEBRUARY 5TH

On February 5th American Baptists celebrate the arrival
on this continent of Roger Williams, their American
founder. He landed February 5, 1631. Williams came to
the Massachusetts colony from Wales, where he had been
born in 1607. It did not take him long to find himself in
unresolvable difficulties with the Puritans there. The trouble was due to Williams' stout contention that the civil
authorities had no right to punish a man for any but civil
offenses. Most people would accept that position calmly
enough today, but it did not suit the Massachusetts fathers. They wanted to regulate every part of a man's life
that they could.

The Puritans admitted no distinction between crime
and sin. A good example, which reached its peak some
years later, was their burning of witches. The state, they
held, could execute someone found guilty of a deal with
the devil just as it could execute someone found guilty of
murder. The state's function covered everything. Williams did not agree with this idea, and he was just as hard
to convince as the Puritans were. The argument led to a
court trial in 1635, in which Williams, of course, didn't
have a chance. He was banished from the colony.

With four companions he proceeded to what is now
Providence, and after a few years of negotiation for land
with both the Indians and the crown, he became the
founder of the Rhode Island colony. With Roger Williams
as their brilliant, courageous, and stubborn leader, the
people of Rhode Island were the first to establish a Baptist congregation on this continent, and the first to build
up a community based on the principle of absolute religious liberty.

Japanese Martyrs Remembered

FEBRUARY 5TH

St. Francis Xavier first took Christianity to Japan in 1549 and for a generation the new faith flourished there. But in 1588, under the angry leadership of the Emperor Tago-sama, an era of horrible persecution began. Thousands of Christians of all ages were tortured and put to death. They were burned, beheaded, crucified, and suspended head downward over pits of burning sulphur. The persecutions continued for many years until it finally appeared that there was not a Christian left in the whole of Japan. But the authorities were quite mistaken. What had really happened was that the Christians had gone underground.

The strength of the invisible church was dramatically proven some three hundred years later, when Christianity was again permitted in Japan. A priest, saying Mass at the altar, was startled when a stranger came and knelt beside him and whispered, "My heart is with your heart." Puzzled, the priest asked questions and learned that this simple lovely statement had for three centuries been the secret password by which Christians recognized each other. The faith had been kept alive through all these years. On February 5th the Japanese martyrs are remembered in the Roman Catholic calendar, particularly St. Peter Baptist and his twenty-five Companions, who were put to death on February 5, 1597.

The Patron Saint of Toothache Sufferers

FEBRUARY 9TH

People who pale at the prospect of having to go to the dentist should think of St. Apollonia and relax a little.

What happened to her makes even such tortures as being burned at the stake or thrown to the lions sound almost pleasant. There are two somewhat different stories about St. Apollonia, but from either of them it is easy to see why she is the patron saint of those who suffer from toothache. If Apollonia didn't know how teeth can hurt, no one ever did.

Both stories agree that it was on the 9th of February in the year 250 that St. Apollonia died for her Christian faith. The daughter of a prominent family in Alexandria, she had enraged her father by becoming a Christian, and he turned her over to the heathens who were at that time carrying on a violent persecution. One version of what followed is that the pagan fanatics tied her to a column, pulled her teeth one by one, and then burned her. The other is that they hit her so hard on the jaw that all her teeth were broken, but that she denied them the final satisfaction of burning her by jumping into the flames herself while her persecutors were momentarily off guard. In either case, the torture and the end result were much the same.

St. Apollonia's symbols in Christian art are, naturally, pincers and a tooth, and she is sometimes pictured with a golden tooth on a chain around her neck.

She Kept Him Out All Night
FEBRUARY 10TH

St. Scholastica was the twin sister of St. Benedict, founder of the great Benedictine monastic order. They lived in Italy in the sixth century. When Benedict started his monastery, Scholastica founded a convent five miles away, modeling the convent life on the same strict rules that had been inaugurated by her brother. (See St. Benedict,

March 21st.) Brother and sister broke their seclusion once a year, tradition says, and met at a half-way point to engage in deep spiritual conversation.

Gregory the Great tells a story about one of the meetings—the last one. Scholastica, so the story goes, had a premonition of death, and knowing that this would be the last time she would see her brother, hoped to prolong the interview. As evening closed in, she begged Benedict to spend the entire night in discussion with her. Horrified at the idea of staying away from his monastery after hours, Benedict stoutly declined. Whereupon Scholastica, in an early demonstration of the principle of never-underestimate-the-power-of-a-woman, simply lowered her eyes, and was silent for a few moments. Immediately there came a thunderstorm of such violence and intensity that Benedict had no choice in the matter. He stayed. Three days later, on February 10, 543, Scholastica died.

The Feast of Our Lady of Lourdes
FEBRUARY 11TH

Among Roman Catholics February 11th is the feast of Our Lady of Lourdes. This feast commemorates the first of several appearances of the Blessed Virgin Mary to a peasant girl, fourteen-year-old Bernadette Soubirous. The appearances occurred in 1858 near the French town of Lourdes. As all the world knows by now, these visions led to the establishment of one of the most famous of all shrines: every year more than 600,000 pilgrims come to the Shrine of Our Lady of Lourdes. At the place where the visions were seen—a grotto on the edge of town—a spring miraculously appeared. Over the past century millions of persons have visited this place and many have been healed of all kinds of ailments. For some time it was

thought that the spring-water itself had some special cur-
ative property, and people supposed that their recoveries
came from bathing in these waters. Analysis, however,
has shown that there is nothing unusual in the chemical
content of the water, and the explanation of the many
cures must be found in the realm of faith rather than of
medication.

The Slave Who Founded a Church
FEBRUARY 11TH

On February 11th, the African Methodist Episcopal
Church honors the memory of its founder and first bishop,
Richard Allen, who was born February 11, 1760. He
was the son of slave parents living in Philadelphia. It
would have been difficult for any young man, slave or
free, to have done what Richard Allen did in colonial
America. The fact that he educated himself to the point
where the Methodist Church was willing to license him
as a preacher was in itself a feat for a slave boy. The
greatest mystery is how he managed to amass $2,000 and
purchase his own freedom by the time he was twenty-six
years old. That would be the equivalent of $15,000 or
$20,000 today, and even in these times of freedom and
opportunity not many young men of twenty-six have accumulated such a sum. But intelligence and ability will
assert themselves under any conditions and by 1786
Richard Allen was a free citizen, leading a Negro congregation which met in the city of Philadelphia on Sunday afternoons in St. George's Methodist Church. This
was only a beginning. Within a year, Allen, who was not
willing to have his congregation become a patronized ap-
pendage to a white man's church, personally bought a lot
and moved onto it an old blacksmith shop. There began

America's first church for colored people. Members of the church were known as Allenites.

The energetic young Negro was only getting started. His church soon had a charter from the Pennsylvania legislature, and plans were under way for a new church building. The building, completed in 1794, was dedicated by the great Francis Asbury, first Methodist bishop in America. Allen's acceptance by the white man's church was complete when in 1799 he was ordained to the Methodist ministry.

By 1816 the Methodist work among the Negroes had grown so tremendously, and Allen was so insistent on the rights of his people, that the time seemed right for the organization of a Negro church on a national scale. In this, as in everything else, Allen took the lead, and when the new church was created it was only natural that he should be its first bishop.

He Thought Satan Had Owned America

FEBRUARY 12TH

The Reverend Cotton Mather, who was born February 12, 1663, is remembered chiefly for his fanatical persecution of witches in Salem, Massachusetts. Probably only history students know that he was a brilliant scholar who entered Harvard when he was twelve years old and was graduated at fifteen. He was pastor of Boston's largest Congregational Church from the time he was twenty-five until he died. And he was for many years one of America's most influential men.

Mather, according to his own lights, had real cause to worry about witches. He believed that before the Pilgrims came to America the whole continent had been the unchallenged realm of Satan. What was more logical, therefore, than the belief that the devil should bitterly resent the godly invaders, and that he should do his best to take possession of as many of them as he could? Reasoning thus, Mather felt it was his Christian duty to go to Salem and work with all his energy to expose and destroy all who had sold out to Satan.

Forgotten, too, are the facts that Mather was one of the first exponents of vaccination for small pox, and that it was through his persuasion that an English merchant named Elihu Yale gave the money to start a college at New Haven, Connecticut.

Old Roman Festival

FEBRUARY 13TH

On this day each year ancient Romans began an eight-day festival, called the Parentalia, in honor of all their deceased relatives. Roman festivals were usually wild and rowdy, amounting, even when they were supposedly religious, to little more than a general nation-wide spree. But this one was quiet, serious, and wholesome. Everything, even the temples of the gods, closed up for the week. People decked graves with flowers and put food in the cemeteries in the belief that the spirits of the departed came and ate it. The poor brought meager provisions . . . salt and a little flour mixed with wine; but the rich set out elaborate banquets. The best thing about Parentalia was that at the end of the week the last day was devoted to forgiveness and the restoration of friendships broken during the past year. This day was called the "Feast of Peace and Love."

It is a terrible commentary on the religion of a nation to note that the people of that nation were at their best when their temples of worship were closed.

The Lovers' Saint

FEBRUARY 14TH

Poor old Valentine, a third century priest who was clubbed and beheaded on February 14th, in the year 270, would certainly be surprised to find himself a lovers' saint. Nobody actually knows why lovers exchange their sentimental greetings on this particular day, but there is one plausible theory: that the Church used the day of St. Valentine's martyrdom in an attempt to Christianize the old Roman Lupercalia, a pagan festival held around the middle of February. Part of the ceremony consisted of putting girls' names in a box and letting the boys draw them out. This, supposedly, paired off couples for a whole year—until the next Lupercalia.

Following its usual strategy of retaining a pagan ceremony but changing its meaning, the Church substituted saints' names for girls' names. The participant was supposed to model his life during the ensuing year after the life of the saint whose name he drew. However, the old pagan custom gradually worked its way back and by the sixteenth century, the girls had regained possession of the name-box. It was the introduction of inexpensive postage that brought about the kind of St. Valentine's Day we now know. Before that time, everything had to be left to the "drawing." But low postal rates made it possible for the poorest lad to by-pass the drawing and let his real choice know how he felt about her. And, of course, there was a certain amount of privacy about it, which helped those who were of a shy nature.

Some say there were two saints named Valentine—some even say there were three. All were martyrs—all are associated with February 14th. St. Valentine, or perhaps

"Saints" Valentine, is the patron of engaged couples and all who wish to marry. Legend says that St. Valentine has the power to patch up lovers' quarrels. This is probably the easiest assignment ever given to any saint. Also for some reason he is invoked against epilepsy, plague, and fainting diseases.

St. Simeon

FEBRUARY 18TH

When the Apostle James, who was also the first Bishop of Jerusalem, died, the remaining Apostles immediately elected his brother Simeon to take his place. James and Simeon were first cousins of the Lord. At the end of His ministry, just before the Crucifixion, Jesus had predicted that the Temple would be destroyed. "There shall not be left here," He had said, "one stone upon another." (St. Matthew, chapter 24 verse 2.) And it was during St. Simeon's time as bishop that the destruction not only of the Temple but the entire city took place. The terrible Titus, Emperor of Rome, moved in with his armies and almost literally left no stone upon another.

When this happened Simeon and his little congregation got out of the way of Titus' armies. When the shooting was over they crept back into the ruined city and found, to their surprise and delight, that one of the few buildings still standing was the one that contained the sacred "Upper Room." This was the room in which the Last Supper had been eaten, in which the Lord had first appeared after His Resurrection, and in which the Holy Ghost had come upon the Apostles. They settled down to rebuild city and church. They went along for thirty years or more, never really in trouble with the Roman authorities, and never quite out of it. But even after so long a time the Romans still worried about Simeon. Being related to Jesus, Simeon was a member of the royal Jewish line, and, therefore, the Romans thought, a possible pretender to the throne. In the year 107 they arrested him. After torture and crucifixion he died, at the great age of one hundred and twenty.

Blessed Robert
FEBRUARY 21ST

In the Roman Catholic Church there are three separate degrees of honor for members who during their lifetime have been conspicuously devout and virtuous. First, a person of heroic virtue may be called *venerable*. Secondly, after an examination of his life has been made and it has been established that at least two miracles may be attributed to him, he may be beatified. A declaration is then made by the Pope in which it is stated this person deserves to be regarded as now residing in heaven. The prefix "blessed" is added to the person's name. The third honor, of course, is *sainthood*—which is often, but not always, reached by those who have been beatified.

In the second group is Blessed Robert Southwell, a high-born Englishman of the sixteenth century, who is remembered on February 21st, the anniversary of his martyrdom in 1595. Southwell lived in the time of Elizabeth I, when loyalty to the Roman Church was enough to place an Englishman in jeopardy. Admitted to the Jesuit order and ordained to the priesthood in Rome, Southwell was sent in 1586 on a mission which was in those dangerous times known as the "English mission." Not daring to wear clerical garb, he lived in London for six years and there functioned as a priest in disguise. After being discovered and arrested in 1592, he was subjected to thirteen separate tortures until finally he was hanged, drawn, and quartered.

The Holy Grail in England
FEBRUARY 22ND

February 22nd is dedicated to St. Joseph of Arimathea. He was the wealthy man who provided the tomb in which the Lord's body was laid after the Crucifixion. St. Joseph was at first a secret follower of Jesus. A man of high rank among the Jews, he was afraid that an open acknowledgment of his allegiance would cost him his position. With the Crucifixion, however, all thought of personal prestige apparently vanished. He went boldly to Pontius Pilate, asked for the body of Christ, and took it himself to a new tomb which he owned.

Joseph's fears were well-founded. When they learned that he was a Christian, they exiled him, and one of the most interesting of all Christian legends is about that exile. The ancient story is that Joseph went from Jerusalem to what is now England, taking with him the Holy Grail—the cup that had been used at the Last Supper. All the famous tales of King Arthur and the Knights of the Round Table were based upon this legend. The Grail had been lost and the Knights devoted their lives to recovering it. Although the details were lost long ago in the dim mists of antiquity, many historians are inclined to believe that Joseph actually did go to England. As to the part of the story about the Holy Grail, no one, of course, can say what the facts are.

And there is an even more dramatic story connected with Joseph. For centuries people in England have said that he was the uncle of Jesus, and that once when he came to the British Isles to inspect some of his tin mines there he brought with him his Nephew, Who was then about ten years old. The idea was widely believed that the Lord Himself was once in England. This fascinating idea has been the inspiration for a wealth of English literary material, as, for example, in William Blake's poetic speculation, "Milton,"

> "And did those feet in ancient time
> Walk upon England's mountain green?
> And was the holy Lamb of God
> On England's pleasant pastures seen?"

He Took the Place of Judas

FEBRUARY 24TH

February 24th is St. Matthias' Day. You can read in the first chapter of Acts, verses 15 to 26, how Matthias was elected to fill the place that was vacated when the traitor Judas committed suicide. After the Ascension, St. Peter stood up among the apostles and disciples and stated that the number of the "inner circle" should be restored to twelve. Everyone apparently agreed, and they proceeded to a kind of election known as "casting lots." Two nominations were made—Matthias and Joseph. Each voter wrote one of these names on a slip of paper and all the slips were put into a box. Then, instead of counting the votes, they simply drew one name out of the box and declared the man whose name it was, elected. "And the lot fell upon Matthias, and he was numbered with the eleven apostles." Almost nothing at all is known about Matthias. His only fame rests upon the fact that he took the betrayer's place. No other mention of him is made in the Bible. Legend says that he carried Christianity to Ethiopia and was martyred there in the year 64.

Leap Year Privilege

FEBRUARY 29TH

This date, which occurs only once in four years, brings up the subject of leap year. The right name for the year with the extra day is "bisextile year." It is necessary under our present calendar system because the year is actually 365 days and four-plus hours long. The extra day every four years brings about a partial correction, thus preventing a discrepancy between the calendar and the seasons. Nobody seems to know why bisextile years are called leap years. There are many guesses, the best of which probably is that February 29th, having no legal status as a day in English courts, was missed or "leapt over" as far as court records were concerned. Whatever happened on February 29th was dated February 28th.

Women's special privilege of doing the proposing in leap years is traced to an old story about St. Patrick and St. Bridget. This was, of course, in the days long before celibacy was mandatory for either priests or nuns. Bridget, who was in charge of a group of nuns, came to Patrick in tears, saying there was much unrest and anxiety among her women because of the unfair custom that prohibited women from taking the initiative in matrimony. The great man, sternly celibate himself, was sympathetic. He offered to grant the ladies the right to do their own proposing one full year out of every seven. Bridget, evidently good at bargaining, talked him into giving them one year out of every four—and the longest one at that. Then, because the agreement was immediately in effect, Bridget proposed to Patrick. He begged off, on the ground that he had taken a vow of celibacy, but his natural gallantry made him soften his refusal a bit by giving Bridget a kiss and a silk gown. Anyone who doubts this story is referred to the fact that up to the last century or so it was an unwritten law in the British Isles that any man had to pay a forfeiture of a silk dress to the lady he turned down.

In Scotland, it was required that a woman who was thinking of taking advantage of the leap year privilege must let her intentions be known by wearing a scarlet flannel petticoat. The edge of the petticoat must be clearly visible in order to give the wary male a sporting chance to get out of the way. This is obviously a man-made rule.

VARIABLE HOLIDAYS AND OBSERVANCES

Race Relations Sunday

Each year on the Sunday nearest Lincoln's birthday, Race Relations Sunday is observed by the Protestant churches of the United States under the sponsorship of the National Council of Churches. The reason for the connection of this special day with the Great Emancipator of the Negro slaves is obvious.

Strictly interpreted, Race Relations Sunday is intended to deal with relations among all races, not only those between white and Negro. But in the United States, by far the most important race problems center around the tensions between white and black, and therefore this particular situation receives most of the emphasis in churches on this day.

Brotherhood Week

When the United States added the words "under God" to its oath of allegiance it provided not only a perfect theme for that year's observance of Brotherhood Week but also a complete statement of everything that Brotherhood Week has always stood for. "One nation under God"—is as deep and straightforward and concise a way as anyone could find of saying that all men are brothers.

Every year since 1934 Brotherhood Week has been proclaimed by the President, sponsored by the National Conference of Christians and Jews, and observed by the whole country on an ever-increasing scale. It began when a priest in Denver, Msgr. Hugh McMenamin, made the simple suggestion that it would be a good thing to have a week each year in which people of all faiths would consider together the implications of the basic brotherhood that underlies their differences. The idea caught on immediately.

Each year in thousands of American communities, schools, churches, synagogues, civic groups, and all sorts of organizations observe Brotherhood Week by bringing together people of different faiths and backgrounds. This provides an opportunity for the people to explain their differences to each other and, also, to see that these variations do not in any way interfere with the fundamental fact of human brotherhood.

For human brotherhood is, after all, a fact and not an ideal. It is actually a mistake to talk as we do about building brotherhood. It was built when man was created. The problem is not to build it, but to recognize it, and to stop acting as though we were not all members of one universal family. That is why it is important for America to call itself officially, "one nation under God." If a nation is one under God, it is one not only under a Master and Judge, but also one under a common Father. And if that is true, the next conclusion is inescapable; it is one family. So Brotherhood Week is not about a nice idea that ought to be true; it is about a true fact that men ignore at their peril. And if the willingness to face facts is a sign of maturity, perhaps America is growing up, for America has faced, at least officially, the fact that it is "one nation under God."

Brotherhood Week is always set for the week in which George Washington's birthday occurs. The first president is a symbol of America's resolve to be free of racial and religious prejudice. When he was President he wrote a letter to the Hebrew congregation in Newport, Rhode Island, in which he assured the congregation that in this country there would be "to bigotry no sanction, to persecution no assistance." This quotation which is famous today has practically become a slogan to the National Conference of Christians and Jews, and it has seemed appropriate to center Brotherhood Week each year around the anniversary of the author of this quotation.

The National Conference, with headquarters in New York, was established in 1928 by Charles Evans Hughes, former Chief Justice of the Supreme Court; Newton D. Baker, Secretary of War during World War I; and the Rev. S. Parkes Cadman, famous New York clergyman. Their purpose was to promote friendship and understanding among Protestants, Catholics, and Jews. Although Brotherhood Week is the largest single project, the Conference is also engaged in a continuous program of education in interfaith relations. The Conference warns that Brotherhood Week does not mean one week of brotherhood per year in America—it means rather a week of emphasis on and rededication to right relations throughout the year.

Pre-Lent

The Sunday called *Septuagesima* is the beginning of a season with the sole function of preparing for another season. The eighteen-day period from Septuagesima to Ash Wednesday is called Pre-Lent. Pre-Lent can be considered a warning of the solemn time that is approaching, a time of preparing oneself for the stern self-discipline of Lent.

There are three Sundays in the Pre-Lenten season, and all of them have jawbreaking Latin names. The first Sunday is *Septuagesima;* the next is *Sexagesima;* and the following one is *Quinquagesima.* In English the names of the three Sundays mean seventieth, sixtieth and fiftieth, respectively, and the idea (which will not stand up mathematically) is that they are seventy, sixty and fifty days before Easter. Since they are only seven days apart they could not possibly bear out this kind of figuring, but people were not concerned about precision in matters of this sort in the olden days.

For many years there was no Pre-Lent season. The happy Epiphany season, which begins January 6th, continued right up to Ash Wednesday, and these three Sundays were known only as the last three Sundays in Epiphany. As Lent developed and grew in importance it became rather abrupt to skip straight from a season of joy into the year's deepest fast. To prevent this rapid change the transitional period was set aside.

Shrove Tuesday

Take your choice of names for this big day in the Christian year: Pancake Tuesday, Carnival, Fat Tuesday, Mardi Gras, Fastnacht, Doughnut Tuesday, or Shrove

Tuesday. What a person calls this day depends largely on his ancestry. But to every Christian it is the last day before the long fast of Lent. Shrove Tuesday, the best known of the day's many names, comes from the custom in the olden times of people making their confessions and being "shriven" just before Lent began. The other names, with the exception of *Fastnacht* (Eve of the Fast), and the Italian *Carnival* (farewell to meat), all have to do with the problem of using up forbidden foods before the Lenten prohibition took effect. Fats, eggs, and butter were put into doughnuts, pancakes, and other rich concoctions by thrifty housewives, and the day became one of excessive eating, and, of course, merrymaking.

The same general tone prevailed on the preceding two days of the week, and Sunday and Monday were days of feasting, leading up to the big revel on Tuesday. Taken together the three days were called Shrovetide. In England, Monday was devoted to getting rid of all the meat in the house. It was called Collop Monday, a "collop" being a slice of meat.

Ash Wednesday

Ash Wednesday has for fourteen centuries been the beginning of the solemn season of Lent, which is a time of self-examination and penitence in preparation for Easter. A deep principle in Jewish religious custom has always been that for every big day there must be enough time for proper means of preparation. This principle was carried without question into Christianity, a direct inheritance from Judaism. In the case of Lent, this time of preparation was at first only the forty hours preceding Easter Day. Soon it expanded to an entire week, then to thirty days, and in 325, to forty days. But, with the idea of a forty-day period definitely established, there was still some confusion because the Sundays during the period (all Sundays being feast days) could not actually be considered as fast-days. But if they were omitted the count was thrown off.

Finally, Gregory the Great, in the latter part of the sixth century, moved the beginning of Lent ahead to the Wednesday before the first Sunday and thus straightened out the inaccurate mathematics of the season. Gregory is also credited with having introduced the ceremony that gives the day its name. In the Roman Catholic Church and in other churches where Catholic tradition is preserved, the faithful will present themselves before the altar and the priest will mark each forehead with a cross of ashes, saying as he makes the mark, "Remember, man, that thou art dust, and unto dust thou shalt return."

When this custom started, the ashes were not given to everyone, but only the "public penitents"; that is, convicted criminals, who were brought barefoot before the church door. As time went on, however, relatives and friends began to show their humility and their affection for the culprits by joining them and asking to be marked as sinners, too. Finally, the number of these extra, self-condemned penitents grew so large that the administration of ashes was extended to the whole congregation, and the ceremony developed into its present form.

Lenten Season

Lent, the season all of Catholic Christendom and many Protestant denominations enter at this time every year, is not an ancient season in its present form . . . at least not as time is measured in a 2,000-year-old religion. In the early Church, that is, in the days of the Apostles and in the time immediately following, Christians led up to Easter with a strict fast from Good Friday to Easter morning . . . no one ate anything at all. This was done in accordance with St. Luke, chapter 5, verse 35: "But the days will come when the bridegroom shall be taken away from them, and then shall they fast in those days." Obviously, the time betwen the Crucifixion and the Resurrection was the time when the Bridegroom was taken away.

The trouble developed as the Church moved further away from Apostolic times and the intensity of the people's piety began to lessen. By the fifth century leaders were casting about for something that would deepen the devotional approach to Easter, the climax of the Christian year. With local variations, a pattern was developing in many places. The time approaching the Easter peak was being used for varying degrees of fasting and preparation, over varying lengths of time, from several days to several weeks. By the ninth century there was general agreement, at least in the western part of the Church. The right length of time seemed to everyone to be forty days. It was there that the Lenten season finally evolved as forty days with Sundays omitted.

The number forty always has been important both in Old and New Testament times, and it was especially appropriate in connection with a fast. Moses had been, presumably, without food for forty days on Mt. Sinai. The children of Israel had wandered forty years, on minimum rations, in the wilderness. Elijah had fasted forty days, and so had Jesus, between His Baptism and the beginning of His ministry. Gregory, the great sixth century Pope, had stated a further reason for a forty day season of penitence. Following up the ancient idea of the tithe, the setting aside of ten per cent of material possessions for God, Gregory had said, "Offer unto Him also the tenth of your days." Forty days are approximately ten per cent of the year. This is why Lent has sometimes been called "a tithe of the year."

The Philosophy of Fasting

But why should Christians practice self-denial in a period of preparation for the greatest day in their calendar? Why should they go without certain types of food? The answer is not that they believe God is pleased by human discomfort. Fasting always has been a basic principle in most of the great religions. It is an instrument of self-discipline. "The world," says Wordsworth, "is too much with us," and religion has always taught that the scramble for physical necessities and pleasures preoccupies man and diverts him from attention to the things of the spirit.

Christians believe, therefore, that a season set aside for the de-emphasis of the physical is essential to man's spiritual development. It provides a time when all people support one another in a general effort to free themselves for concentration on matters of the soul. In earlier times, incidentally, the money saved by abstinence from expensive food was expected to be given as alms.

This season is known as Lent in the English language only. The word comes from the Anglo-Saxon *lencten,* which means just what it sounds like: "lengthen." It is the season of the year when the days are "lengthening." The French call the season *Careme;* the Italians call it *Quaresima.* Both words come from the Latin *Quadregesima,* which means "forty."

First Friday in Lent

On the first Friday in Lent each year millions of women in every part of the world join together in a World

Day of Prayer. Women of many nations unite to form a "circle of prayer" around the globe. The same service is used everywhere, translated, of course, into local language, and the same general plan of operation is followed everywhere. In each community one church is selected for the service, and throughout the day women of all denominations come and go, each woman staying as long as she wishes, to take her place in this world-wide bond of faith.

The Feasts of Lots

The 14th and 15th of Adar constitute the happy festival of Purim, in which Jews all over the world celebrate their nation's deliverance from a fiendish plot which, if it had worked, would have completely exterminated them. In the days six hundred years before the Christian era, when nearly every Jew was in slavery in Persia, the Persian prime minister Haman was seized with uncontrollable rage against the Jews. The king had married the beautiful Jewish girl, Esther. This had offended Haman's strong feelings about segregation, especially when Esther's relatives at court failed to show him the proper deference. With sly cunning Haman cajoled the weak king into giving him permission to destroy all the Jews.

To find out which day would be best for his diabolical project, Haman cast lots, and the lots told him things would go especially well on the 14th of Adar. This is why the festival is called Purim—*Purim* means "lots." But neither Haman nor whatever pagan gods were controlling the lots were a match for Esther and her clever cousin Mordecai. Under Mordecai's guidance Queen Esther appealed to the king and persuaded him to rescind the permission he had given Haman and to grant the slaves the right to defend themselves. The end result was that Haman and his sons swung from the gallows that had been prepared for the Jews.

Scholars nowadays are quite doubtful about the accuracy of the account in the book of Esther. Many of the details seem impossible to reconcile with known historic facts. But in the larger sense, the story of Purim has been true over and over again in Israel's long and stormy history, and this festival is in reality a rejoicing over the many occasions when the Jews have outlasted all the Hamans and the Hitlers who set out to destroy them.

While no religious ritual has been prescribed for Purim, there are many customs and traditional observances. As with all Jewish festivities, food is an important element. For Purim two of the main delicacies are triangular cakes, one called *kreplach* and the other called "Haman's cap." The idea that has grown up over the years is that the shape of these cakes is an imitation of the three-cornered hat worn by the evil prime minister. Beans and peas are also special Purim foods. The background of this is the story that Esther, unable to get kosher food in Persia, confined her diet to these two vegetables.

CHAPTER III

‑‑‑‑‑‑‑‑‑‑‑‑‑‑‑‑‑‑‑‑‑ · ‑‑‑‑‑‑‑‑‑‑‑‑‑‑‑‑‑‑‑‑‑‑‑

March

‑‑‑‑‑‑‑‑‑‑‑‑‑‑‑‑‑‑‑‑‑ · ‑‑‑‑‑‑‑‑‑‑‑‑‑‑‑‑‑‑‑‑‑‑‑

The Patron Saint of Wales

MARCH 1ST

Each of the countries in the British Isles has its own patron saint. England has St. George; Ireland, St. Patrick; Scotland, St. Andrew. The patron of Wales is St. David, and March 1st, which is supposedly the anniversary of his death, is a big holiday for the Welshmen. St. David, a sixth century prince's son, began his religious life as a hermit. After a while he started a monastery, where he gained a reputation as an austere taskmaster. His monks had to live on bread and water. They were not allowed to use oxen to pull their plows—they pulled them themselves. For all his severity, there must have been a sweetness about David, for the people adored him. They came from miles around for counsel and for material help. They called him their father and their teacher.

A legend about him tells of an instance when the
bishops of Wales had called the people together to hear
a pronouncement about doctrine. They found that the
crowd was so big that no man could possibly make his
voice heard by everyone. After much shouting and failure,
they sent for David, who spoke in his normal voice and
was easily heard by all. As he spoke, the ground under
him rose, until finally he was standing on the top of a
new mountain. Fantastic as legends sometimes sound,
there is usually some truth at the core of them. What this
one probably means is that David, the father and teacher
of the people, made the faith plain to all, not by volume
of sound but by the clarity of his expression. David ended
his days as Bishop of Menevia. After he died they
changed the name of Menevia to St. David's, and it is
there that the great Welsh Cathedral of St. David's still
stands.

The Society of Friends

MARCH 4TH

It was over two hundred years ago that William Penn
received from Charles II a grant of American land that
subsequently became the Quaker colony of Pennsylvania.
There are over 158,000 Quakers in this country. The
quiet people, who call themselves the Society of Friends,
had their beginning in England. This beginning was in
the preaching and organizing genius of George Fox, who
in 1647 began adding his contribution to the general protest against the empty, over-formalized religion of the
time. Fox taught a simple idea: that creeds and special-
ized learning were unimportant in religion. What really
counted was the "Inner Light," that is: Christ in the
heart of man as man's guide in thought and conduct.
No ordained ministry seemed necessary to Fox. The

Church, to him, was just a gathering of friends who were guided by the Inner Light. Thus, they were able to guide each other.

Almost immediately these quiet, sturdy "Friends" set to work on things that were wrong with society. They renounced war; they worked for the abolition of Negro slavery; they brought about prison reform; and they championed temperance, and improved education. In their early days they set themselves apart from the rest of the world by their dress and speech. Although they no longer dress in black or speak in the Biblical "thee and thou" style, their concern about social matters is as deep as ever. The American Friends Service Committee is at work today all over the world, wherever human need or human misery exist.

The name "Quaker" is a nickname, but it is more familiar to most people than the real name: Society of Friends. Fox's journal records that in 1650 "Justice Gervase Bennett first called us Quakers because we bid him tremble at the word of God."

St. Perpetua and St. Felicitas

MARCH 6TH

The whole story of St. Perpetua and St. Felicitas covers only a few days. Little is known about their lives. It is the way they died that helps the world remember them after seventeen centuries. In all Christian history there is no better example of the unshakeable conviction of the early Christians or the limitless cruelties of those who persecuted them. Perpetua was a twenty-two year old matron of high social position in Carthage. Felicitas was her slave. When they were arrested for the crime of Christianity they had not yet actually become Christians. They were, however, receiving instructions for holy baptism, and they did not think of offering any resistance to the arrest. They were baptized on their way to prison. Felicitas at the time had a baby in arms; Perpetua was within a month of becoming a mother. Both were sentenced to be thrown to the lions. Before the sentence was to be carried out Perpetua had her baby. Both children were taken by the officers; what became of them is not known.

The story of the execution is gruesome almost beyond belief. Instead of being fed to the lions the two women were wrapped in a net and exposed to the goring of a savage cow. Felicitas died quickly, but Perpetua lived so long that the crowd tired of the torture and demanded that she be killed by the sword. To make the matter even more heartrending, the swordsmen appointed turned out to be a youth just learning to be a gladiator, and his nervous timid stabs did nothing but add to the agony. Perpetua herself finally had to help him guide the blade by which she died. St. Augustine made a lovely play on the names of these two Saints when he said they are now in "perpetual felicity."

The Founding of the Paulists
MARCH 6TH

On March 6th, 1858 in New York City, there began "The Missionary Society of St. Paul the Apostle," usually called the "Paulists": one of the smallest, but certainly one of the most active and effective orders in the Roman Catholic Church.

The founder, Father Isaac Hecker, wanted to prove what he had long believed—that America was as much a possible mission field as any South Sea island or Chinese province. Father Hecker and several companions got the necessary permission from the Pope and set up their new organization, stating as their chief purpose the conversion of non-Catholics, particularly in America. For nearly a century now the Paulists Fathers have been bringing converts by the thousands into the Roman Catholic faith.

"The Big Dumb-Ox"
MARCH 7TH

Saints are not usually saints because of their intellectual attainments but rather because of their godliness. The fame of St. Thomas of Aquin, however, rests mainly on his reputation as a theologian and thinker, and in a way this is too bad, for along with his giant mentality St. Thomas had a piety and a devotion that would have made him a saint under any circumstances.

It is no wonder that the world remembers Thomas for his scholarship. Even as a precocious five-year-old he was confounding his teachers with his constant question, "What is God?" Throughout his school days, which went on until he was twenty-seven, his silent deliberate ways and his great hulking body may have deceived his fellow-students into nicknaming him "the big dumb-ox," but his professors knew they were dealing with one of the great minds of all time. One of them said one day to the students, "Someday this 'ox' will let out such a bellow of instruction that it will sound to the four corners of the world." And indeed he did. His profound writings, particularly his *Summa Theologica,* have furnished the standard basis of Roman Catholic thought down through the centuries.

Thomas was well-born. His father was a count—the Count of Aquin. But, after the manner of saints, the boy cared nothing for wealth and position. At the age of nineteen he horrified his aristocratic family by joining the Dominican order of mendicants (beggars). His sister at that time found out what it was to match wits with him. Trying to reason him out of the religious Order, she found that instead she reasoned herself into one. She finished her days as a nun.

All through Thomas' short adult life—he died in 1274 at the age of forty-nine—he taught and wrote and made himself generally indispensable in the intellectual life of the church. What the world forgets is that his theological writings meant little to him compared to the hymns and devotional material he wrote, and none of it meant anything at all compared to the visions he had from time to time. In fact, the great *Summa* itself was left unfinished, because it became, he said, worthless in comparison with what had been revealed to him in his visions.

It is not amiss to point out that the intellectual pursuit of truth can by itself alone make a great spiritual contribution to life. In a time like our own, when one man's fact may be thought another man's falsehood, a Thomas Aquinas might by his insistence on absolute truth do much to save us from our mental and spiritual chaos.

How an Army Invaded America

MARCH 10TH

Under the headline "Missionaries to America," the New York Herald Tribune of March 11, 1880, reported a strange "invasion" of the United States. On the previous day, eight persons—one man and seven women—arrived from London on the steamer Australia and proceeded immediately to set up the kind of street-corner evangelistic meeting now familiar to all Americans, who have become accustomed to the ways of the Salvation Army. To

New Yorkers in 1880, the Salvation Army was a brand new thing under the sun. Fifteen years before in London's roaring East End, a young Methodist revivalist by the name of William Booth had begun to hold religious meetings for the rough and ready people of that slum section. He held them wherever he could—in dance halls, in warehouses, and sometimes even in a tent erected in a cemetery. He called his effort the "Christian Mission."

By 1878 he was calling it the Salvation Army. It was eight officers of this new Army who landed in New York on March 10, 1880, and surprised the town with the tambourines, flag, and uniforms that are now so much a part of the American scene. On their flag was the legend "N. Y. No. 1." That one post has now grown into 1,400 posts in the United States, and instead of eight hardy pioneers, there are 5,000 members. All over America today the Salvation Army is bringing "spiritual and material benefits"—in the form of lodging houses, farm colonies, fresh air camps, day nurseries, Christmas dinners, free clinics, etc.,—"to those whom the conservative religious bodies do not reach."

Orchards' Patron Saint

MARCH 11TH

Although "Johnny Appleseed" wasn't a saint, he is known as "the patron saint of American orchards" and he certainly was one of the most quaint and interesting characters of American pioneer times. His memory lives today in the calendar of national, if not religious, figures. He was born John Chapman, in Boston, in 1774, but his real name and his Boston background were soon forgotten. When he came paddling down the Ohio river from Pittsburgh in 1806, John Chapman was a young man with a purpose. He had two canoes lashed together and filled

with one of the strangest cargoes ever seen: appleseeds.
For the next forty years he tramped over the Ohio, In-
diana, and Illinois wilderness, starting apple orchards on
river banks and in clearings beside the settlers' cabins.
From time to time he would come back to every orchard,
to prune it and to take care of it.

He was a deeply religious and much loved man. Indians who would have nothing to do with any other
white man welcomed Johnny Appleseed. Through the
forests filled with wild animals and snakes Johnny plod-
ded, barefoot and unarmed. Whenever possible, he came
to rest at the end of the day at someone's cabin, and
there spent the evening reading the Bible and Emmanuel
Swedenborg's writings to the pioneer family. Most of
Johnny's trees are gone now, but in the early days of this
country's westward movement many a homesteader was
delighted to find that the "patron saint" had been there
ahead of him and had left a well-kept orchard for his
family's pleasure and nourishment. Chapman died in In-
diana, near Fort Wayne, on March 11, 1847.

A Saint's Sainted Son

MARCH 12TH

Roman Catholics on March 12th honor a saint who was
also one of their most illustrious popes: Gregory, called
"the Great." He lived from 540 to 604, and was pope for
the last fourteen years of his life. Gregory was in a large
measure responsible for the beginning of the rise of papal
power, and has therefore been called the first representa-
tive of medieval Catholicism. Built on foundations laid by
him, the earthly power of the Bishop of Rome climbed
during the next two centuries to the peak which it maintained throughout the Middle Ages. By the year 800 the

pope, as head of the Holy Roman empire, ruled over nearly all the known world.

For all his executive skill, Gregory was a devout and humble man. He was the first pope to sign himself "the servant of the servants of God," a title that has been attached to the Papacy ever since. Much medieval church music is called Gregorian, but it is doubtful that Gregory himself actually inaugurated the use of the musical form that bears his name. Gregory's mother was a saint, too: St. Sylvia, whose day is celebrated on November 3rd.

Soldier with a Spear
MARCH 15TH

From as early as the fourth century it has been believed that St. Longinus was the "soldier with a spear" in John, chapter 19, verse 34, who pierced the side of Jesus as He hung on the Cross. It is not for this act, of course, that Longinus is a saint. The tradition, however, is that as the water and blood came from the spear wound some fell on Longinus himself, with a double result: he was both cured of an eye ailment and converted to the faith of the One he had pierced.

The spear itself, minus its point, is still preserved, although it has been through many hazards. It was in Jerusalem until the seventh century. St. Antonius of Piacenza reported having seen it there in 570. In 615 the Persians captured Jerusalem and for some time the spear was in their hands. But it was recovered and now, although the point seems forever lost, the rest is in St. Peter's in Rome.

St. Patrick
MARCH 17TH

In most cases, if there is uncertainty about a saint it is because we have so little information to go on, but with

the great Patrick of Ireland it is just the other way. There
is a vast amount of material about him—but it doesn't
jibe. Where was he born? Was March 17th the date of his
birth, or his death, or both? There are so many conflict-
ing stories about such details that many scholars now
think there must have been at least two Patricks, and
probably more, and the stories about them have become
terribly mixed up. Nevertheless, it must also be true that
there was once in Ireland one great commanding figure,
so magnificent that all myths and legends gravitated toward him even though they were really about other men.
And the best tradition is that this one personage was a
man named Magnus Sucatus Patricus, son of Calpur,
born in Glastonbury, England, about 386. His father was
a Christian and a high-ranking official of the town.

Young Patrick had little interest in religion and certainly none at all in Ireland until, at the age of sixteen,
he was captured by pirates and sold as a slave in Northern
Ireland. There for six years he lived the quiet contempla-
tive life of a shepherd and the great truths of God began
to be clear to him. When at twenty-two he escaped, his
only thought was to be ordained and go back to Ireland
a freeman and a missionary. And this he did, in 432. Ireland by then was partly Christian, but the Druids were
there and they opposed Patrick with all their magic and
their cunning. One time, for example, they poisoned his
wine, but he was too smart for them. By a miracle he
froze the wine, poured off the poison, thawed the wine
and drank it—to the Druid's frustrated astonishment.

It is thought that Patrick died either in 461 or in 493.
If it was the latter year he would have been over one hundred, which is, of course, entirely possible. His bones
have not been preserved. The only relic of him that is left
today is his handbell, which may be seen in the National

Museum in Dublin. His staff was kept in the church at Armagh until the sixteenth century, when the Protestants burned it as an object of superstition.

Of all the stories about the great St. Patrick of Ireland, the most frequently heard is the one about his having rid the island of all snakes and vermin. There is a legend-within-a-legend about a miracle that happened on the day when this extermination was accomplished. It seems that wherever St. Patrick went he always had a big bass drum with him—tradition does not say whether he had a drummer boy or whether he whacked away at the instrument himself.

On the day appointed for the banishment of the snakes, great crowds of people sat about on the hillside, waiting to see the show. The saint arrived amidst a tremendous roar of drumbeating appropriate to such an occasion. As he proceeded up the hill the drum was beaten with such vigor that it burst, and when this happened, a wave of disappointment swept over the crowd, for it was their secret opinion that without his drum St. Patrick would not have much power. And to make their suspicions even worse, a huge black old snake was seen gliding down the hillside shaking as if it was convulsed with laughter. But there the miracle occurred. An angel came down and patched the drum. The sermon of banishment was preached, the drum was beaten, and the snakes disappeared and have not been seen since.

Of all the traditional St. Patrick's Day parades in America, the greatest and best known is that of the Friendly Sons of St. Patrick in New York City. Since 1784 these happy Irishmen have been making the city gay on March 17th in honor of their patron saint. It is more than likely, however, that most of the Friendly Sons of today would be amazed if they knew that their first president, back in 1784, was a Presbyterian.

St. Patrick, as every Irishman knows, converted Ireland to Christianity, and so transformed a scattered horde of barbaric tribes into an enlightened nation. That was in 432. A man named Palladin had tried it the year before, and must be given credit for being the first missionary to Ireland. But the wild tribesmen were too much for him and he soon left. Nothing really happened until Patrick arrived.

As we have already noted, Patrick rid the islands of its snakes, but there is a persistent legend that says he missed one. In Lake Dilveen there was one old serpent that gave the saint a lot of trouble. Not having time to finish him off in one day, Patrick told him he would be back to take care of him on Monday. But the good saint forgot to come back. The whole thing just slipped his mind. So, the folks in the neighborhood say, the old snake still waits for the forgotten appointment to be kept. Every Monday morning he rises to the surface of Lake Dilveen, and he looks around for a while and finally calls out "It's been a long Monday, Patrick," and then he goes back down for another week.

Sheelah's Day
MARCH 18TH

Everyone knows that March 17th is a great day for the Irish, but few outside the lovely green island know that the next day is Sheelah's Day. Who Sheelah was is not certain. Some say she was St. Patrick's wife; some say she was his mother. All agree that her memory is to be maintained along with that of the great Patrick, and that the shamrock worn on St. Patrick's Day is to be kept and worn throughout this day, too, and it is finally "drowned" in the last glass of the evening. It will sometimes happen that a man will—quite accidentally, of course—drop his shamrock into a glass and drink it down before the drowning ceremony takes place. The only thing he can do is get a fresh shamrock and another glass. A careless fellow may use up quite a few shamrocks this way.

St. Joseph

MARCH 19TH

All that is really known about St. Joseph, the foster father of Jesus, is what appears in the New Testament, but it is, after all, enough to give the definite impression that he was a kind parent, a devoted husband, and a man of upright character. He was a descendant of King David. He worked as a carpenter in the town of Nazareth. And he was, at least four times, under the direct guidance of the angels. An angel appeared to him in a dream to assure him of Mary's purity, (Matthew, chapter 1, verses 19-21). Angels told him to take his Family to Egypt to escape Herod's slaughter, (Matthew, chapter 2, verse 13). Angels appeared to tell him when the danger was over and it was safe to return home, (Matthew, chapter 2, verse 20). And, finally, angels guided him to Nazareth, where the Holy Family made their home, (Matthew, chapter 2, verse 22).

Besides this recorded history, there is a lovely legend that tells how Joseph won Mary as his bride. It is said that Mary had many suitors, and that the old priest Zacharias called them all together and informed them that he had been told in a vision that God had put it up to him to make the selection for her. He asked them all to leave their staves or walking sticks with him overnight. In the morning, Joseph's staff was found to have budded

leaves and blossoms, and it was obvious to all that God
had chosen Joseph.

"Doctor Livingstone, I Presume"
MARCH 19TH

On March 19th many Protestants observe the birthday
of one of the greatest of modern Christians: the Scotch
doctor, David Livingstone. A century ago in Africa he
set the pattern for much of our present missionary work.
Livingstone was not a clergyman. He was among the first
of what we would now call medical missionaries, that is,
doctors who go into backward lands to carry on a Christian ministry of healing. Also new was Livingstone's idea
of teaching natives not only Christian theology, but the
whole modern culture. You don't stop at telling a native
the Gospel story; you also teach him farming, sanitation,
and all the things he needs to build a social framework
for the new religion.

Among the doctor's contributions to the development
of Africa was his discovery of waterways and water
power. He was the first white man to see Victoria Falls,
the Zambesi, and Lake Ngami. In 1871, H. M. Stanley,
New York newspaperman, arrived in Africa with his
famous greeting: "Dr. Livingstone, I presume," and with
his backing of American wealth. Together, the two men
carried on explorations that would have been impossible
for Livingstone alone. From a religious point of view,
Livingstone's greatest contribution was the common-
sense example he set for all Christian missions. He taught
the Church to measure missionary success not in number
of converts, but rather in terms of development of a total
Christian culture in primitive and savage lands.

The Father of the Blessed Virgin

MARCH 20TH

St. Joachim, father of the Blessed Virgin Mary, was an old man when his illustrious daughter was born, and is always shown as an old man in Christian art. He and his wife, St. Anne, had been married twenty years when their prayers for a child were answered. They had vowed if they could be blessed with a baby they would consecrate it, boy or girl, to the service of God. Little did they realize the extent to which that consecration would reach. Joachim must have been well-to-do, though his business or profession is not known. Certainly he was a devout man. The real depth of a man's religion can usually be gauged by what he does with his money. Joachim divided his income into three parts: one third for the Temple, one third for the poor, and one third for him and Anne to live on. The portion they kept for themselves appears to have been adequate.

A beautiful legend tells that Mary learned, by miracle, the moment when her father would die, and sent angels to help him through his last agony. From these angels the old man learned in his final moments that his daughter was to be the mother of the Messiah. It is hard to imagine any happier deathbed news.

The Father of Western Monasticism

MARCH 21ST

St. Benedict, who was born in 480, was the father of western monasticism, that great movement which kept alive the literacy and culture of Europe through the Dark Ages and tremendously affected European history. As a youngster, Benedict went to Rome to study, but he was so shocked by the loose living he encountered in the metropolis that he fled to the mountains and took up a solitary life in a cave. His cave is now known as the Holy Grotto. The record says Benedict's whereabouts was known only to a monk named Romanus, who brought him food. But there must have been a leak somewhere, for his reputation for sanctity spread and he was elected abbot of a monastery at a place called Vicovera. He went there but did not last long. He and the monks disagreed; they tried to poison him, and he went back to his cave.

From then on, people came to him in great numbers. In his neighboring territory he set up twelve monasteries. His main achievement in this line, though, was when at the age of forty-eight, he established the famous abbey of Monte Cassino. He presided over the abbey until he died in 543. It is the "Benedictine rule" for which he is most renowned: he required of his monks absolute obedience, charity, and voluntary poverty. They must devote seven hours a day to manual labor and two hours to spiritual reading. They could have no animal food, and they must refrain from laughter. This was the severest of all monastic rules, but it was eventually adopted by nearly all orders.

The Blind Hymn-Writer

MARCH 24TH

On this day in 1820, Fanny J. Crosby, one of the greatest of all Protestant hymn writers was born. Although she was blinded at the age of six weeks, Fanny Crosby taught school, married, and led a perfectly normal life. Over her long lifetime—she died at ninety-five—she produced more than 5,000 poems, hymns, and secular songs. Four generations of American Protestants have sung Fanny

Crosby's hymns, the best known of which are "Safe in the Arms of Jesus" and "Rescue the Perishing."

God's Greatest Messenger

MARCH 24TH

All angels and archangels are messengers of God, but the Archangel Gabriel has had the most important assignments given so far to any of the heavenly host. On four occasions he has brought man word of the coming of the Lord. Twice he explained to Daniel the meaning of visions that prophet had had about the Messiah. (See Daniel, chapter 8, verses 16 to 26, and chapter 9, verse 21.) He appeared to Zacharias (Luke, chapter 1, verses 11 to 20) to tell him about the birth of John the Baptist, who would be the forerunner of the Christ. And, most important of all, he announced to a Hebrew girl that she would, while still a virgin, be the mother of the Lord Jesus.

Saints are customarily honored in the calendar on the day of their death, but since Gabriel never died his day is the one before the day of his fourth and greatest assignment. The name *Gabriel* means "man of God."

Annunciation of the Blessed Virgin Mary

MARCH 25TH

March 25th is called the Annunciation of the Blessed Virgin Mary. It should really be the Annunciation "to" . . . , for it celebrates the occasion when the Archangel Gabriel appeared to the young Jewish maiden and announced to her that she was to be the mother of Jesus. (St. Luke, chapter 1, verses 26 to 38.) Although the Church began very early to commemorate this event, the date itself cannot have been fixed before the date of Christmas was established, which was sometime late in the fourth century. The two dates are dependent on each other, because they must normally have been nine months apart. The English called this day "Lady Day of March," to distinguish it from four other Lady Days in the Christian calendar; that is, four other days on which the Blessed Virgin is honored. These four are: her Purification, February 2nd; her visit to her cousin Elizabeth, July 2nd; her birth, September 8th; and her conception, December 8th.

Annunciation usually falls during Lent, and is kept as a feast day in the midst of the Lenten fast. If, however, it should happen to come on Maundy Thursday or Good Friday it is transferred to a date after Easter. Popular medieval superstition held that if Annunciation and Easter happened to come together it was the omen of national misfortune. In a primitive figure of speech, that seems a little shocking in this more sophisticated age, they said,

> "When Our Lady falls into Our Lord's lap
> Then England beware of great mishap."

Such a coincidence of dates did happen in 1951, however, without any catastrophic result to England.

A Day of Many Facets
MARCH 25TH

This day was for several centuries the biggest, fullest day of the year, with more meanings attached to it than any day should have. Primarily, of course, it was the day on which the Incarnation (the earthly life of Jesus) actually began—His conception was considered to have taken place at the moment when Mary, in response to Gabriel's announcement, said, "Behold the handmaid of the Lord; be it unto me according to Thy word." Next (because medieval scholars loved to have everything come out with mathematical precision), the belief grew up that March 25th was also the date of the Crucifixion—the completion of the cycle, with the Lord's death occurring on the date of His conception. Then, reaching all the way back, people decided that this was not only the day on which Christ's earthly life began—it was the day everything began, the day of Creation itself. From here it was a very short step—an almost unavoidable one—to the idea that March 25th must be the beginning of the year, and from the twelfth century until the calendar reform in 1752, March 25th was New Year's day.

The Good Thief

MARCH 25TH

A further March 25th event is found in St. Luke, (chapter 23, verses 39 to 43) where there appears the brief but eloquent story of the "two malefactors" (St. Matthew and St. Mark call them "two thieves") who were crucified with Jesus. One of them joined with the crowd in reviling the Lord; the other, repentant, was promised "Today shalt thou be with me in Paradise." This "Good Thief," who popularly has been called Dismas, though the name is much in doubt, is honored in the calendar on this day. Since a saint's day is normally the anniversary of the saint's death, this is the same as saying that the Crucifixion took place on March 25th.

And since the Annunciation is commemorated on this day, too, it is also the same as saying that the length of the Lord's earthly life, from conception to death, worked out to an amazing mathematical nicety. People used to attach a tremendous mystical significance to making things come out even in this way. Greek tradition, though following the same line of thought, had a different idea. It was the Resurrection that took place on March 25th. The Crucifixion and the memorial of the Good Thief were on March 23rd.

St. Dismas is the patron of persons condemned to death, and, more widely, of prisoners in general. In the United States the National Catholic Prison Chaplains Association, by special permission from Rome, observes the second Sunday in October as Good Thief Sunday, with masses in American prisons in honor of St. Dismas.

VARIABLE HOLIDAYS AND OBSERVANCES

Mid-Lent Sunday

The fourth Sunday in Lent is known by several names, the most widely used of which is "Mid-Lent Sunday." In the Roman Catholic calendar it is called Laetare Sunday, and in the Anglican (Episcopal in the United States) it is Mothering Sunday. The origin of Mothering Sunday is actually older than Christianity itself. The ancient Romans had a festival of Hilaria, "the mother of the gods," each year at the Ides (the 15th) of March. One feature of the festival was that the people brought offerings to the temple. When Christianity began to be powerful enough to take over the pagan culture, it was always the Church's policy to adapt old festivals to the new order rather than to abolish them, and this is what happened in the transition of the Festival of Hilaria into Mothering Sunday.

As the Christian calendar took shape, this Sunday became stabilized not at mid-March but at mid-Lent. The English people used to have a happy custom in connection with Mothering Sunday. Young men and women living away from home, as apprentices, servant girls, etc., were given the day off to visit their parents. It was a day of family reunions.

The fourth Sunday in Lent, is also sometimes known as Rose Sunday, because of an old but little-known Roman Catholic custom. Beginning in the eleventh century, it has been the annual practice of the Pope on this Sunday to bless a rose made of gold. Occasionally, but not every year by any means, the rose is sent to some parish in recognition of special devotion to the church, or to some Catholic ruler or other distinguished person who has been conspicuous for his Catholic spirit and loyalty. Most often, however, the rose is put away after having been blessed, for it represents so great an honor that there are few who are worthy to receive it.

There is an old superstition that the Golden Rose brings bad luck to its owner. Probably this idea had its beginning in what happened to Joanna of Sicily, the first queen to whom the rose was sent. She was soon dethroned and strangled by her nephew. In those days, that sort of thing was fairly likely to happen to a queen whether she had the Golden Rose or not, but Joanna's fate was apparently enough to start the superstition. Rose-colored vestments are worn in Roman Catholic churches on this day, in place of the usual purple ones that are worn on other Sundays in Lent.

Passion Sunday

The fifth Sunday in Lent is generally known as Passion Sunday. The name comes from the fact that on this day, for the first time in Lent, mention is made of the Lord's Passion; that is, His suffering and death. The Epistle (one of the Bible readings in the Mass) for this day is from the ninth chapter of Hebrews. It deals with the voluntary self-offering of Jesus on the Cross. Because it introduces this note, this Sunday is considered the beginning of the last part—and climax—of the Lenten season. The week that follows Passion Sunday is called Passion Week. It is not to be confused with the last week in Lent, which is called Holy Week.

Rabbi Isaac Mayer Wise

On the last Sabbath in March each year, Reform Jews of America honor the memory of Rabbi Isaac Mayer Wise who in 1873 organized the few scattered liberal congregations in the United States into what has become the powerful 150,000-member Union of American Hebrew Congregations. This day is known among Reform Jews, therefore, as Isaac Mayer Wise Sabbath.

Coming from Hungary to America, Rabbi Wise (no relation to the famous Stephen Wise) first served a congregation in Albany, N. Y., and then moved to Cincinnati. Because of a growing conviction that Judaism must be liberalized to make its greatest impact within the new American culture, he issued a call to all like-minded Jews to join with him in presenting a united front through a formal nation-wide organization. Besides the Union of Congregations, Rabbi Wise also founded the great Hebrew Union seminary in 1875. (It is now merged with the Jewish Institute of Religion.) In 1879 he founded the Central Conference of American Rabbis.

Isaac Mayer Wise Sabbath commemorates both the birth and death of the pioneer rabbi, since he died within a week of his eighty-first birthday. He was born in 1819 and died in 1900.

➤➤➤➤➤➤➤➤➤➤➤➤➤➤➤ · ⫷⫷⫷⫷⫷⫷⫷⫷⫷⫷⫷⫷⫷⫷⫷

CHAPTER IV

April

➤➤➤➤➤➤➤➤➤➤➤➤➤➤➤ · ⫷⫷⫷⫷⫷⫷⫷⫷⫷⫷⫷⫷⫷⫷⫷

The First "April Fool"

APRIL 1ST

Even All Fool's Day has sometimes been thought to have a connection with religion, or rather with incidents recorded in the Bible. For example, a writer in the *London Public Advertiser* for March 13, 1769, advanced the idea that Noah started the whole thing. It was, said this writer, on the first day of the Jewish month that corresponds to April that Noah mistakenly sent out the dove from the ark to find out if the waters had gone down. This is recorded in Genesis, chapter 8, verses 8 and 9. When the dove returned without having found any dry land, Noah thereupon became the first "April Fool." Such a story is, of course, nonsense. But the custom of setting apart a day of the year on which people try to make fools of each other is probably as old as Noah. And the custom has

been followed in many countries and all ages. There just
seems to be something basic in all of us that enjoys making even our friends look silly.

The ancient Romans had such a day, but it was not in
April. They played tricks on each other during their
Saturnalia festival—in December. In Hindustan they have
a very old celebration called the Feast of Huli, which always ends on March 31st. This is the closest anyone else
comes to our April date. These people spend March 31st
trying to send one another on absurd errands.

The April date is, in fact, a fairly new thing. It probably comes from France, where the Gregorian calendar
was adopted in 1564. New Year's Day was at that time
officially moved from March 25th to January 1st. Jokers
continued to make mock New Year calls after the old
March date and thought they made fools of the people
who forgot about the change and received them seriously.
If this is actually the origin of April Fool, it could not
have come into England or the American colonies until
the middle of the eighteenth century, for England waited
until then to adopt the Gregorian calendar.

Hebrew University Day

APRIL 1ST

With the movement of Zionist Jews back to Palestine
after World War I, there came many problems. The new
settlers were starting "from scratch" in every phase of
their community life. Business, building, agriculture, re-
forestation—everything had to be developed. One of the
biggest problems was the diversity of cultures represented.
The population of the new country had come from many
parts of the world, and though they were all Jews, it

would not be an easy task to weld them into a cultural unit.

One big help in the creation of unity would be the use of their common ancient language in the education of the young. Starting with the primary and secondary schools, all classes were taught in Hebrew. By 1925 the point had been reached where young people, already familiar with the language, were ready for college, and on April 1st of that year the Hebrew University in Jerusalem was opened and dedicated. The university stands on a hillside overlooking the site of Solomon's Temple. Jews, not only in Israel, but throughout the world, observe the anniversary of its opening as Hebrew University Day.

The Founding of the Mormon Church

APRIL 6TH

In 1820 and again in 1823, Joseph C. Smith, a devout man living near Palmyra, New York, was visited by visions of the angel Moroni. In 1827, the angel delivered to Smith an additional book of the Bible, called the Book of Mormon, in which was revealed a record of the early inhabitants of the American continent. The Book, written on plates of gold, stated that America had been populated by migrations of Jews from the Holy Land, and that these people had been visited by Christ after his Resurrection.

While Smith and a friend, Oliver Cowdery, were engaged in the translation of the plates, John the Baptist, on May 25, 1829, appeared to them and ordained them priests after the order of Aaron, who was the brother of Moses and the first priest of Israel. (See Exodus, chapters 28 and 29.) Less than a year later, three Apostles; Peter, James, and John, also appeared to the two men and ordained them to an even more ancient order of priesthood, that of the Melchizedek. (See Genesis, chapter 15, verses 18 and 19.)

On April 6, 1830, Smith and Cowdery, with a group of followers, organized under New York state laws the Church of Jesus Christ of Latter Day Saints, which is popularly known as the Mormon Church. This date is celebrated annually by nearly a million Mormons.

Salvation Army Founder's Day
APRIL 10TH

This day is celebrated by the Salvation Army as Founder's Day. It is the birthday of William Booth, the Methodist minister whose concern for the underdog led him to establish that famous, worldwide organization on the premise that "a man may be down but he's never out."

Born in England, April 10, 1829, Booth went to London at the age of twenty and began a program that scandalized his conservative Methodist brethren. Feeling that the underprivileged people of London's slums were prevented by their condition from understanding the usual presentations of the Gospel, Booth went out into the streets and into prisons, theatres, and factories, with brass bands, with popular songs adapted to religious themes, and with an informal type of preaching never heard before in sedate London. He also offered shelter and breakfast to the needy, and advocated social reforms that would put the slum people into a position where the Gospel could have meaning for them. The energetic evangelist's militant attitude brought upon him and his co-workers the name "Salvation Army," and by 1878 he had organized his movement after the pattern of the British Army. The Salvation Army extended to America in 1880, to Australia during the next year, and after that, to all the world.

The Visions of Bernadette

APRIL 16TH

April 16th is the anniversary of the death, in 1879, of a French peasant girl named Bernadette Soubirous. Bernadette lived a short life—thirty-five years—and was ill and bedfast much of the time, but her influence has reached almost every corner of the world. For it was through the visions of Bernadette Soubirous that the world's most popular shrine, the shrine of Lourdes, came into being. Gathering firewood near the town of Lourdes with her sister and a friend on February 11, 1858, fourteen-year-old Bernadette was astonished beyond belief to see, in a crevasse by the river bank, an apparition of a lovely young girl not more than a year or two older than she. The vision wore a white veil, a white robe, and a blue sash, and carried a rosary. Dreading the publicity that would surely follow, Bernadette did not mention the strange occurrence to her companions, who obviously had not seen what she had seen, but other visions followed on succeeding days. On February 27th the Lady said to her, "Go tell the priests that a chapel should be built here." At this point there was nothing for the shy Bernadette to do but to obey the order.

The news spread, of course, and everyone demanded proof. A test was arranged and the date of March 25th was agreed upon. On that day many of the clergy, and thousands of the curious, gathered by the river to see whether Bernadette's story was true, or was, as generally suspected. the hallucination of a sick mind. What happened was enough to convince them, for even though only the child saw the vision and heard her say, "I am the Immaculate Conception," there could be no doubt in the minds of the witnesses that something tremendous was going on—especially when Bernadette, in response to a command heard only by her, touched the dry earth and a spring gushed forth. A chapel was built on the spot four years later, in 1862.

Bernadette entered the convent of the Sisters of Charity at Lourdes immediately after her visions—nineteen altogether—and when she was twenty-two, finally was admitted to the Order. She died a year after having taken her perpetual vows.

San Jacinto Day
APRIL 21ST

San Jacinto Day is a great day in Texas, but it has nothing to do with the good Saint Hyacinth of whose name Jacinto is the Spanish version. St. Hyacinth was a young slave in Rome who was burned to death for her faith sometime around 257. In Texas this day is the anniversary of a famous and all-important battle fought in 1836, the outcome of which was that Mexico was forced to recognize the Republic of Texas. Only a few weeks earlier the Mexican general, Santa Anna, had besieged a Franciscan mission known as the Alamo at San Antonio, Texas. On March 6th he captured and massacred the entire company of its defenders, including a man by the name of Davy Crockett.

Flushed with victory, the Mexican proceeded eastward until, at a place called San Jacinto near the present city of Houston, he met up violently with General Sam Houston himself. When the smoke and dust had cleared away, Santa Anna was a prisoner and his army was scattered. This was the end of Mexico's effort to keep Texas. The Lone Star republic was established, and the hero, Sam Houston, became its President. The battlefield is now a state park, and San Jacinto day is celebrated with great enthusiasm annually in Texas, especially at Houston and San Antonio.

St. George and the Dragon
APRIL 23RD

The most famous legend about St. George, who is the patron saint of England and whose day is celebrated on April 23rd, is the story of how he killed the dragon. Back in St. George's time (third century) there lived, in a lake near the town of Silene in Lybia, a dragon so ferocious that the townspeople were kept in mortal terror. Every day he would come up to the city gates looking for food. At first the townspeople sent soldiers out against him, but his breath was so poisonous that one blast from his flaming nostrils would destroy a battalion. For a while the people managed to stand him off by throwing out two sheep each day, but there came a time when they had no more sheep. Then they were reduced to giving him their children.

One morning St. George, an officer in the Roman army, came riding by the lake, and on the shore he found a beautiful maiden, sitting there sobbing, waiting to be eaten. (There is no case on record of any dragon ever eating an ugly maiden.) The monster rose out of the lake, and started for his breakfast. But St. George held him at bay with his lance, and instructed the girl to put her belt around the dragon's neck. She did so, and they went back to the town, with the venomous beast trotting along on his leash like a spaniel. Inside the city walls

George struck off the dragon's head and thus lifted the terrible siege. George made it plain to the people that it was the power of Christ that made him able to save them, and the entire population, from the king down, was converted and baptized. The origin of this fanciful tale is impossible to determine, but it was accepted and carried in the Missals and Breviaries of the church until Pope Clement, in the sixteenth century, caused it to be dropped.

The fact that there is no such thing as a dragon has never hurt this legend in the least. Nor has anyone, apparently, ever been bothered about the staggering mathematics of the baptisms at Silene—20,000 in one day, which would be 800 per hour, 13 per minute, in a full 24 hour day.

Another of St. George's legendary feats was his appearance centuries after his death, as a giant warrior, towering in the midst of the Christian armies during the Crusades and frightening off the Moslem foe merely by the awful majesty of his presence. So many stories of these apparitions were brought back to England by returning Crusaders that St. George was, by popular acclaim, declared the patron saint of England.

The great historian Gibbon had serious doubts about even the character of this famous George. Gibbon identified him with a quite disreputable bishop of Cappadocia named George, and said it is a shame a person of such unsavory reputation "has become transformed into the renowned George of England, patron of arms and chivalry." Not many scholars agreed with Gibbon, however. One may dismiss the legends, but it is impossible to get around the fact that there was in the third century some giant of the faith named George, whose activities were so conspicuous and so important, that he captured men's imaginations and their hearts. Nothing will ever dethrone him now.

Feast of the Three Holy Maries
APRIL 24TH

In southern France they say that Lazarus, whom Jesus raised from the dead, Mary and Martha, his two sisters, and several of the Lord's other close friends came there to live very soon after the Resurrection. The legend is that this group was forced into a small leaky boat and set adrift at the Holy Land end of the Mediterranean, and that by Divine Providence the craft was not only kept afloat but also guided to land on the French shore. Thus, miraculously rescued from death, the little company set about converting the natives. It seems quite unlikely that the story could be true, but, on the other hand, it is not completely impossible.

Besides Lazarus' sister Mary, two of the other women are said to have been named Mary, and on April 24th in this part of France everyone still keeps the Feast of the Three Holy Maries. The belief is that these three holy women lived together, that they preached Christianity to all who came their way, that they were all buried together, and that the sick can still be healed by touching such of their bones as remain. Their relics are made accessible to the sick on this day.

Over the centuries the Feast has come to have a special importance for the gypsies, of whom there are many in that part of France. The idea has grown up that one of the Maries was herself a gypsy. Ignoring the utter impossibility of such a notion, the gypsies join in and add their color to the ancient festival.

St. Mark

APRIL 25TH

Probably a great many people if asked to name the
Twelve Apostles would start out with Matthew, Mark,
Luke, and John, the writers of the four Gospels. They
would be wrong about two of them: Mark and Luke. St.
Mark, whom the Christian Church commemorates on
April 25th, was much too young to have been an Apostle,
although it is likely that he was often among the Lord's
followers and was well-known to Jesus Himself. He may
have been there the night Jesus was arrested, though the
story on which this guess is based is no credit to young
Mark, if it is true. In chapter 14, verses 50 to 52 of
Mark's own Gospel, he tells about a young man who was
so anxious to get away from the scene that when one of
the soldiers grabbed his cloak he slipped out of it and
ran away naked. Tradition has always inclined to the belief that this frightened young man was Mark himself.

He is remembered mainly, of course, for having written
one of the four Gospels. His is, in fact, the earliest of the
four, even though Matthew's is placed ahead of it in the
New Testament. Mark was a close friend of the great St.
Peter, who refers to Mark as "son," meaning, probably,
that Peter baptized him. Mark traveled with St. Peter
and scholars think it was from Peter that he got most of
the material for his Gospel.

In England there was once a grim superstition about
St. Mark's day. It was thought that the ghosts of all who
were destined to die during the coming year could be
seen entering the church on this day.

Adviser to Kings

APRIL 30TH

Catherine of Sienna lived only thirty-three years, but in that short time she became one of the greatest women in the calendar of saints. There are no picturesque legends about her. Her story is simply a story of goodness. The eighteenth child of a poor Italian family, this fourteenth century girl was sought as a counsellor by kings and popes. It started on a small scale. Catherine's friends and neighbors found that she could not only heal their physical illnesses but also straighten out their problems and quarrels. Her reputation spread from her own neighborhood to the whole continent, and before she died the most important people in the world were bringing their problems to her.

During the great plague of 1374 Catherine performed tremendous miracles of healing. Her devotion, then and all through her life, to the poor and the sick, especially those with the most dread diseases, has resulted in her being called the forerunner of modern social workers. Some of the people Catherine helped did not show any sign of appreciation, and her friends advised her to have nothing to do with such ingrates. Catherine impatiently replied, "Do you think our Lord would be pleased with us if we left works of mercy undone because our neighbor is unthankful?"

A Night of Demons

APRIL 30TH

The night of April 30th is Walpurgis Night, when anything is likely to happen. Centuries ago people believed that on this night before the first of May witches, war-

locks, and demons were loose upon the countryside,
stealing cattle, casting spells on domestic animals, bringing blight on the fields, plague to human beings, and dis-
aster to the community in general. So it was a night of
worry and fear. People fought the supernatural villains
with the most potent charms they could devise. Houses
were purified with juniper; bouquets of herbs were hung
over cowshed doors; other herbs were tied to poles and
burned. At a signal in the night, church bells were rung
and all the villagers rushed out into the streets screaming
to frighten off the unearthly visitors. Then they lighted
bonfires and scattered the ashes on the fields. By these
ceremonies they thwarted the goblins' evil intent. However, the charms did not last long. It all had to be done
over in June—on Midsummer's Eve. (See June 24th.)

VARIABLE HOLIDAYS AND OBSERVANCES

Holy Week

From Sunday through Saturday before Easter is the
Christian Holy Week, observed by Protestants and Catholics alike as the most solemn, most significant moment
of the Christian year. These seven days commemorate the
final week of Jesus' earthly life, in which He came to
Jerusalem, met and challenged ecclesiastical leaders, was
betrayed and crucified, and placed in His tomb. Every
one of these days has through the centuries accumulated
its own customs—and sometimes superstitions. The Germans call Holy Week "Still" or "Silent" week, and some
Americans (mistakenly) call it Passion Week. The way to
understand this week best is to look at it as a whole. Some
days are more important than others, but every day provides its own chapter in the story of Holy Week.

Palm Sunday

The first day of the week was the day on which He rode into Jerusalem in what appeared for the moment to be great triumph. Later events proved that his Sunday popularity was without any real depth. This was the time of the Jewish Passover, when the city was filled with holiday pilgrims. It is believed that Jesus deliberately chose this time for His final encounter with the Jewish ecclesiastical authorities in order that the showdown might come in the presence of the year's largest crowd. Because of the overcrowded condition of the city at Passover, many pilgrims found lodging for the nights outside Jerusalem and came in during the days. This is what Jesus and His friends did. They spent Sunday, Monday, and Tuesday nights in the village of Bethany, a few miles away. Matthew, chapter 21, beginning at the eighth verse, tells that the happy crowd, many of whom probably knew Jesus as a popular rabbi, made a special event of His arrival, cheering and throwing down palm branches for Him to ride over.

Palm Sunday as a Christian observance goes back to about the tenth century. In thousands of churches on Palm Sunday, palm branches are blessed and carried in processions. The greatest of present-day Palm Sunday processions is the one in Rome where each year the Pope, carried in St. Peter's chair on the shoulders of eight men, appears to bless the palms. Some of the branches are kept back to be burned to make the next year's Ash Wednesday ashes. The rest are given to the people to take home. These palms were treasured as charms against evil, particularly against storms and lightning. One old custom which seems to be reviving in America, was to make little crosses out of the pieces of palm. In England, until comparatively recent times, there was the quaint and happy Palm Sunday custom of the Pax Cake (*pax* is Latin for "peace"). People who had quarreled during the past year sought each other out and ate the little Palm Sunday cakes together. They said "Peace and good will" to each other and resolved their disagreement. The idea was that they did not want to go to their Easter Communion with anger or hatred in their hearts.

Monday of Holy Week

On Monday there was the famous clash with the money-changers, when Jesus overturned their tables and drove them out of the temple. The rest of the day he spent quietly, preaching and healing.

Tuesday of Holy Week

On Tuesday the Jewish leaders took the initiative and tried to trap Him into some statement that would either discredit Him or enable them to charge Him with blasphemy. It was Tuesday of Passover Week that gave us the famous "render unto Caesar" incident that has become a part of our everyday language. (See Luke, chapter 20, verses 22 to 25.) On Tuesday He made His last public appearance as a rabbi. Things were moving rapidly now. Jesus spent part of the day teaching in the Temple. Toward evening, he stood with his disciples on a hill outside Jerusalem, where weeping and looking down at the city, He foretold the city's destruction in one of history's saddest soliloquies.

Wednesday of Holy Week

Wednesday is sometimes called "Spy Wednesday," because it was the day on which Judas Iscariot made his shocking deal with the Jewish priests, promising for thirty pieces of silver—about $20 (the price of a slave)—to bring them to the place where they could arrest Jesus without exciting the populace.

Maundy Thursday

Thursday is known as Maundy Thursday. The word *maundy* is an English corruption of the Latin *mandati*. The day was called "dies mandate"—the day of the mandate—from the fact that on Thursday evening Jesus gave His followers "A new commandment—that ye love one another." (See John, chapter 13, verse 34.)

The great importance of Maundy Thursday, however, lies in the fact that it was on this day that the Last Supper—Christianity's central sacrament—was instituted. Jesus and the Twelve Apostles had gathered in the evening to eat the traditional Passover meal, as hundreds of other groups were doing at the same time all over the city of Jerusalem. It began, therefore, as simply the observance of a familiar Jewish custom.

But the Apostles soon saw that their Master was turning it into something quite new. As He took the ancient symbols, the bread and wine, and explained them as His own Body and Blood, the Apostles quickly grasped His meaning. The Jews had been saved from bondage in Egypt by the blood of a lamb smeared on their doorposts. Here Jesus was saying that all mankind was to be saved from the bondage of sin by His own blood, freely, voluntarily offered. He was the sacrificial lamb.

It is recorded also (John, chapter 13, verse 5) that at this supper Jesus washed the feet of the Apostles. This act of humility has appealed to the imagination of Christians since early times. Kings and emperors, bishops and cardinals used to wash the feet of persons of inferior position—sometimes even beggars—on Maundy Thursday. The King of England, for example, used to have poor men brought to him, one man for each year of his age. The king then washed their feet with his own hands, and gave them food, clothing and money. Special new coins, called "Maundy money," were used for the occasion. Although the ceremony itself was last performed by James II, who reigned 1685–1688, part of it still survives in the Queen's distribution of new coins to the poor in London on this day.

Good Friday

Scholars are not sure why this anniversary of the crucifixion is called "good" when actually it is the blackest day in all history. Some say it is because of the good things gained for man on the Cross; others say the word "good" is a corruption of "God's"—it was originally called "God's Friday." At any rate the day has been in the Christian calendar since the very beginning of the Church, even before Easter was observed. It was of what happened on Friday that St. Paul wrote the familiar "Christ our Passover is sacrificed for us," now mistakenly sung in many churches on Easter.

Long neglected by Protestant churches, Good Friday has again come into almost universal observance. From noon to three o'clock churches of all denominations in all parts of America hold the "Tre Ore" (Three Hour), a service of meditations on the seven utterances, called the

Seven Last Words, which Jesus made from the Cross. This service is held from twelve to three to coincide with the time during which the Lord actually was on the Cross. St. Matthew, chapter 27, verse 45, establishes it as the period between the sixth and ninth hours of the day, which, in modern terms would be noon to three P.M.

To find all seven of these "words" one must comb through all four of the Gospels. They are as follows:

1. Father, forgive them, for they know not what they do. (Luke, chapter 23, verse 34.)
2. Today shalt thou be with me in paradise. (Luke, chapter 23, verse 43.)
3. Woman, behold thy son (to Mary). Behold thy Mother (to John). (John, chapter 19, verses 26 and 27.)
4. My God, my God, why hast thou forsaken me? (Matthew, chapter 27, verse 46—Mark, chapter 15, verse 34.)
5. I thirst. (John, chapter 19, verse 28.)
6. It is finished. (John, chapter 19, verse 30.)
7. Father, into Thy hands I commend my spirit. (Luke, chapter 23, verse 46.)

Holy Saturday

Saturday brings the week, and the season of Lent, to a close. This was the day for baptisms in the early church. Christians in early times were prepared for baptism during Lent and brought to this sacrament on the day before Easter. Many churches, especially the Episcopal, still hold large baptismal services on Holy Saturday.

Easter Day

Easter, the commemoration of Christ's Resurrection, is the principal feast of the Christian year, greater even than Christmas, because to Christians it is the climax of

God's plan for man's salvation. It is also the most joyous
of all Christian days. Indeed, it was at one time known
as the "Sunday of Joy." Christians rejoice over the tremendous fact that Jesus rose from the dead. They are
happy, too, over the ending of the long stern season of
Lent. And Easter comes at what has always been the
happiest time of the year—the springtime, when after
months of gloom and difficult living, man sees all life
being renewed before his eyes. One wonders what it must
be like in the Southern Hemisphere, where Easter comes
in the autumn. Perhaps there would be some advantage
to such an opportunity to consider the Resurrection at a
time of year when Nature seems to be denying it.

For many years, in America, the observance of Easter
was not by any means general. This was because of the
Puritan anti-festival influence, which was very strong in
many parts of this country. It was not until the Civil War,
when so many American homes were struck by the loss
of their young men, that the Resurrection came to have
an irresistible significance to the whole nation. Actually
the New Testament account does not specify the time of
day that the Resurrection took place; it only states that
on the first day of the week—"early while it was yet dark"
—Mary Magdalene discovered that it had happened. (See
John, chapter 20, verse 1.) And supposing the Lord had
risen only moments before Mary's arrival at the empty
tomb, the elapsed time would have been about forty
hours—less than two days. The traditional "three days"
is one of those peculiar time measurements that occur frequently in the Scriptures.

It took the Christian Church three centuries to settle
the question of a date for Easter. The Council of Nicea,
in 325, decided it should always fall on the first Sunday
after the first full moon on or after the vernal equinox

(March 21st). Therefore, its possible dates range all the way from March 22nd to April 25th.

Eastern Orthodox Easter

Sometimes the gap between the Eastern and Western Easter is one week, sometimes more than one week, and once in a while the two coincide. The reason for the difference is extremely complicated—so mathematical, in fact, as to be not very interesting. Aside from the complex arithmetic involved, it all has to do with the fact that the Easterners still use the old Julian calendar, which the West gave up, nation by nation, from two hundred to four hundred years ago. When England (and the American colonies) adopted the present (Gregorian) calendar in 1752 the two were eleven days apart. Now the discrepancy is twelve days. Both East and West use the same formula for reckoning the date of Easter each year, but because they use different calendars it is not more than once or twice in a lifetime that both come up with the same date.

National Christian College Day

Since 1941, the last Sunday in April has been designated as National Christian College Day in many American Protestant churches. The purpose of the day is to develop among church members a concern that American college education be carried on within a specifically Christian frame of reference. Church leaders believe there is an important difference between teaching in which subject matter is related to the sovereignty of God and teaching which maintains a spiritual neutrality. The church college, leaders say, is the best guarantee of a God-centered higher education.

The population of the United States is increasing rapidly, but the number of college students is growing even faster. By 1970 it is estimated that there will be six million, possibly nine million, young men and women in American colleges and universities. State-supported institutions do not need to worry about these statistics. To church educators, however, they are alarming, for the church college is financially dependent entirely on voluntary gifts. National Christian College Day is therefore partially an appeal for financial support of the colleges. Local congregations on this day are not only encouraged to see the importance of Christianity in higher education and to send their best young people to college where such education is available, they are also asked to include denominational colleges in their annual budgets.

Day of Deliverance

In the Jewish calendar the Sabbath just before Passover is called *Hagodol,* or Great Sabbath. It commemorates the Sabbath that preceded the escape from Egypt, of which Passover is the memorial. This day is notable because it was the day on which the tremendous and horrible miracle occurred that made the escape possible. Each Jewish family had been ordered by Moses to set aside a lamb to be sacrificed, an order which they carried out with considerable fear, because the lamb was held sacred by the Egyptians. As the Egyptians were preparing to punish this sacrilege, God struck their homes and destroyed every first-born son, and in the subsequent confusion the Jews were able by the following Thursday, to make their famous getaway, ending a 430-year period of slavery. It is because of this miracle that this day is observed as the Great Sabbath.

Passover
(Pesach)

The Jewish Passover has been known as the Festival of Freedom ever since the Jews escaped from slavery in Egypt more than 3,000 years ago. This event is regarded as the real beginning of Israel as a nation and a religious community, and Jews through the centuries have celebrated it each year as a commemoration of their solidarity. But even before the deliverance from Egypt, while they were still nomadic shepherds in the desert with no thought of a national identity, the Jews had a spring festival at this time of year. At this season they sacrificed a lamb or a young goat, believing this offering would avert plagues, misfortunes, and all manner of evils.

The name *Passover* and the festival's present meaning came into use when God sent His angel to slay the first-born son in every Egyptian household, while "passing over" the homes of the Jews (See Exodus, chapter 12). The fact that some sort of Jewish festival existed at that time is evidenced by the fact that the Jews' homes were marked for the angel with the blood of a lamb sacrificed at an already traditional observance. The Egyptians, momentarily paralyzed by the magnitude of the tragedy, allowed the Jews to slip away to freedom.

Since that time Passover has been an expression and a reminder not only of the birth of the Jewish nation, but of some of Judaism's deepest beliefs: that God works in human history; that man has rights over tyranny because God, not any king, is master over His people; and that God cares about the plight of the oppressed. With such doctrines for its foundation, Passover has become a festival of hope and confidence as well as the "Festival of Freedom."

While the Temple still stood in Jerusalem, every Jew who could possibly manage to do so made a pilgrimage to the Holy City for Passover. After the Temple was destroyed, Passover became, as it is now, mainly a home festival, the chief feature of which is a ceremonial meal at which the family gathers to hear the Passover story read and to partake of symbolic foods and wine.

The Seventh Day of Passover

The seventh day of Passover is the next-to-last day of the eight-day festival. By ancient tradition this is the day on which the Red Sea waters miraculously opened to let the Israelites cross over, but closed again on the pursuing Egyptians, drowning the entire Egyptian army. Hebrew lore tells that when the fleeing Israelites saw that they were caught between their pursuers and the sea, four solutions to their predicament were offered: One faction proposed group suicide—they should all plunge into the sea. Another faction wanted to fight it out with the Egyptians, although the odds against them were staggering. Others were willing to be taken back into slavery, which would, of course, have been made a more severe and oppressive condition than the one they had just escaped. And some thought that by creating a great uproar they might deceive the Egyptians into thinking they were outnumbered, and so turn them back.

Moses alone said that deliverance would come from God, and Moses, it turned out, was right. Rabbis for centuries have used this legend to show that there is a lesson here for all ages and for all mankind, not only Jews. In the desperate and seemingly hopeless situations in which man continually finds himself he will not find his solution in self-destruction, in his own power, in submission, or in demonstrations. He would do well to place his confidence in the final triumph of God and the right.

The Last Day of Passover

The eighth day of the festive Passover season is the day of *Yizkor,* that is, memorials for the dead, which are said at the morning synagogue services. Jews who are unable to attend services are permitted to recite the memorial prayers at home. An interesting feature of Passover is that it is kept, by decree of the rabbis, seven days in Israel and eight days in all other lands. With this eighth day the Passover comes to an end everywhere. The last restriction, which deals with the eating of unleavened bread, ends when the stars appear in the evening, and the joyous "feast of freedom," is officially concluded.

CHAPTER V

May

May Day
MAY 1ST

May Day has never been a great day in America, mainly because the Puritans frowned on such frivolity and never let the celebration get started in the early days of this country. But our European ancestors made a great thing of it, and in many places it is still observed. It goes back to very ancient times. All civilizations, in their primitive agricultural stages, expressed their joy and their gratitude to the gods each year when the fertility of nature was renewed. The May baskets of flowers and the May pole dances, with which we are at least somewhat familiar, came from the old Roman Floralia—the festival of flowers.

The Christian aspects of May Day, and of the whole happy month of May, are—to be perfectly honest—an after-thought. All the pre-Christian religions, with their worship of nature, made May the time of their prayers for a good growing season. The Druids used to have a great May festival in honor of the god Bel. Bel was the same as the fertility god, Baal, who is mentioned in the Bible. Baal is said to have sometimes lured the Israelites away from their devotion to Jehovah.

There are still places in the British Isles where May Day is celebrated with bonfires on the hilltops, recalling the time when the Druids built fires on which they laid sacrifices to Bel, in the hope that he would give them good crops during the coming summer. Other ancient peoples sacrificed children to Moloch for the same purpose. In Sweden, and in other parts of Europe, the big event of the day is a sham battle between two husky youths representing winter and summer. To everyone's great joy, summer, of course, always wins, and winter is buried in effigy.

The Romans, not usually a gentle people, were certainly milder than usual in the way they welcomed the month of May. They dedicated the month to Flora, their (and the Greeks') flower-goddess, and they spent the first day of May gathering flowers as offerings to her. In ancient times Roman children made little images of Flora and decorated them with flowers on this day. Later, as Christianity began to take over the pagan festivals, these May dolls were turned into crude childish likenesses of the Blessed Virgin Mary.

The First Apostle
MAY 1ST

May 1st is also St. Philip and St. James day. Both saints were Apostles, but it is not known why they are honored on the same day. St. Philip may have been the first man

to follow Jesus. The record (St. John, chapter 1, verse
43) indicates that Peter and Andrew were invited to become Apostles a day before Philip was, but they went
home to put their affairs in order, and Philip went with
the Lord before they returned. One tradition says that
Philip was the anonymous man whose request to be allowed to go and bury his father before joining Jesus
brought forth the famous "Let the dead bury their dead."
(Luke, chapter 9, verse 60).

There is a great deal of confusion about St. James. At
least three men named James—perhaps five—were prominent in the New Testament, and tradition has mixed
them up somewhat. It is fairly clear, however, that this
day is intended to honor St. James the Less; that is,
the younger of the two Apostles of this name. St. James
the Less was some sort of kinsman of Jesus. According to
one legend, Judas had to kiss Jesus to identify Him to
the soldiers because of the strong family resemblance between Jesus and James.

James became the first Bishop of Jerusalem. He was
put to death in 62 A.D. by angry Jews. They threw him
down from the top of the Temple and, when that failed
to kill him, stoned him and beat him until he died.

Father of the Faith

MAY 2ND

On May 2nd the Christian Church remembers a man who
sixteen centuries ago spent his life "planting trees under
which men of a later age might sit." You and I, whether
we know it or not, sit under his trees today. For St.
Athanasius, bishop of Alexandria, Egypt, in the fourth
century, fought, almost single-handedly, a fight that allowed the still new Christian faith to proceed on its way

without alterations that might have changed it into just another of the many ideas that have appealed to men for a while and then faded out. Most saints are saints because of visions or self-denial or lives of simple devotion, but sometimes a great intellectual defender of the faith rises up and becomes a saint because through him the Christian religion itself is enabled to resist intellectual attacks that might ultimately dilute it.

Such a man was Athanasius. He had the bad luck to be Bishop of Alexandria at a time when a brilliant priest named Arius was disturbing the entire world with his teaching that Jesus was not actually God—not equal with the Father. Alexandria in those days was the world's center of learning. What Alexandria said, the world listened to. And kings as well as the clergy listened to Arius and inclined to accept a doctrine that would have reduced Jesus to little more than an inspired human prophet. Athanasius, through merciless persecution including four exiles, stood fast and won out against the Arian heresy, and has gone down in Christian history as one of the great figures in the formative period of Christian doctrine. He is one of the "church fathers" to whom modern Christians are indebted for the present definiteness and purity of the faith they have inherited.

The Wood of the Cross

MAY 3RD

May 3rd is called the Invention (finding) of the Cross, and commemorates the discovery by St. Helena, in 326, of the Cross on which the Lord was crucified. Helena was the mother of the great Roman Emperor Constantine. Besides the Cross, Helena is said to have found the four nails that were used in the Crucifixion, and the small plaque that bore the sarcastic inscription "The King of the Jews." There are many ancient legends about all these grim instruments of history's most infamous act.

For example, there have been many notions about the kind of wood from which the Cross was made. People of some Middle European countries believed that it was made from an elder tree, and so repulsive was this tree to them that these people would go without fuel to heat their homes and cook their food rather than burn elder wood, which was often quite plentiful even when other wood was scarce. There was a superstition in these lands, not always supported by experience, that a person caught in a thunderstorm was sure to be safe under an elder tree because lightning would never strike the tree of which the Cross was made.

Another tradition said the Cross was made from an aspen tree, and this theory gave rise to two ideas about the constant motion of aspen leaves. One was that ever since the Crucifixion the aspen has trembled at the recollection of its awful guilt; the other was that because the aspen was the only tree that did not tremble on the actual day of the Crucifixion, it was doomed to quiver forever thereafter.

Still another notion was the Cross was made from the wood of the mistletoe. This legend said that up to that time the mistletoe had been a fine tree, tall and sturdy, but for its part in the Crucifixion it was punished by being reduced to the small, parasitic condition in which it is now seen.

St. Helena is said to have started home from Jerusalem with four nails. One of them she threw into the Adriatic sea when her ship was tossed by a storm. The storm abated instantly. The other three were taken to Rome to the Emperor Constantine.

"Furry Day"

MAY 8TH

The Archangel Michael, generalissimo of the armies of heaven, has had a habit of appearing on earth from time to time for many centuries. May 8th is kept—in the Roman and some other churches—in commemoration of the time when he appeared in 492 to a rich Italian cattleman to tell him where he wanted a church built in his honor. There are numerous other legends about early appearances of this glamorous member of the heavenly host.

One of the least-known visits of Michael to earth is also one of the most interesting. In the English county of Cornwall, there is a town called Helston, and it is said that the name comes from Hellstone, or stone of hell. The legend is that there once was in the yard of a tavern in this town a huge block of granite which in earlier times had been the stone that blocked off the entrance to hell. The story tells that Satan one night picked up the stone at hell's gate and started off with it on some nefarious errand known only to him. His journey took him across Cornwall, and there he had the bad luck to run into Michael. Naturally, a tremendous fight ensued, and Satan, when he saw he had the worst of it, fled, leaving the stone.

Every May 8th there is a big celebration among the townspeople of Helston. The big rock has long since been broken up into building stones and used for local construction, but the people still turn out on this day and rejoice together over the Archangel's great victory. They call the day "Furry Day," nobody knows quite why. The term may be a corruption of "fair day"—the day of the fair, or it may even be a version of Flora's Day, referring all the way back to the original May goddess of flowers, the Roman Flora.

He Couldn't Stand Success

MAY 9TH

Some people can't avoid having honors heaped upon them. Even if they try to hide, fame tracks them down. That is the way it was with St. Gregory of Nazianzus, whose exquisite writings have enriched Christian literature for sixteen centuries. St. Gregory, whose father was Bishop of Nazianzus in the fourth century, was shy, sensitive, and deeply spiritual. He was fitted for the life of the literary hermit and, more than anything else, that was exactly the life he wanted. Instead, he rose, resisting at every step of the way, to one of the highest positions in all Christendom. He did not want to be a priest, but his father forced him to become one. He did not want to be a bishop, but when the diocese of Sasima was created, his friend Basil, another bishop, cajoled, persuaded, and forced him to accept the new office. He stood the limelight as long as he could and then went back to Nazianzus, where he spent several years helping his aging father.

But the terrifying prominence at Sasima was nothing compared to what was coming. The church at Constantinople, riddled with heresy, somehow persuaded Gregory to come to them and win the people back to orthodoxy. Almost before he knew it they had made him Patriarch of Constantinople, which was one of the five loftiest positions in the whole Christian Church. The spectacular success only made him more miserable. In less than a year he retired again to his boyhood village of Nazianzus, where he died in obscurity in 391.

"Saint" Tammany's Day

May 12th

Ever since he appeared in their midst during the Crusades, St. George, patron saint of England, has had a reputation for looking after British soldiers. American troop-
ers during the Revolutionary War were more amused
than impressed by the idea that their foe boasted a patron
saint, and to poke fun at the redcoats, the revolutionists
adopted a patron of their own—a somewhat disreputable
old Indian chief named Tamanend who had lived earlier
in what is now eastern Pennsylvania.

They called him "Saint" Tammany, selected May 12th
as his festival, and celebrated the day with pompous and
ridiculous ceremonies. Tammany societies appeared in
many American towns. After the war, most of the societies
died out, but the one in New York City—Tammany Society No. 1—continued to flourish. The famous Aaron Burr
developed it into the strong political machine that is still
known as Tammany Hall. On May 12, 1789, the group
formally organized itself into the more dignified Columbian Society, but the name Tammany held on, and still
does to this day.

"Frost Saints"

May 11th, 12th, 13th

These three days are the festivals of St. Mammertus, St.
Pancras, and St. Servatus. In the wine-growing part of
France occasionally a severe cold spell strikes just at this
time of year, working great damage on the grapevines,
which by this time are far developed. Scientists say the
unseasonable frost is caused by air currents blowing off a
late breakup of polar ice in the north. But the peasants

have a different idea. They believe it is caused by the
anger of one of these three saints, whom they have somehow irritated. It is impossible to know in any given year
just which saint is the offended one, so they call them all
the "frost saints."

French peasants have been known, when the thermom-
eter took a plunge on these days, to retaliate by flogging
the statues and defacing the pictures of Mammertus, Pancras, and Servatus. In Germany, too, these saints are held
in dubious honor by people whose livelihood depends on
agriculture. There they call them "the three severe lords,"
and farmers and gardeners say that nothing is safe until
their days are past.

First Episcopalians

MAY 13TH

This day is the anniversary of the Episcopalians' beginning in America. On May 13, 1607, a party of 105 persons
landed at what is now Jamestown, Virginia, and began to
establish the first permanent colony on this continent.
With the group was Chaplain Robert Hunt, who therefore became the first resident Anglican clergyman in
America and set up the first church. The famous Captain
John Smith described this church in his memoirs. "We
did hang an awning," he wrote, "to three or four trees.
This was our church. Yet we had daily Common Prayer
morning and evening, every Sunday two sermons, and
every three months the Holy Communion."

Shrine of St. Dymphna

MAY 15TH

In all the world there is no other town like the Belgian
town of Gheel. On any day you happened to be there you

could find at least 2,500 mentally ill people in residence. Anyone you meet on the street may be a mental patient. These people are all visitors in Gheel, and they are welcomed there by the townsfolk and taken into their homes and cared for. This strange situation is the direct result of a seventh century tragedy. A lovely Irish princess named Dymphna, whose father was wildly insane, fled in panic from home in Ireland and arrived eventually in Gheel. The king, however, was not so badly deranged that he could not pursue and find her. Cleverly following her trail of Irish gold money, he caught up with her in the Belgian town and brutally murdered her with a battle-ax.

Since that horrible day Dymphna has been invoked against insanity. A shrine of St. Dymphna was soon erected at Gheel, which through the centuries has drawn thousands of pilgrims and produced many miraculous cures. One is tempted to suspect that one of the shrine's greatest miracles is the caring, unterrified attitude of Gheel's citizens toward the poor disturbed folk who come there. Perhaps this friendly acceptance is a big factor in the cures that are effected at St. Dymphna's shrine.

St. Brendan's Voyage

MAY 16TH

Perhaps if it hadn't been for St. Brendan you and I would not be Americans. That statement requires some explanation, for which it is necessary to go back to the sixth century, when St. Brendan with a crew of monks set out from Ireland on a voyage that lasted seven years. No one, including Brendan himself, knew quite where he had been when he returned, but the stories of this great voyage continued to grow and accumulate legendary additions for many centuries, one of which is that the voyagers actually discovered America and started other explorers thinking there was a land of wonders beyond the Atlantic waters.

The voyage seems to have been divided into two parts. First, they had come, in only forty days, to a group of islands full of singing birds. Then, they went on for the great part of the journey, and after years of sailing came to Paradise (America?). The Middle Ages found the story fascinating. Maps and charts of Brendan's voyage were widely circulated. When Portuguese sailors discovered the Azores, they took it for granted that they had found Brendan's islands, "the fortunate isles where the birds sing."

The maps and charts were especially interesting to one young man who thought he saw something far beyond the Azores. From the moment they came into his hands he pored over them, entranced, and he could not rest until he himself had tried a greater voyage. The young man's name was Christopher Columbus.

Swedes' Patron Saint
MAY 18TH

On May 18th Swedes in the United States, as well as in Sweden, will be remembering their great twelfth century king, Eric, whose virtues have made him their patron saint even though the church has never officially canonized him. Eric was ahead of his time. In an age when women were regarded as property—like horses and hunting dogs—Eric made laws that dignified their position and gave them legal rights. He took his Christianity seriously. When Finnish pirates menaced the coasts of Sweden, Eric did not attack them with arms. Rather he converted them, thus stopping the piracy and at the same time establishing a friendship between the two nations that has endured to the present day. St. Eric, the protector of Sweden, died in battle (against Denmark) on May 18, 1160.

The Pope Who Resigned
MAY 19TH

St. Peter, a hermit who became Pope Celestine V, was born inconspicuously in an Italian village in 1215, and remained inconspicuous in a cave on the side of Mt. Magella until he was seventy-nine years old. Then, suddenly, one day he found a cardinal, an archbishop, and two bishops prostrating themselves before him on the floor of his cave. The old hermit had been elected pope. What had happened was that two elections had deadlocked in an effort to find a pope who would be satisfactory to all factions that were tearing the church apart in those days. After a year of getting nowhere, the cardinals in desperation elected Peter, and at once they began to wonder whether or not they had done the right thing. Peter was amazed, the cardinals were dubious, but the people were overjoyed. As the new pope with the papal robes over his ragged sackcloth rode into nearby Naples, 200,000 wildly enthusiastic Italians lined the streets to welcome him.

Naturally the terrified old man was hopeless as a pope. He was too naive and inexperienced to head the complicated affairs of the Holy Roman empire, and too old to learn. He lasted just five months and could stand it no longer. In December, 1294, he abdicated and went happily back to his tattered hermit's robe. He died on May 19, 1296.

He Grabbed the Devil by the Nose
MAY 19TH

St. Dunstan, to whom May 19th is dedicated, is not a well-known or important saint, but there is an interesting

story about him. He is the patron saint of blacksmiths—
you will soon see why. A tenth century Englishman, St.
Dunstan was so good that he kept the devil worried.
Satan felt that the saint's activities had to be watched all
the time. One day, when Dunstan was working at the
monastery forge, he looked up and saw old Nick peering
at him through the window. Quick as a flash he pulled the
redhot tongs from the coals and grabbed the devil's nose
with them. The victim, howling and writhing, ran and
dipped his nose in nearby Tunbridge Wells to cool it off.
And that is why the water in Tunbridge Wells to this day
is sulphur water.

Conversion in Aldersgate Street
MAY 24TH

May 24th is a very special day for the world's twelve million Methodists. It is known as the day of the Aldersgate
Experience, and is the anniversary of John Wesley's conversion. John Wesley, at thirty-five, was a clergyman in
the Church of England. He had been in America (Georgia) preaching to the Indians, and had been a faithful
and energetic servant of God and church. But he desperately felt that his own religion was dry and barren. "I
have preached conversion to the Indians," he said, "but
who will convert me?" He was convinced that true Christianity was not in the formal rules and practices of the
church, but in each man's personal experience of the living Christ in his heart.

On the evening of May 24, 1783, Wesley went to a
house in Aldersgate Street, London, where a small group
of people had gathered to read Luther's preface to the
Epistle to the Romans. Wesley says in his account of the
evening that at about a quarter to nine, as Luther's de-
scription of the change that God works in man's heart

through faith in Christ was being read, "I felt my heart strangely warmed." From then until he died in 1791, at the age of eighty-eight, John Wesley never ceased to tell all men of the Christ Who had warmed his heart, and to lead them to the same experience. The fire that was kindled in Aldersgate Street that night rose in the next fifty-three years to a flame that made Wesley the dominant religious figure of the eighteenth century.

St. Augustine

MAY 26TH

St. Augustine was the first Archbishop of Canterbury. It is the position now occupied by the man who is official head of the thirty million Anglican Christians throughout the world. History does not show that Augustine had the usual qualifications of a saint. He left no record of great piety and he was not really a humble man. There is only one story of a miracle performed by him: he healed a blind man, but he did it to show he had more power than some other bishops. His place of honor in the church calendar comes mainly from the great importance of the organizational work he did.

There had been Christians in England before St. Augustine's time, but when the Angles and Saxons invaded the island in the fifth century, they drove everything before them, including a feeble, poorly-organized Christian Church. Bishops, priests, and people took refuge in the west, beyond the reach of the barbarian invaders. In 596, Pope Gregory the Great, having seen some of the handsome blonde Angles in Rome, felt that the Gospel must be carried to their land. He selected Augustine, a local priest, and sent him off on the mission, with a small group of monks accompanying him. Halfway along the journey the little band began to hear such hair-raising tales of the ferocious barbarians they were going to visit that they sent a messenger back to the Pope with a request that the whole thing be called off. The request was not granted.

When they arrived, however, it was not nearly so bad as they had expected. It turned out that the queen (Bertha, daughter of the King of Paris,) was a Christian, and that the king, Ethelbert, was completely friendly. Ethelbert gave them as headquarters an old church, which the British Christians had abandoned in their flight, and was himself soon baptized. Many of the people followed the king's example, and Augustine's mission flourished.

Besides bringing Christianity a second time to England, and organizing the English Church into much the same structure it still has after thirteen centuries, Augustine made other vital contributions to the life of England. He brought the remote little island into contact with the cultural influences of the civilized world, and into communication with other Christian nations. The disciplinary rules by which he and his clergy lived have been adopted by Roman Catholic religious orders, both men and women, known as Augustinians. (This Augustine is not to be confused with Augustine of Hippo, one of the all-time "greats" of the Church, who lived nearly two centuries earlier.)

The Angels Carved His Tombstone
MAY 27TH

May 27th is the day in honor of the Venerable Bede, an obscure but very important saint. There are no records of any miracles performed by Bede, nor are any stories of great piety told about him. This eighth century English monk was only a quiet scholar who was never outside the county in which he was born. The reason he is a saint is his great contribution to the Church in England. Without Bede's *Ecclesiastical History of the English Nation* the English Christians would have known nothing at all of their ancestors in the faith.

Why does the writing of such a book make a man worthy of sainthood? Because the unity of one age with all other ages, both past and future, is one of the most vital aspects of Christianity. It is important that today's Christians know where their heritage came from, and that they feel their connection with those from whom the inheritance comes. It keeps the family together across the centuries. God used Bede to see that this unity was kept in England.

Bede was not called "the venerable" during his lifetime; but a legend tells that after his death a stone-cutter who was carving his tombstone was unable to think of a fitting adjective for the inscription. He had carved, in Latin, "In this tomb are the bones of _____ Bede," leaving a blank space to be filled in when the right word should come to him. The next morning the stonecutter awoke to find that during the night angels had filled the blank space with the word *venerabilis*—"the venerable."

The Maid of Orleans

MAY 30TH

May 30th is St. Joan's Day everywhere in the world except in New Orleans, Louisiana. There they honor her on May 9th. This strange girl was one of the most important women in all recorded history. Before she was twenty, she had been burned at the stake as a heretic, but in her short lifetime she led and inspired an army to almost supernatural military achievement and restored most of France to its king.

Born about 1412—the exact date is not known—Joan was apparently like any other child until she was thirteen. Then she began to hear voices speaking to her, which she said were the voices of St. Michael, St. Catherine, and St. Margaret. In May, 1428, these saints told her to go to the Dauphin, or prince (Charles VII) and help him recover his kingdom from the English, who had invaded and taken over much of the country. Within fifteen months most of the land had been retaken. Joan herself was captured by the king's enemies, turned over to the English, burned on May 30, 1431. This is why May 30th is St. Joan's Day. It was, however, on May 8, 1429, that Joan saved the city of Orleans, for which our American New Orleans is named. That is why New Orleans keeps the following day, May 9th, as its own special St. Joan's Day.

Twenty-five years after St. Joan's death her trial was reviewed at the request of her mother and brothers, and the verdict reversed. It is hard to see what good this would do, though the family apparently considered it important to clear Joan's memory of a charge nobody had really believed in the first place.

This peasant girl, Joan La Pucelle, from the village of Domremy, must have been a very strange girl. Depending on your point of view, it would probably have been very easy to see her as either a saint or a witch, for it was obvious that some spiritual forces were at work within her. Perhaps it is only legend that there were some standing by when she was burned as a heretic and her ashes were thrown into the river Seine who said, "We are lost. We have burned a saint." But it is certain there were many who were not satisfied that justice had been done.

St. Joan's canonization came in 1920, five centuries

after her death. It would not be too far wrong to say that Joan is the best known of all the saints. More than 2,000 plays, biographies, and articles have been written about her.

The Double Purpose of Memorial Day

MAY 30TH

Memorial (or Decoration) Day does not appear in the calendar of any church. It is a patriotic holiday, but its religious overtones are so strong that it has a definite effect on sermons, hymns, and prayers in many churches on the preceding Sunday.

The day itself has undergone an evolution since its inception in 1869. In that year, Gen. John A. Logan, commander-in-chief of the Grand Army of the Republic, designated May 30th as a day on which the graves of Union soldiers were to be decorated. Over the years the honor was extended first to include the graves of Confederate soldiers and finally the graves of American soldiers of all our wars. In recent years Congress has further enlarged the scope of Memorial Day by proclaiming it as a day when the nation shall pray for peace.

Thus it now not only honors those who have died for their country, but also looks forward to the time when, by the help of God, there shall be no more war. The southern states that do not participate in the May 30th observance hold their Memorial Day on April 26th.

VARIABLE HOLIDAYS AND OBSERVANCES

Month of Mary

In the Roman Catholic Church the month of May has since the late eighteenth century been set apart as the

"Month of Mary," and special devotions have been offered
to the Blessed Virgin all through the month. The ultimate
background of this may be the early Church's clever
switch of people's devotion from the Roman Flora to the
Christian Mary, but the more immediate reason is that a
Father Latonia, a Jesuit in Rome two hundred years ago,
promoted the emphasis on the Blessed Virgin in order to
set up a discipline and counteract a looseness of living
among the students at the Jesuit College. The idea of May
as the Month of Mary has since spread throughout the
Roman Church.

National Family Week

All three major faiths in America (Protestant, Catholic
and Jewish) observe National Family week. The observances are of a simultaneous rather than a joint nature,
with each faith following its own customs and methods
in emphasizing the fact that a nation is only as strong as
the families that make it up, and that the strength of the
family is religion. Church members are encouraged to ex-
amine their own lives from the standpoint of their individual contributions to the religious quality of their
homes. Congregational groups will analyze and discuss
ways of correcting social conditions that have an adverse
influence on American family life. National Family Week
always begins on the first Sunday in May and leads up to
Mother's Day and the (Protestant) Festival of the Christian Home.

Mother's Day

Probably no observance ever spread faster than the one
proposed in 1907 by Anna Jarvis of Philadelphia, who
suggested a day in honor of mothers. By 1911, "Mother's

Day" was being celebrated not only in every state in the
United States, but also in Canada, Mexico, South America,
Africa, China, and Japan. In 1914 Congress authorized President Wilson to set aside the second Sunday in May as an
official holiday in honor of mothers and motherhood.
Thus, although most of the day's activities are centered
in church services, it is really a national rather than an
ecclesiastical holiday. The original proclamation stated
that the American flag should be displayed on Mother's
Day.

Mother's Day has gone through an interesting, though
sometimes disturbing, evolution. There was a time in the
history of this day when sentimental excesses turned
many people against it. Ministers read the morning lessons from their mothers' Bibles and preached sermons
that left hardly a dry eye in the congregation. Soloists
tore their listeners' heartstrings. The day developed a sac-
charine quality that was distasteful to many serious people, who felt that such sentimentality was actually a
reflection on the real dignity of motherhood. In most
Protestant churches, Mother's Day has become the Festival of the Christian Home, and the emphasis extended to
include not only honor to mothers but also a recognition
of their responsibilities in building family life on a proper
religious foundation. Another desentimentalizing influence
has been the fact that Mother's Day now follows National
Family Week.

Rural Life Sunday

The denominations belonging to the National Council of
Churches observe Rural Life Sunday, a day of emphasis
on the religious aspects of agricultural life. Since the Middle Ages, the Monday, Tuesday, and Wednesday before

Ascension Day have been known as Rogation Days (from *rogare*—to pray) and the Sunday preceding them is called Rogation Sunday. Originally these were days of general prayer, without any specific reference to farming, but because they occur at this time of year it was only natural that prayers for the newly planted crops came to have a special prominence in the people's petitions.

Some churches call this day "Soil Stewardship Sunday," which goes deeper into the matter than merely praying for good yields. To talk about stewardship of the soil reminds man of his responsibility to cherish and care for the land because it is owned by Almighty God and only loaned to man. The conservation of the soil is properly a religious question—a matter of a relationship between God, Who owns the earth, and man, who uses it.

In many denominations urban and rural ministers will exchange pulpits on this day, and in country churches farm organizations like the Grange and the 4-H clubs attend services in a body.

Ascension Day

According to the book of Acts, Jesus "showed himself alive after his passion by many infallible proofs, being seen of them (the Disciples) forty days." On the fortieth day He left them by ascending into the heavens—"a cloud received him out of their sight." For this reason the fortieth day after Easter (always a Thursday) has since very early times been observed as Ascension Day by the Christian Church, commemorating the Lord's departure from earth and His return to His heavenly source. Tradition says this day must always bring fair weather, for it is the day on which Jesus "kissed the clouds." Some churches call this day Holy Thursday, which causes some confusion because others, notably Roman Catholics, use the name Holy Thursday as referring to the Thursday before Easter.

The site of the Ascension (see Acts, chapter 1, verses 1-12) has always been assumed to have been Mount Olivet, just outside Jerusalem. An ancient legend told that on the stone of this hill there were plainly visible the footprints Jesus made on the rock as He left the earth. Early Christians constantly made pilgrimages to the spot to kiss these sacred marks and even the reliable Jewish historian Josephus mentions these footprints as if they and their miraculous presence were common knowledge. He says that all the passing and repassing of the Roman armies failed to wear them away.

The Knights Templar, whose ritual involves the key events in the life of Jesus, make a special point of attending church services in a group on the Sunday following Ascension Day.

Folk-traditions have grown around this holiday. One interesting old Ascension Day ceremony, still surviving in some remote parts of England, was the custom of "well-dressing." Frames and trellises were erected around the wells and decorated elaborately with flowers. After a morning service in the church, priest and congregation would walk in formal procession, singing psalms and hymns and visiting every well in the countryside. This was a Christian adaptation of an even more ancient Roman celebration called Fontanalia, an annual flower festival at this time of year honoring the spirits that were thought to be in charge of springs, streams, and fountains. It is just one more of the many examples of the Church's fine sense of public relations back in the early days of Christianity. The pagans loved their festivals, and the Church had the wisdom to keep the traditional dates but at the same time to put a new and Christian meaning into them.

Armed Forces Day

Armed Forces Day, proclaimed by the President each year, is always the second Saturday in May. The primary purpose of the day is to pay tribute to persons serving in the nation's Army, Navy, and Air Force. Secondly, it aims at promoting the unification of the three branches of the service. Many churches throughout the country observe the next day as Armed Forces Sunday. The reason for the churches' concern with Armed Forces Day is that the military leaders of the country have requested it. Recognizing the place of religion in American life, the sponsors of Armed Forces Day each year ask the Chaplain's Board to prepare a special prayer to be used by all chaplains on this occasion. Chaplains are also asked to focus the attention of their men on the spiritual aspects of the day.

Since all American churches have both clergy (chaplains) and lay members in the armed forces, it is natural that parishes back home would want to join in giving religious meaning to the day and to make use of the special prayer. No particular ceremony or type of service is prescribed. Each church determines its own way of emphasizing the close connection between church and nation in American life.

The Counting of the Omer

In the Jewish calendar there is a day called *Lag B'Omer,* which is literally "33 omer." A day with such a name needs some explaining and this is the explanation: between Passover and the next Jewish festival (Shabuoth) there are fifty days. In the book of Leviticus, chapter 23, verses 10 to 16, the people were commanded by Jehovah to make an offering of a sheaf of barley on each of these fifty days. A sheaf is the same as an omer. So, on each of the days an omer was offered, the days were counted, and every evening, after the service, the number of the day was solemnly announced. This ceremony, in time, came to be known as "the counting of the omer."

Passover was the time of the barley harvest and Shabuoth was the time of the wheat harvest. You would think that the interim period would have been a time of joy and merrymaking as harvest time has always been among primitive peoples. Remember, this goes way back into Jewish history, to an era when the Jews were greatly influenced by pagan neighbors on all sides. But it did not work out that way. Instead of being happy during this period, the Jews—their scholars do not know why—decided they should be in a state of semi-mourning. So without any really substantial explanation there are no feasts, no joyous events, no marriages, and among the especially devout not even any haircuts, all through the fifty days—except on Lag B'Omer! On that day, for some reason that is lost in antiquity there is a break in the season and a person may take time out.

Actually, Jewish scholars believe, the 33rd day of this period is connected with ancient rites that were going on among the pagans long before the Jews really got themselves separated from the heathen life around them in the "Promised Land." Somewhere back in pagan history, there was an ancient festival of the forest at this season—and somehow it got taken into the calendar of the primitive agricultural Jews just settling into a new land.

Scholars have tried to give this midharvest day some

Jewish significance by relating it to actual events in Jewish history. One story is that a plague which had broken out among the pupils of the famous Rabbi Akiba's school suddenly and miraculously stopped on this day. This alone would have been enough to make it a special day among students.

Another story deals with another rabbi, Simeon ben Yohai—whose birth and death are both said to have occurred on Lag B'Omer. In the times when the Romans were occupying the land of the Jews, the emperor issued an order forbidding the teaching of the Jewish religion. Rabbi ben Yohai defied the order and had to flee for his life. For twelve years he lived in a cave in the mountains of Galilee.

His students continued to visit him in his mountain hideout, and to avoid arousing the suspicion of any Roman soldiers who might be lurking about, they always carried bows and arrows to give the impression that they were only going hunting. The bow and arrow, therefore, have come to be the symbol of this holiday. In many countries Jewish children and their teachers go to the woods for picnics and for games, especially games in which the bow and arrow are used.

CHAPTER VI

June

St. Elmo's Fire
JUNE 2ND

Sometimes on stormy nights at sea, sailors will see a pale brush-like spray of electricity at the tip of the mast. Naturally, this phenomenon was known long before the time of any Christian saint. The Greeks had a word for it—three words, in fact. They called it Helena if it appeared as a single jet, or Castor and Pollux when it was double. In the Middle Ages sailors had a superstition that these fires were the souls of the departed, rising in brilliance and glory. And since St. Elmo was at the time the most popular of sailors' patrons, it was thought that the souls were achieving this happy condition through his intercession. So they called the electrical display "St. Elmo's Fire."

There is, however, some confusion from this point on.

This day that is called St. Elmo's Day is really St. Erasmus' Day, in honor of a third century Italian bishop who suffered martyrdom on June 2, 304. He was a patron saint of sailors and was especially popular just at the time St. Elmo came along. Elmo was a thirteenth century Dominican who had spent much of his life working among the sailor-folk along the Spanish coast. It was this second friend of theirs to whom the sailors referred when they talked about St. Elmo's fire. Over the centuries he and the earlier patron, Erasmus, became so coupled together in the sailors' minds that eventually no distinction was made between them, even as to name.

The Tomb of Eve

JUNE 3RD

The Arabs say that Eve is buried in the graveyard of the temple in the city of Jiddah which is the seaport for Mecca. No burials have been made here during the last 1,000 years. Tradition there says that Eve was more than 200 feet tall. Her tomb is a shrine, to which pilgrimages are made every seven years by certain tribes of Arabs known as Ishmaelites.

June 3rd, according to Arab legend, is the anniversary of the murder of Eve's son Abel, by her other son Cain. The Arabs say that the doors of the temple at Jiddah cannot be kept closed on this night. No matter how securely they are fastened they continually fly open, and wails of anguish come out—obviously from a re-enactment of the world's oldest crime.

Ireland's Third Saint

JUNE 9TH

Everyone knows St. Patrick is the patron saint of Ireland, and many people know he shares that position with St. Bridget. But hardly anyone realizes Ireland has three patron saints. The third is St. Columba (or Columcille) whose memory is honored today. And a very great man he was—every bit as gifted and impressive as St. Patrick, with his tremendous stature, his booming voice that could be heard a mile off, and his depth of piety and learning.

Columba was an Irishman born and bred, which Patrick was not. He was born in Dongela in 521, about sixty years after Patrick had died. His family, on both sides, was of royal blood. This is not to disparage St. Patrick, but rather to say it is strange he should so greatly have overshadowed as important an Irishman as Columba.

Columba, a priest at twenty-four, spent fifteen years traveling up and down Ireland organizing churches, schools, and monasteries just as his famous predecessor had done. Then, suddenly, with twelve companions—all relatives of his—he exiled himself from his beloved country and went to the rocky island of Iona, off the coast of Scotland, where he set up a monastic community. He landed on Iona on the eve of the festival of Pentecost.

The reason for this self-imposed exile is not really known, but there is a persistent legend about it. The story is that Columba had a feeling of guilt over his part in starting a battle in which three thousand men were killed and, to settle his conscience, he resolved to go to another country and win at least three thousand souls for Christ. The accuracy of the legend cannot be verified but there

is no doubt that Columba greatly exceeded his goal of
three thousand converts.

There are many stories of how the robin got his red
breast, but one of the loveliest comes from the lore connected with St. Columba. "Have you a song, redbreast?"
the good man said to a robin which had alighted on his
window sill, and the robin sang to him of how on the
day of the Crucifixion he had been in his nest near the
Cross of Calvary. The Lord looked at him with eyes so
full of pain and sorrow that the robin flew to Him and
pulled out the thorns piercing His forehead. In this act of
mercy the bird's breast was covered with the precious
blood, and that is how the robin got his red breast.

St. Barnabas

JUNE 11TH

All that is known about St. Barnabas is what can be read
in the Acts and some of St. Paul's Epistles, but it is
enough to place him as one of the foremost figures in the
early Church. He is said to have been one of the "Seventy" the Lord sent out (Luke, chapter 10, verse 1) on
the first practice run for itinerant Christian preachers.
Although he is not named in any list of the Twelve Apostles, verse 14, chapter 14, of the Acts refers to him as an
apostle. Some people believe he was also the writer of the
Epistle to the Hebrews.

Barnabas' real name was Joseph, but his friends in the
Church renamed him. Several translations are offered for
the name Barnabas. The King James version makes it
"son of consolation;" others have thought "son of encouragement" more accurate; but it probably meant "son of
prophecy." From this probability has come the tradition
that St. Barnabas had the gift of prophecy.

One very important thing this saint did was to vouch for St. Paul when that notorious persecutor of Christianity showed up in Jerusalem after his conversion. The last the Jerusalem Christians had heard of him he had been "breathing out threatenings and slaughter" against them, and they were in no mood to welcome him into the fold. See Acts, chapter 9, verse 27. Barnabas reassured them and Paul was accepted, to the great enrichment of Christian history.

As a member of the economic community created by the early Church, Barnabas conformed to the rules by selling his land and turning the money over to the apostles. His contribution must have been quite a sizeable one, for he is the only contributor mentioned by name. See Acts, chapter 4, verses 36 and 37.)

It was with Barnabas that Paul began his famous missionary journeys into the Gentile world. They must have been an impressive team. At the town of Lystra Paul healed a lame man, and the people were convinced that these missionaries were gods. Paul, they were sure, was Hermes (Mercury) and Barnabas, who was probably taller and more dignified, they thought was Zeus (Jupiter). It was all the two could do to keep the townspeople from sacrificing a bull to them. Unfortunately Paul and Barnabas had a falling-out, as even saints will do, and went their separate ways. Legend says Barnabas was finally stoned to death by the Jews on his native island of Cyprus.

St. Anthony of Padua
JUNE 13TH

St. Anthony of Padua, who lived in the thirteenth century, was the greatest miracle-worker of his time. For reasons that are no longer clear, he became and remains the patron saint of all careless people, especially those who lose things—a category that takes in almost the entire human race. In European countries when anything goes astray—an article, an animal, or a child—prayers are raised to St. Anthony. In our own country many a good Catholic is grateful to him for the recovery of things lost or carelessly misplaced.

He is also the patron of animals. In the days before automobiles everyone in Rome from Pope to peasants sent his horses and mules to St. Anthony's Church on June 13th to be blessed.

Anthony was a friend and companion of the great Francis of Assisi, and legend indicates that the two had much in common. Everyone knows the famous story of how St. Francis preached to the birds. There is a similar one about how St. Anthony, who, when the people refused to hear him, preached to the fish, which gathered around with their heads out of the water and listened attentively. So great was Anthony's reputation for holiness and miraculous power that he was elevated to sainthood only a year after his death. Pope Gregory IX canonized him in 1262.

St. Vitus

JUNE 15TH

Everyone has heard about St. Vitus, because of the disease which bears his name, but scarcely anything is known about the saint himself. He is said to have been put to death on June 15, 303, for being a Christian. Tradition indicates that he was very young at the time, for two others who died with him were Modestus, his tutor, and Crescentia, his governess.

There are various explanations of how his name came to be associated with the disease properly known as chorea. One story is that there was a shrine of St. Vitus in Germany and that people believed that anyone who danced before this shrine on St. Vitus' Day would be assured of good health for the coming year. Some dancers danced with such tremendous enthusiasm that their jerky hysterical movements resembled those of patients suffering from chorea. St. Vitus is, of course, the patron of all who have chorea or epilepsy. He is also invoked against rabies and sleeping sickness.

Dogs Named for Saint
JUNE 15TH

St. Bernard of Menthon is heard of nowadays mainly because of the big dogs that bear his name. Everyone knows about the immense, kind-faced animals that go out with little kegs of rum fastened to their collars and rescue travelers lost in the Alpine snows. The headquarters from which these dogs operate are two mountain hospices that were founded by Bernard at two particularly hazardous passes, which have come to be called Great St. Bernard pass and Little St. Bernard pass. Both passes, more than 7,000 feet above sea level, are choked with snow the year round.

The hospices were really a sort of afterthought or by-product of the saint's original project. He was disturbed about the ignorance and paganism of the people who lived in the rough mountain villages, and he gave up wealth, position, and the prospect of marriage to devote his life to the instruction and conversion of these people. Soon familiarity with the country showed him that these two passes were death traps for hundreds of travelers, and he resolved to do something about it. He built the

two hospices, about the year 962, and turned them over
to the Augustinian monks. Now, as then, about forty
monks from these two houses of mercy go out with their
big trained dogs to look for wayfarers lost in the heavy
mountain storms. If they find a traveler alive, they bring
him in and give him food and shelter until the storm is
over and he is ready to continue his journey. The dead
are given decent burial.

St. Botolph

JUNE 17TH

Hardly anyone would suspect that the Puritan fathers
who founded the city of Boston, Massachusetts, named
it after a saint. Probably they didn't even know it themselves, for they were thinking of the town of Boston in
Lincolnshire, England. But that ancient town was named
for St. Botolph. Boston is actually "Botolph's Town."

Back in the seventh century there were two British
brothers, Adolph and Botolph, who became so interested
in what little they had heard of Christianity that they
went to Gaul (France) to find out more about it. The
instructions they received in Gaul changed them from
interested inquirers into delicated workers. Adolph became a bishop and a great teacher of the faith. Botolph
went back to England and asked the king for land on
which to build a monastery. The king granted the request and Botolph built his monastery at the spot where
the town of Boston still stands.

Little is known about the good saint himself. It is somewhat ironical that his memory should have been, even
unintentionally, perpetuated in the name of a great American city established by men whose religion fanatically
abhorred the very idea of saints.

The Signing of the Magna Charta

JUNE 19TH

June 19th is the anniversary of the signing of the Magna Charta (great charter) at Runnymede, England in 1215. Although it does not appear in the official calendar of any church, it is a day of great religious significance throughout the English-speaking world. It was on this occasion that the English nobility forced the tyrannical King John I to sign a document giving them—not everybody, just noblemen—forty-eight new personal rights and liberties; chief of which was freedom of worship. The opening words of the Magna Charta were "The Church of England shall be free."

To Americans, long accustomed to liberty, the mere loosening of a few restrictions for a small group of dukes and earls may not appear to be much of a step toward freedom. The point is that it was *a step*—perhaps it might even be considered the first one. The religious meaning here was that the basic Christian idea of the value of the individual human being began at Runnymede to find at least some meager, limited expression in the structure of government.

New Church Day

JUNE 19TH

Many Christians look forward to the Second Coming of the Lord, but to one group the Second Coming has already happened. June 19th, according to the Swedenborgians, is the anniversary of that event. Followers of the eighteenth century Swedish mystic Emanuel Swedenborg believed that in the year 1757 there was a great judgment in the spiritual world, with the result that the evil

spirits were separated from the good, and a new Heaven
was set up. Then, because it was necessary that new doctrines be preached in the new Heaven, Jesus called His
Apostles together and put them to work again just as He
had put them to work on earth seventeen centuries earlier. And it was on June 19th and 20th that this reassembling and recommissioning took place.

Without being conscious of the importance of the date,
a number of Swedenborg's disciples met on June 19, 1770
and organized themselves into the Church of the New
Jerusalem, which soon came to be called, as it is now,
simply "The New Church." It was some years before they
began to realize that they were always, apparently quite
by chance, holding their really important meetings on the
19th of June. Then they perceived the significance of this
day, and named it New Church Day.

St. Alban

JUNE 22ND

St. Alban's life as a Christian was a short one, but he was
the first, and perhaps the best known, of all English
saints and martyrs, and his name is still honored in England. Alban was living quietly as a genial pagan in the
town of Verulam in 304, when a Christian priest, hotly
pursued by Roman persecutors, begged for refuge in his
house. Alban took him in, and it was not long before the
priest had converted him and baptized him. This must
have happened in a matter of only a few days, or even
hours, for the Romans had not yet given up the chase.
Alban changed clothes with his guest and went out and
gave himself up as the priest. Naturally, the deception
was quickly discovered, whereupon the new Christian
confessed his faith and was himself sentenced to death.

What happened to the priest is long forgotten, but several legends are told about Alban's last hours. In the first place, they had to take him across a river to reach the place where he was to be beheaded. But the bridge was too small for the large crowd that had gathered to watch the execution. Not wishing to see the populace denied their fun, Alban said a prayer and caused the waters to divide, so that all went across dry-shod. At the place of execution the martyr asked for a drink of water, and a spring gushed forth from the ground in front of him. The story tells, too, that the soldier who was appointed to kill Alban refused to carry out the order, and was beheaded along with the saint.

A shrine was erected almost immediately, and many miraculous cures were attributed to it. The fame of the shrine soon overshadowed any reputation the town may have had, and Verulam became known as St. Alban's, which is its name to this day. There was nothing in the life of St. Alban that would have made him prominent for sixteen centuries. His real importance is in the fact that he was England's first martyr.

St. Paulinus

June 22nd

Many towns have patron saints and many of them pay elaborate homage to their patrons, but only St. Paulinus has anything like "The Lilies of Nola," an elaborate spectacle in his little Italian town of Nola. Many years ago this ceremony was, although lovely and colorful, quite a simple one. The people carried lilies in processions through the streets. That was all there was to it. But somewhere along the way, somebody began to make changes and embellishments—until today the "lilies" are great structures eighty or ninety feet high, weighing as much as three tons. Still called lilies, they are much like parade floats, some even providing a deck to accommodate a band of trumpeters.

St. Paulinus himself is almost lost in all these goings-on. And the chances are he would not mind. He was a quiet, poetic sort of person back in the fourth century, attractive, genteel, and greatly beloved, but not at all given to display. Hardly any facts are known about him. It is not unlikely that he would have been forgotten if Nola had not developed the lavish celebration in his honor.

St. John the Baptist
JUNE 24TH

Here is a day that tried to replace an old pagan festival and almost got lost in the process. St. John the Baptist's Day was placed on June 24th when Christmas was set as December 25th, because according to the New Testament (St. Luke, chapter 1, verse 36) John was just six months older than Jesus. But if it was to be exactly six months, why didn't they pick June 25th? Because the 25th would never have had a chance. Midsummer's Eve, the great pagan festival of the summer solstice, had for centuries been celebrated on June 24th, and the Christians' best strategy was to try to take this date over and put a new meaning into it. Any saint's day placed on the day following a day and night of wild heathen revelry would have been dominated right out of existence before it even got started.

Even with their realistic approach the Christians were not too successful in making the substitution. One example will show how Midsummer's Eve had more influence on the saint's day than the saint's day had on it:

The pagans, in their worship of the sun, had developed many of their superstitious Midsummer's practices around the building of bonfires, with the bonfires, of course, symbolizing the sun. Dancing around these fires, leaping through them, or saving their ashes were considered charms against disease and witchcraft. There was no chance of doing away with the bonfires, so the Church reinterpreted them. The Lord had once called John the Baptist "a burning and shining light," (St. John, chapter 5, verse 35) and the Church insisted that this was the real symbolism of the fires. But all that happened was that St. John the Baptist was let in on the superstitions, and began to be invoked along with the bonfires against the misfortunes the fires were supposed to prevent. June 24th, incidentally, celebrates St. John's birth rather than, as is usual with saints' days, the anniversary of his death.

John the Baptist was never actually a Christian and therefore cannot be classified as a Christian martyr. He did not die for his faith in Christ. Nevertheless, as the forerunner of Jesus he has always occupied a very high place in Christianity. In the Eastern Church he is second only to the Blessed Virgin Mary.

John is the patron saint of missionaries because he was sent to prepare the way of the Lord. To his own followers, however, he was much more than simply the precursor of some greater figure. He was to them the prophet of the Messianic age, with his own disciples, his own religious groups, and his own traditions and legends.

Episcopalians' Cross

JUNE 24TH

In San Francisco there is a special observance on June 24th, especially among Episcopalians. It was on June 24,

1579 that the Reverend Francis Fletcher, Sir Francis
Drake's chaplain, read the first English service ever heard
on this continent, and of course he read it from the
Church of England prayer book, which is substantially
the same as the *Book of Common Prayer* used by Episcopalians today. A granite cross, called the Prayer Book
Cross marks the spot where this service was held. Many
California churchmen make pilgrimages to this cross each
year.

Pontius Pilate

JUNE 25TH

June 25th is St. Pontius Pilate's Day—in the Coptic
(Egyptian) and Abyssinian Churches. And the idea of
Pilate as a saint does make a weird kind of sense. It is
based on the notion that he was only doing his part in
the great drama of salvation, which God had planned
from eternity. Someone had to take this role, and Pilate
was appointed. Not many Christians would look at it this
way, but a few do.

A further reason for making Pilate a saint is the legend
that he became a Christian and was martyred for the
faith. No one actually knows what happened to him. The
last authentic information is that he was called back to
Rome about six years after the Crucifixion. From there on,
legend takes over. It is worth noting that none of the
Gospel writers is at all severe on Pilate in the New Testament accounts of the trial. Where we might well expect
bitterness toward the man who sentenced the Lord to
death, we find instead a lenient and at times almost sympathetic portrayal of his character. It is not entirely beyond the actual possibilities to believe that Pilate might

have ended as a follower of the Man he condemned to
the cross.

A Mormon Anniversary

JUNE 27TH

June 27th is an anniversary—and not a happy one—among
the Mormons. It was on June 27, 1845, that the founder
and leader of Mormonism, Joseph Smith, and his brother,
Hyrum, were killed by an angry mob at Carthage, Illinois. Smith and his followers had settled in the nearby
village of Commerce City six years before, renaming it
Nauvoo, which, they said, was a Hebrew word meaning
"beautiful place." Nauvoo was to have been to Mormonism what Salt Lake City finally became. By 1844 headquarters had been established there, a temple had been
built, and a university planned. But the Mormons had
trouble with their "Gentile" neighbors and it all came to
a climax on June 27, 1845 with the assassination of the
Smith brothers.

The immediate result of their leader's death was that
the Mormons split up in disagreement over who should
be his successor. One faction favored Smith's son; another,
and larger, preferred a man, prominent in the church, by
the name of Brigham Young. All agreed, however, that it
was necessary to leave Illinois. Smith's group moved to
Independence, Missouri, where their descendants still
maintain their church headquarters, under the name of
The Reorganized Church of Jesus Christ of Latter Day
Saints. Young's adherents went to the territory of Utah,
where they have flourished numerically and financially
ever since. Eighty-five per cent of all Mormons belong to
this part of the church.

One strange by-product of the death of Smith was the

establishment of the only monarchy that ever existed within the boundaries of the United States. After Smith's death, during the intense competition for the position of leadership, one of the elders of the church, a dynamic, red-bearded man named James Jesse Strang, produced a letter which he said had been written by Smith, expressing the wish that Strang should succeed him. The letter was not considered genuine, and Strang's ambitions were thwarted.

But only temporarily. In anger, he gathered a following of his own and left Nauvoo, going to Beaver Island, an island at the northern end of Lake Michigan. Here he set up a colony based on the doctrines and principles of Mormonism. The colony grew and prospered under Strang's genius, and in 1850 he allowed himself to be crowned king of Beaver Island. The King Strang hotel, in the present Beaver Island summer resort, still bears witness to the fact that a kingdom once existed here.

Heavenly Gate-Keeper
JUNE 29TH

June 29th is St. Peter and St. Paul's Day because of the tradition that both saints were martyred on the same day —at Rome, in the year 64, or perhaps 65. But St. Peter gets most of the attention. In the Anglican calendar St. Paul has dropped entirely out of the picture, and the day is simply St. Peter's Day. St. Peter is known in folk-lore, and in many a funny story, as the keeper of the gates of heaven. There is scriptural ground for this. In St. Matthew's Gospel, chapter 16, verse 19, the Lord said to Peter "and I will give you the keys of the kingdom of heaven." It is hardly likely that Jesus was assigning to Peter the task of examining every applicant for admission, but that is the way a literal-minded world has interpreted the gift of the keys.

No one has more patron saints than fishermen do, and St. Peter is one of these. There are two good reasons for this. One is that Peter himself earned his living by fishing. The other is that Jesus said to him (and to his brother, Andrew), "follow me and I will make you fishers of men." Matthew, chapter 4, verse 19.

It was on June 29th, nearly nineteen centuries ago, that the famous *Quo Vadis?* incident happened. According to the legend, St. Peter, who had been condemned to death, had escaped from prison and was hurrying along a road outside Rome, putting as much distance as possible between himself and those who were determined to kill him. To his great surprise he met the Lord, carrying a heavy cross. *"Domine!"* said St. Peter, who by this time apparently spoke Latin, *"Quo Vadis?"* (Where are you going?) And Jesus replied "To Rome to be crucified again in thy stead." Whereupon Peter, desperately ashamed, returned to the city to face his martyrdom. The story also says that he asked to be crucified head downward, as a symbol of his unworthiness to suffer the same death as his Lord. Roman Catholics and Lutherans also commemorate the death of St. Paul on June 29th.

VARIABLE HOLIDAYS AND OBSERVANCES

Feast of Corpus Christi

In the Roman Catholic Church, and in parts of certain other churches, the Thursday after Trinity Sunday is the Feast of Corpus Christi (Body of Christ). This colorful festival honors the sacrament of the Mass (also called Eucharist, Holy Communion, and Lord's Supper) in which the Body of the Lord is received by man. It is always on a Thursday because Jesus instituted this sacrament on the Thursday of Holy Week, the day before His crucifixion.

Both the day and its name are the direct result of the doctrine of transubstantiation, which was rejected by Luther and most other non-Roman Christians. This doctrine states that the consecrated bread in the Mass becomes in substance the Body of the Lord. Although widely believed for many centuries the doctrine was not made official until 1215. Immediately after the official pronouncement people began to feel that it should be the occasion of a great new holy day.

It is said that a Belgian nun named Juliana, soon after 1215, had a vision in which she saw the moon, brilliant except for one dark spot, and was told that the dark spot referred to the Church's lack of a festival in honor of transubstantiation. She went at once to her bishop and persuaded him to authorize such a festival, for which she had written a service. By 1264 the day was universally observed throughout the Western Church.

In all Catholic countries Corpus Christi customs are—and have been since the beginning—some of the most beautiful of the whole year. The feature of the day is the great procession through the streets, in which the sacred Host (consecrated bread) is carried and the path ahead is strewn with flowers.

Children's Day

Most American holidays, except political ones, have their roots in the Old Country, and so it is with Children's Day, which is observed by many Protestant churches. In parts of Europe, May Day, that is May 1st, was confirmation day for Roman Catholic and Lutheran children. One feature of the day was that the youngsters carried to church bouquets of the wildflowers that were in season at that time of year.

As an American observance, Children's Day began in June 1856, at the Universalist Church in Chelsea, Massachusetts. June was a much better time for flowers than May in the northerly Massachusetts climate. Roses were in bloom then in Chelsea, and as the children's special Sunday became an annual event, it was at first known as Rose Sunday. By 1868 the Methodist Church had officially set the second Sunday in June as Children's Day on a national basis. Other denominations soon followed. The day is now part of the calendar of the National Council of Churches.

Father's Day

Father's Day, which began in 1909, has achieved an importance almost equal to that of Mother's Day. There is now a National Father's Day Committee, with headquarters in New York City, which sponsors the day and tries to put into it a deeper meaning than a mere annual pat on the back for Dad. For example, the Committee adopts a theme of some spiritual depth each year and promotes this theme throughout the month of June.

Father's Day is not an official church day, any more than Mother's Day is. But one great evidence of the essentially religious character of our country is the fact that American family celebrations seem quite naturally to lead the family to church. Many a happy Dad sits in church on Father's Day morning with Mother and the youngsters, bursting with pride and trying to appear casual about it.

The Fast of the 17th of Tammuz

The fast of the 17th of Tammuz is in sad commemoration of the day the Roman army broke through the wall of Jerusalem, in the year 70, and the doom of the city and the Temple was sealed. It was the beginning of the end. It had happened once before, six-and-a-half centuries earlier, when Babylon conquered Israel, destroyed the Temple, and carried almost all the population off into slavery, and this day's mourning includes the sorrow of that earlier occasion. But the second destruction was a greater calamity than the first, for the first had a happy ending. After seventy years the people returned and re-built the Temple and this second edifice had lasted through all the years. This time the destruction and the dispersion of the people had a tragic finality about it. The Jews were scattered over the face of the world and they are still scattered.

The fast of the 17th of Tammuz (*Tammuz* is the name of a month) is, however, one of the four fasts which Zechariah (chapter 8, verse 19) said will someday be turned into days of joy and festivity. Jews have faith that this day will not always be a day of gloom.

Also commemorated on this day is another tragic event in Jewish history: the occasion recorded in Exodus, chapter 32, verse 19, when Moses, coming down from Mt. Sinai carrying the stone tablets on which the Law was engraved, found the Israelites worshipping a golden calf, and in his rage and indignation smashed the sacred stones to bits.

Feast of the Harvest

On the Sixth of Sivan, fifty days after Passover, comes *Shabuoth*, the Feast of Weeks. It is the festival that ends the seven weeks of the grain harvest, and was originally named the Feast of the Harvest. The harvesting of grain began in the spring with the reaping of the barley crop and ended with the cutting of the wheat. Nothing could have been more natural to a nation of farmers than a time of rejoicing when the hard labor of this season was over, and nothing could have been more natural to a religious people than the offering of a sacrifice and prayers of thanksgiving. The agricultural tone of the festival dates it in Jewish history: it must have begun after the Jews settled in the Promised Land and became tillers of the soil.

Of course Shabuoth could not remain a farmer's festival after the Jews lost their homeland and stopped being farmers. So, instead of dying out, it adjusted to the changing situation. It took on a new historical significance and a new spiritual content. It came to be considered the anniversary of the time when God first entered into His covenant with man and gave the Law—the Ten Commandments—to Moses. And that is the chief meaning of Shabuoth today—an annual commemoration of the day the Jews first received the Law, their greatest spiritual treasure. Its message is about the Jews' distinctive, God-given appointment. It holds before them the fact that they are a people set apart for a spiritual purpose. It reminds them that the Law, though entrusted to them, is for the whole world, and that it is their responsibility to see that the world receives it.

It is appropriate that Shabuoth has become in Conservative and Reformed synagogues the traditional time for confirmation. In confirmation the Jewish child is dedicated to Israel's great spiritual mission.

Pentecost, the alternate name of this festival, was given to it by Greek-speaking Jews. It means in Greek, "fiftieth,"

and refers to the fact that Shabuoth falls on the fiftieth
day after Passover.

The Birthday of the Church

It was on the Jewish feast of Pentecost, the fiftieth day
after Passover, that the Christian Church began. Most
Christian bodies still call the day by its ancient Jewish
name, although Anglicans (Episcopalians) have their
own name for it: Whitsunday. What happened on this
day is recorded by St. Luke in the second chapter of the
book of Acts. The Holy Spirit came upon the Apostles
with fire and the sound of "a mighty rushing wind," and
they immediately hurried to the Temple and began to
preach about the risen Christ. Three thousand persons
clamored for baptism, and the Christian Church had become a reality. This was the birthday of organized Christianity.

St. Luke, throughout the rest of the Acts, makes this
day the key to the whole story of how the Gospel spread
across the world. And it was indeed the turning point, for
whatever we may mean by "the coming of the Holy
Ghost" (and there are various interpretations) there can
be no doubt that it changed the Apostles from a frightened little group, huddled in an upstairs room in Jerusalem, into a vigorous company who recklessly charged
out at the risk of their lives and carried the Christian
message boldly—even defiantly—to all within earshot.

There is a significance, often overlooked, in the fact
that this new beginning took place on the day of Pentecost, for according to tradition it was also on this day,
centuries earlier, that the Jewish religious community had
its formal foundation. This was the day on which Moses,
standing on the smoky top of the volcano, Mt. Sinai, had

received the Law, and Israel had become a nation set apart to carry out a divine mission. The meaning here was that the Old Covenant, given in the wind and fire of the volcanic mountain top, was now superseded by a New Covenant, given amidst the same awe-inspiring display of flame and the wind's ghostly invisible power. Here, too, was the fulfillment of the Baptist's prediction, recorded in Luke, chapter 3, verse 16, that the One who would come after John would baptize with the Holy Ghost and with fire.

From a purely practical standpoint, this was an excellent time to get wide circulation for anything one might have to say in Jerusalem. The city was full of pilgrims who were in town for the Pentecost holiday. Any new idea presented to them would be sure to spread with them as they returned to their home territories. The British name for this day, Whit or White Sunday, comes from the white garments that were worn on Pentecost by the newly baptized. The day before Easter was traditionally the time for many new Christians arrayed in white robes to be baptized, but in England's northern climate it was much too cold for such a ceremony at Easter. They therefore waited until the weather was milder and held their baptismal services on Pentecost.

Pinkster Day

The Greek word *Pentecost* took some rather strange forms when it reached Northern Europe as part of the Christian calendar. In Germany it became *Pingsten,* which is far enough from the original, but the Dutch went even further. To them it was *Pinkster.* So it was that in early New York, populated by Dutch settlers, the feast of the beginning of the Christian Church was Pinkster Day. And to the Dutch settlers it was a gay time, with the day itself and several days thereafter being devoted to an exchange of neighborly visits, for which everyone rode in flowerdecked buggies or wagons. In the pioneer communities there were games and booths and general festivities beginning on Monday and lasting throughout the week. Albany was a sort of special center of this celebration. The part of the city now called Capitol Hill was once known as Pinkster Hill, because it was here that the carnival took place. By some strange, unexplained development it became the custom for the Negro population to take over the merriment on Tuesday, and because the Negroes at that point in our country's history were still very close to their African origin, the whole occasion soon deteriorated into almost a jungle orgy, with native drums and dances that struck terror in Dutch hearts. By 1811 Pinkster Day had been legally prohibited by the state legislature.

The Ember Days

Four times a year, at the beginning of each of the natural seasons, come the Ember Days. These are three days of fasting—always Wednesday, Friday, and Saturday of the week following, respectively, the first Sunday in Lent, the day of Pentecost, September 14th, and December 13th. The name Ember is a corruption of the German word *quatember,* which in turn comes from the Latin *Quattor Tempora,* meaning "the four seasons."

The origin of these days is quite obscure and much debated. Some scholars connect them with the old pagan purification rites that always took place at the seasons of planting, harvest, and vintage. The Ember Days have come to be associated, particularly in the Roman Catholic Church, with ordinations to the sacred ministry. Each of the four weeks in which the Ember Days fall is called an Ember Week.

Trinity Sunday

Big days in the Christian calendar are commonly connected with some saint or historic event. Trinity Sunday is the single exception in the whole year: a day in honor of a purely theological concept. Beginning with the season of Advent, the Church, in a sequence of observances, runs through the Lord's life, His birth, baptism, ministry, passion, death, resurrection, ascension, and finally, the coming of the Holy Spirit. All these are celebrated as ways in which God has revealed Himself, His purposes and nature, in actual historic happenings. Now the sequence is brought to a conclusion with a day of summing-up, a statement of what He is, not only in history, but through all eternity: three persons in One God, a Trinity.

There is no reason to suppose that we could explain the doctrine of the Trinity, when no one else in Christian history has ever been able to do more than come fairly close, but we can say that it is man's attempt to deal with the three ways in which he has encountered God. God, in His love, has shown Himself to us as our Creator, our Redeemer, and our Sanctifier—or, to put it in other but equally conventional terms, as the Father, Son, and Holy Spirit. What this means is that man sees God in the fact that the universe exists, in the person of Jesus of Nazareth, and in the daily presence of God in human affairs. This statement fails to explain the Trinity, just as all others have failed—but it does say that man has experienced God in three ways and needs to use some triple form of expression to talk about Him.

It was late in Christian history—the tenth century—before it occurred to anyone to set up a festival in honor of so abstract a concept, and even then it took several more centuries for the feast to get into the Church's calendar. Started by Stephen, Bishop of Liege (Belgium), around 910, Trinity Sunday was quickly taken up in the Low Countries, Germany, and England, but it was not until 1334 that it became a universal observance.

The Church now begins its longest season, the Trinity season, which continues until Advent—around December 1st. The symbolism of this lengthy season refers to the long period of the Church's life under the guidance of the Holy Spirit until the final Advent of Christ, when time shall be no more.

CHAPTER VII

July

Feast of the Most Precious Blood
JULY 1ST

July, in the Roman Catholic Church, is the month of the Most Precious Blood, and the first day of July is the Feast of the Most Precious Blood. The reference is, of course, to the blood of Jesus, which ever since the time of the Last Supper has been regarded by Christians as a source of life-giving power. Societies and religious orders of both men and women in the Roman Catholic Church have offered devotion to the Most Precious Blood for centuries, but it was not until a little more than one hundred years ago that the festival became universal and a day was selected for general observance.

The circumstances under which this occurred are interesting. In 1849, Pope Pius IX was forced into exile because Rome was being attacked by the armies of France. One of his companions was a general officer of the Fathers of the Most Precious Blood, who attempted to persuade him to make a vow that if he regained the papal lands he would establish the festival, then kept in some localities, as a universal observance. The Pope, without hesitation, replied that he did not wish to bargain with God but that he would extend the festival to the whole Church regardless of what might happen to his lands. This decision was reached on the day before the first Sunday in July. Pius therefore decreed that every first Sunday in July should thereafter be dedicated to the Most Precious Blood. Pius X subsequently moved the feast to the first day of July.

The Man Behind the English Reformation

JULY 2ND

In line with our modern tendency to oversimplify things, the easy way to explain the English Reformation is to say that Henry VIII brought it about because he wanted to divorce his queen (Catherine of Aragon) and marry his sweetheart, Anne Boleyn. Actually, this explains nothing.

The real power behind the Reformation in England was Thomas Cranmer, Archbishop of Canterbury, who was born on this day in 1489. As did many other priests, he found himself caught up in the wave of religious reform that was sweeping Europe at the beginning of the sixteenth century. But Cranmer was no ordinary priest. He was under a compulsion to be a spokesman for the new movement, to lead his whole branch of the Church into freedom from Roman domination.

Cranmer was a statesman (one could even say a politician) as well as a clergyman. He was astute enough to seize the propitious moment and use the king's domestic confusion as a chance to put himself in a position where his word would really count for something. He could and did say, without any sacrifice of principle, that Henry's marriage to Katharine was not valid. She had been his brother's widow, and there was a church law against such marriages. The logical conclusion, therefore, was that the marriage was null and Henry was free to marry Anne.

Naturally, such logic pleased the king and it was not long before Cranmer, with Henry's influence behind him, was Archbishop of Canterbury and Primate of All England. From this lofty station he was able to bring about the reforms and changes he considered proper. Henry's marital troubles were not the cause of the English Reformation; they simply provided Cranmer with his opportunity.

The changes came to a climax in 1534. Twenty-two years later Cranmer was deposed by the Pope, tried for treason and convicted by an English court, and burned at the stake. Anglicans (Episcopalians in the United States) remember Thomas Cranmer chiefly for his work in translating the prayers and services of the church from Latin into English and thus developing that great classic, *The English Book of Common Prayer*.

A Famous Visit

JULY 2ND

St. Luke, in his first chapter, verses 39 to 56, tells the lovely story of how the Blessed Virgin Mary, immediately after learning that she was to be the mother of Jesus, went to visit her cousin Elizabeth, who was soon to bear John the Baptist. Elizabeth's home, according to tradition, was in the town of Ain Karin, in the beautiful hill country just west of Jerusalem, a journey of about eighty miles for Mary.

According to the story, Elizabeth's baby "leaped for joy" in her womb at the sound of Mary's voice, and it was at this moment, so the Roman Catholic Church teaches, that John the Baptist was cleansed from original sin and filled with heavenly grace. It is the first recorded instance of the Lord's use of His mother as mediator in the sanctifying of man.

July 2nd is observed in commemoration of this event. It is called the Visitation of the Blessed Virgin Mary. Mary stayed three months with Elizabeth and returned home just before John was born. If John's birth occurred on June 24th, the day on which it is universally celebrated, then July 2nd is chronologically wrong for the visitation. This of course is not important. None of these ancient dates is ever exact.

Independence Day

JULY 4TH

Independence Day is not thought of as a religious holiday, but there can be no doubt that it had a deep religious significance in the minds of those men who signed the Declaration of Independence on July 4, 1776. John Adams, just after the signing, wrote to his wife, "It (this day) ought to be commemorated as the day of deliverance by solemn acts of devotion to Almighty God."

Deems, in his book, *Holy Days and Holidays,* says, "To tell the story of Independence Day and leave out religion is impossible." There was a definite religious purpose in the founding of four of the original colonies: Massachusetts, Maryland, Georgia, and Pennsylvania, and the same basic religious meaning was in the minds and hearts of the men who founded the new nation. It is safe to say that no church in America, Protestant, Catholic, or Jewish, fails to emphasize Independence Day in its services on July 4th or the preceding Sunday.

One church, the Episcopal, has made official provision for a service on July 4th itself. Before the American Revolution the present Episcopal Church was a part of the Church of England, a "state" church, in which days of patriotic significance were observed as a matter of routine. It seemed quite natural, therefore, after the Revolution to put something in the new prayer book about the day that might be called the new country's birthday, and a prayer of thanksgiving was proposed "for the inestimable blessings of religious and civil liberty."

Such a prayer would certainly be acceptable to everyone today, but in 1786 it would have been offensive to a comparatively large group of Episcopal clergymen who had never been very enthusiastic about the Revolution in the first place. Its inclusion might have prevented the new prayer book from being adopted. So, tact and diplomacy prevailed; the prayer was withdrawn, and it was not until 1928 that any provision for July 4th was made in *The American Book of Common Prayer*.

The First Official Saint
JULY 4TH

July 4th is St. Ulrich's Day. It is not a particularly important day, nor was Ulrich a particularly important saint. His distinction lies in the fact that he was the first saint ever canonized according to the present formal procedure of the Roman Catholic Church. This happened on February 3, 993. Through all the centuries prior to this, saints became saints pretty much just by popular acclaim in their own localities, always, of course, with the bishop's approval. There was no official or universal ma-

chinery. And as time went on the number of local saints
and their local cults grew to a point of confusion that
amounted almost to chaos.

A saint is a person who has already been received into
the Church Triumphant, a person worthy of veneration
by the Church on earth, and this is a dignity not to be
lightly established. It was therefore only logical that the
time should come when the Pope, as representing the
whole Church, would take to himself the responsibility for
deciding so important an issue. Ulrich, Bishop of Augsburg for fifty years, was the first whose name came up for
this formal consideration, or at least the first approved.
Even in his case the old habits had not yet been entirely
overcome. The people of Augsburg, with the consent of
the new bishop, had already begun to venerate Ulrich as
a saint.

Democracy's Forerunner
JULY 7TH

It is altogether appropriate that the birthday of a Congregational minister by the name of Thomas Hooker
should occur within the week in which Americans celebrate Independence Day. Hooker, who was born on July
7, 1586, and died on the same day in 1657, has been
called by historians "the father of American democracy."

Beginning as a Puritan clergyman in England, Hooker,
to avoid trouble with the authorities of the Established
Church, came to Massachusetts Bay Colony. This was in
1633. Within three years he was having so much difficulty with the church leaders there that he took his entire congregation and moved to what is now Connecticut.

What the trouble was about seems commonplace now,
but in 1636 Hooker's ideas were revolutionary. He main-

tained that all the people—not just the church members—
have the power, from God, to choose their public officials
and to define the powers of those officials. It was this
advanced doctrine that earned Hooker his "father of
American democracy" title. When he moved in 1636, he
and his flock founded both the colony of Connecticut and
the city of Hartford. Hooker remained in Hartford as the
Congregational pastor—which in those days meant head
man of the community—until his death eleven years later.

First Crusader

JULY 8TH

Nearly every Christian alive in those days expected the
world to end on the first day of the year 1000, and many
devout people journeyed to the Holy Land in order to
be there when the last trumpet sounded. When New
Year's Day came and went without incident, a grateful
wave of piety began to sweep over Europe. The age of
cathedral building began. Pilgrimages to Jerusalem, instead of ceasing when the danger was past, increased by
the thousand and continued throughout the whole century.

Peter the Hermit, who died on this day in 1115, was
perhaps the most important of all pilgrims, for out of his
journey came the Crusades, that series of holy wars that
kept Europe in turmoil for two hundred years and
changed the whole course of Western history and culture.
Peter was a man of low birth and little learning, who
lived as a religious recluse in northern France. He had
visions from time to time, and came to regard himself as
God's special instrument, but it was not until he went to
Jerusalem that he knew what God's particular purpose
for him was.

The Holy Land was at that time in the hands of the Mohammedans, and Peter soon saw that it must be taken away from them. Back he came to Rome to tell Pope Urban II of his project. The Pope, enthusiastic, sent the hermit out to raise an army and proclaim the deliverance of Palestine. This was in 1095. By November of that year 100,000 warriors set out, and the army grew to 300,000 as it proceeded. These men, in their devotion to Peter, made him their leader, which was a fatal mistake, for he did not have the ability for this task. The Crusade was a total failure. Nearly all the Crusaders were captured or killed. Peter, however, managed to hide out in Palestine and was on hand to join a later army of Crusaders when they came and successfully drove the Mohammedans out of Jerusalem.

St. Kilian and the Duchess
JULY 8TH

St. Kilian, a seventh century Irishman, came to the same end as John the Baptist, and for exactly the same reason. An angry wife had his head cut off because he had said her marriage was unlawful. This was in the days when the Irish clergy apparently just couldn't stay at home. All through the sixth and seventh centuries, Irish priests went wandering about continental Europe. Kilian was one of these missionaries. He settled in Wurzburg (Germany) finally and had a great deal of success at converting the heathen.

One of his first converts was the duke, Gozbert, who ruled the country, and who was married to his brother's widow, Geilana. Such a marriage was against the law of the Church, and Kilian insisted that it be annulled. Geilana, furious, watched her chance, and when Gozbert was away on a trip she sent an assassin to cut off Kilian's head. The story tells that Kilian made no resistance whatever.

It is also told that when Gozbert returned and asked for the saint, a woman who had seen the murder reported it to the duke, and the murderer confessed. Whereupon Gozbert called the people together and asked them how he should deal with this killer. One of them, prompted by the duchess, said to let him go and see if the Christian's God would avenge the death of His saint. This idea was accepted, and the assassin immediately died of a raging fever.

Martyrs of Gorkum

JULY 9TH

History books record many stories about the difficulties of Protestants in the early days after the Reformation, but they often fail to mention that things were not always easy for the Catholics. For example, in the Netherlands, where Calvinism soon became extremely strong, persecution of Catholics by Protestants equalled anything the mind of man has ever devised in the way of violence. Angry, uncontrollable mobs roamed the countryside, destroying church statues, stained-glass windows, and precious ancient ornaments under the pretext of "purifying" the Catholic churches and ridding them of their "superstitions." They tortured and killed clergy, monks, and laypeople. The little town of Gorkum in Holland was invaded by such a rioting mob in July, 1572. After plundering and wrecking the churches, the Calvinist horde, on July 9th, marched nineteen priests and friars to the gallows and hanged them for the crime of being good Catholics.

He Joked with His Executioners

JULY 9TH

St. Thomas More, who lived from 1478 to 1535, was a man with a very strange sense of humor. When they brought him to the scaffold where he was to be beheaded, he said that if some one would help him up the steps he was sure he could manage to get back down by himself. When he was about to lay his head on the block he lifted his beard so that the headsman's axe would not chop it off, because, he said, the beard was not guilty of anything. And to his executioners he said, "Take care, for I have a short neck, and you have to look to your honor."

Of course it was not his ill-timed clowning that made him a saint. Sir Thomas More was an English lawyer of great charm and ability, and a prominent man in politics. At the age of thirty-two he was a member of Parliament, and from there he rose rapidly to be Lord Chancellor, which would be called Prime Minister today. But when the Church of England broke with Rome in 1534 and declared that the King (Henry VIII) was the head of the Church, More refused to go along. So the witty and popular Lord Chancellor, who had been Henry's favorite, was martyred for his loyalty to the Pope.

Great Theologian

JULY 10TH

This was the birthday, in 1509, of John Calvin, the great theologian of the Protestant Reformation. Nearly all Protestant denominations today trace the origin of their doctrinal systems back to either Calvin or Martin Luther. The Puritans, who so deeply affected American thought (and still do) were Calvinists. Calvin is remembered chiefly nowadays for the sternness of his theology, but there are many stories to indicate that he was just as severe with himself as he was with the rest of the world.

One of his biographers gives a staggering list of Calvin's regularly scheduled activities. Besides his writing, his addresses to the clergy, and his countless conferences and consultations with all who wanted to see him, he prepared and delivered 186 lectures and 286 sermons a year. The writer of the biography says he cannot make up his mind which was the hardier, Calvin or the audience that had to listen to so much talk. Even when he was in his last illness, in 1564, Calvin continued to maintain this heavy schedule. When his friends tried to get him to ease up a bit, he said, "What! Shall the Lord come and find me idle?"

The doctrines of this Frenchman, (whose name in French was Jean Chauvin) have had a tremendous effect on the life of America, although there are few people who would hold them without some modification today. Puritans, Presbyterians, and other religious groups in America's early days believed firmly in such Calvinist teachings as the total depravity of man, salvation by grace alone rather than by good works, and predestination. Best known of these doctrines is predestination, by which Calvin meant that some people are elected or destined to be saved and some are not, and there is nothing any man can do about it either way.

This belief, however, did not, as might be expected, result in utter hopelessness, because Calvin further stated that since no one knows whether or not he is among the elect, everyone must lead a holy life just on the chance that he is one of the favored ones. Besides this, if you find you can keep the laws of God, you may take this ability as a good sign that you belong to the elect.

Calvin, or Chauvin, was born on July 10, 1509. He was educated first for the priesthood and then for the law. In 1532 he experienced a "sudden conversion" and from then on he spent his life in Protestant reform, which at that time was a brand new element in Christianity. In 1533, because of a radical public speech he made, he was forced to flee France. He went to Switzerland, ending up finally in the city of Geneva, where he became an absolute dictator, running the town strictly according to his doctrines and rules of conduct.

St. Felicitas

JULY 10TH

The ancient Romans were a superstitious lot. Whenever anything unpleasant happened to them they were sure it was because the gods were annoyed, and they looked around to see what or who was annoying them. When Christianity began there was no longer any difficulty in finding out why the gods were angry: obviously, it was the Christians who were upsetting them. Whatever happened—flood, epidemic, or crop failure—it was always the Christians' fault, and the only remedy was to throw a few of them to the lions.

Such nonsense was behind the torture and death of Felicitas and her sons, the Seven Holy Brothers. Felicitas was a pious widow, high up in Roman society. Pagan priests told the emperor that the gods were distinctly irritated by the idea of a woman in her position taking up Christianity. It was a bad example to the common people, and the emperor might be sure no good would come of it.

The lady was given a chance to renounce her dangerous doctrines. When she refused, she and her seven sons, also Christians, were brought to trial, and, of course, condemned to die. One son was beaten to death with a whip loaded with lead; one was thrown from a high rock; two were beaten with staves; three were beheaded. The mother, after watching it all and shouting words of encouragement to her sons throughout their ordeals, was herself beheaded. This is supposed to have happened on July 10th, about the year 162. (St. Felicitas is prayed to by expectant women who hope their babies will be boys.)

The entire story is rejected by some parts of the Christian Church as being suspiciously similar to the account in the Second Book of the Maccabees, chapter 7, of the seven sons who were cruelly put to death before their mother's eyes in the second century B.C. by the Syrian king, Antiochus Epiphanes. Their offense was that they refused to eat pork.

Orange Day

JULY 12TH

July 12th is the anniversary of the Battle of Boyne, which took place in Ireland in 1690. Actually the battle was fought on July 1st, but that was when the Old Julian calendar was still in use.

The trouble was between the Roman Catholics and the Protestants of Ireland. Ireland in those days was entirely under English rule, and when James II, a Catholic king of the Stuart line, was deposed in 1668 and his throne was given to William of Orange, Catholic Irishmen remained loyal to James, and Protestants sided with the man from Orange. (Orange at that time was a little independent principality, in what is now the northern part of France.) Each side raised an army of about 30,000 men, and the two collided as only Irishmen can, on the banks of the Boyne River. The Protestants won the battle, which was a decisive one.

And this was the beginning of that complex phenomenon known as Irish politics. The Catholics formed underground societies designed to restore the line of James,
and the Protestants countered by forming the "Loyal
Orange Institution," committed to maintaining the link
with Protestant England. As Irishmen left England for
the New World, lodges of Orangemen were formed in
Canada and in the United States. The political question
of Stuart vs. Orange is no longer a live issue, but there
are still many lodges of Orangemen in America, maintained now for purposes of fellowship, and Orange Day is
still observed, but without the violence of past years.

Our Lady of Fatima
JULY 13TH

It was on July 13th in 1917 that the people of the Portuguese village of Fatima were finally convinced that three
of their village children had really been seeing and talking with the Virgin Mary over a period of two months.
On May 13th of the same year the dos Santos children,
Lucia, Jacinto, and Francisca, had been playing near the
village when they heard the sound of thunder. Looking
up they saw, so they said, "a young girl" standing above
the top of a small tree nearby. "The young girl" spoke to
the children and said that she would meet them again in
six months at the same time.

The children, having no idea that it was Mary whom
they had seen, reported the incident to their parents, and
to others. No one quite believed them, and yet no one
quite dared to disbelieve. And so the story spread. Five
months ahead of the scheduled appointment, the vision
appeared to the young dos Santoses on June 13th, and
this time they were told that this would happen on the

thirteenth of every month. From then on it was clear to the adults of the community that unless the children were deceiving either themselves or their elders, this must certainly be a manifestation of the Blessed Lady herself.

On the 13th of July every one came from miles around to see what would happen. On this occasion only the children could see the vision and only they could make out what she said, but many people heard a "buzzing sound" clearly enough to convince them that there was some reality in what the children had reported. Over the next twenty years the miracle was investigated and authenticated by the bishop and the local clergy and finally given acceptance by the Pope. Since that time July 13th officially has been the day of Our Lady of Fatima.

St. Vladimir

JULY 15TH

Nobody outside of Russia knows much of what goes on inside, but rumors do get out that there is a Christian, anti-Communist underground movement there, that its patron saint is St. Vladimir, and that its symbol is St. Vladimir's cross. If this is true it is certainly logical, for it was this same Vladimir who, back in 986, turned Russia from a pagan country into a Christian one. Vladimir became Emperor of Russia in 980.

At first he was not friendly to Christianity. But he had a tremendous interest in religion and wanted to know about all of them. To his court he invited representatives of Judaism, Mohammedanism, Western Catholicism, and Eastern (or Greek) Catholicism. After hearing them all, Vladimir decided the Easterners had what he needed, and he and all his court were immediately baptized. Then, he ordered the entire population of the country to accept Christianity and be baptized.

Russian Christians today have a name for St. Vladimir which means "the equal of an Apostle," which is indeed what he was to them. They like to dwell on the contrast between the cruel pagan days before his conversion and the gentle happy days that came afterward. They are praying and quietly working that the same change may take place in modern Russia.

St. Swithin's Day
JULY 15TH

Rain is the most important liquid in the world. Man's very life depends upon it. It is natural, therefore, that since the beginning of time the subject of rain—why it comes or doesn't come, how to make it come or how to stop it—has been surrounded by hundreds of theories, ranging from the deeply religious to the darkly superstitious.

One of the greatest rain makers of all time was St. Swithin, the ninth century English bishop, who, according to one of our most popular legends, sent a six-weeks downpour to thwart an attempt to move his bones one hundred years after his death. The superstition still persists, both in England and other parts of the English-speaking world, that

> "On Swithin's Day, if it should rain,
> For forty days it will remain."

There is nothing to support this idea, except that it usually rains a good deal at this time of year in most parts of the Northern hemisphere.

Here is the story behind this superstition. Swithin, Bishop of Winchester, England, in the middle of the ninth century, was a man of unusual humility, even for a saint. Before he died he gave instructions that he was to be buried not in the Cathedral, as bishops were, but in the churchyard like anyone else. And so it was done.

But after one hundred years had gone by, people decided that it was not right to have so great a man buried anywhere except under the altar, and arrangements were made to move the bones, the date being set for July 15th. When the solemn procession started out for the ceremony, there came a storm of such intensity that the project had to be postponed. By the time the storm had gone on for forty days the authorities began to get the idea: Swithin didn't want to be moved. So they called off the move and the rain stopped and the sun came out. The only trouble with this story is that it is not true. Swithin was moved, without incident, on July 15, 971.

There is another story about Swithin and a struggle he and another saint had over a poor sick man they were both trying to heal. The only point of this story is that it shows how people attribute to the saints the childish emotions they feel themselves. For centuries St. Swithin was the most popular healer in England. There were constant pilgrimages to his shrine, and crutches, canes, and sometimes shoes were left there by those who were healed. This legend says that a group of friends brought a sick man on what seemed to be his death bed, but they brought him with the intention of invoking a different saint. They were persuaded, however, to try St. Swithin. As they kept their vigil through the night, finally none of them could stay awake any longer. The sick man dreamed that he was being tugged about and that someone had managed to get one of his shoes off. In the morning when he awoke the man was healed, but the shoe actually was gone and has not been found to this day.

The question still stands: What saint stole the shoe? Obviously, Swithin and his rival saint, jealous and petulant, were pulling and hauling for possession of the sick man during the night, but no one knows which one had hold of his feet.

The Carmelites

JULY 16TH

The Carmelites are the oldest mendicant (supported by alms) order in the Roman Catholic Church, and July 16th is their special day. It is the feast of Our Lady of Mt. Carmel. The actual record of the Carmelites goes back a long time—to 1158, when Italian Crusader Berthold of Calabria established himself and ten companions on the famous biblical mountain.

The legend of the Carmelites goes back even twenty centuries before that. According to their cherished tradition, they really began in the time of the prophet Elijah, who built an altar on Mt. Carmel, in the ninth century B.C. (see I Kings, chapter 18). At that time, the Carmelites say, Elijah had a prophetic vision of the Blessed Virgin Mary—nearly nine hundred years before she was born.

The feast was first kept on the 16th of July about 1330 and extended to the whole Church in 1726. Most of the celebration of this day takes place in Italy and in Italian sections of American cities, where people parade through the streets carrying statues of the Virgin.

The Christian Science Founder

JULY 16TH

Christian Scientists take little notice of birthdays, believing that birth and death are only insignificant transitional points in the course of man's eternal life. Therefore they will not celebrate July 16th, which is the birthday of their founder, Mary Baker Eddy, who was born July 16, 1821, at Bow, New Hampshire. Mary Baker's early religious affiliation was with the Congregational Church.

Mrs. Eddy apparently began the train of thought that led to her new theology when she was engaged in an enterprise of healing in Lynn, Massachusetts. This was when she was in her early fifties. In 1875 when Mrs. Eddy was fifty-four years of age, she expounded her ideas in the first edition (1,000 copies) of her now famous *Science and Health with Key to the Scriptures*. Very soon she gathered a following of students, who called themselves Christian Scientists. Within a year they had formed the Christian Students Association, and by 1879 they had, with Mrs. Eddy's support, obtained a charter as "The Church of Christ, Scientist."

The new church was the subject of many bitter attacks, which in 1883 Mrs. Eddy undertook to answer through a new publication called the Journal of Christian Science.

From 1882 Mrs. Eddy lived in Boston until her death on December 10, 1910. One of her contributions to American life, valued by thousands who are not members of her church, was the founding in 1908 of the great newspaper, the *Christian Science Monitor*.

The basic belief, now held by Mrs. Eddy's half-a-million followers, was that since God created all things, and since God would be incapable of creating evil, it is therefore not possible for evil to have any real existence.

St. Vincent de Paul

July 19th

On July 19th the Roman Catholic Church honors the man who, probably more than any other single individual, is

responsible for organized charity. St. Vincent de Paul, a
French peasant of the seventeenth century, not only led
a life devoted to caring for the poor, the sick, and the
underprivileged—he also saw to it that the good works he
started were continued by others.

Beginning with a concern about people of his own
class, the peasants, de Paul went on to an interest in what
must have been the most pitiable group of his time: the
prisoners. Convicted criminals were used by the government as nothing more than machines, to provide power
for boats, but they were treated worse than a man ever
treats any piece of machinery. They were chained to their
places in the galley when they were able to pull an oar,
or were chained in vermin-infested dungeons if they became too ill or too weak to work and they were kept there
on a diet of black bread and water.

St. Vincent visited them and ministered to them with
a love that won the most hardened of them. And he was
not content to minister to them and then leave them as
they were. He interested others in their plight and
worked to improve their condition. He saw that just starting good works was not enough. Some provision must be
made for maintaining and developing his gains. This was
Vincent de Paul's great contribution, the difference between him and the hundreds of other saints who devoted
their lives to the care of the sick and needy: Vincent de
Paul organized groups that would carry on what he had
started. The best known of the organizations are the
Lazarist Fathers (so named because they were founded at
the town of St. Lazare, in France) and the famous Sisters
of Charity.

Now many a Roman Catholic parish has a branch
(called a conference) of the great world-wide Society of

St. Vincent de Paul. These local societies, following in the spirit of the saint, visit the poor, the sick, and the needy.

St. Margaret

July 20th

The farther back we go in Christian history, the more incredible are the stories about the saints. St. Margaret, who lived in the third century and was one of the "voices" that spoke to Joan of Arc, is said to have been swallowed by a dragon.

Margaret, who is considered the epitome of feminine meekness and innocence, was a girl of striking beauty, the daughter of a pagan priest. When she was converted to Christianity by her nurse, her father would have nothing more to do with her. He drove her away from home, and she took up the life of a shepherdess to support herself. It was while she was herding sheep that she was seen by Olybrius, governor of Antioch, who was so smitten by her beauty that he wanted to marry her at once. She declined his offer, saying that she was committed to Christ. The governor was not accustomed to being turned down, and in his wounded pride he had her thrown into a dungeon.

St. Margaret, like St. George, is always shown in Christian art with a great dragon. It is from her imprisonment that the dragon story comes. The legend tells that Satan appeared to her in the dungeon in the form of a dragon, and that she chased him away by showing him a cross. Another version says the dragon swallowed her, but that inside him she made the sign of the cross and he disgorged her intact. Because of her providential deliverance from the interior of the dragon, St. Margaret—so the story goes—prayed that she might be of help in all precarious deliveries, and it was in this way that she became the patron saint of all women in childbirth.

Stories of this sort, of course, test the credulity of the faithful and bring on the scorn of the unfaithful. But the real point, never to be overlooked, is that they represent a deep and primitive groping for an answer to a deep and primitive human need. Women waiting to be taken to the delivery room, husbands pacing the hospital corridors —all know why St. Margaret was for centuries the most popular saint in the Christian calendar.

After her imprisonment the governor, still relentless, had her tortured and beheaded. In Christian art Margaret is sometimes shown rising from a battered and defeated dragon.

A Day for Elijah

JULY 20TH

On July 20th both the Roman and Greek Churches honor an Old Testament Jew who lived a thousand years before the Christian era began. This day is set aside for Elijah, commemorating the greatest of the prophets, Elijah or Elias, whose name means "Yahweh is God." Jews and Mohammedans, too, although they do not have a day for him in their religious calendars, hold Elijah in high respect. He is thus a universal figure, cutting across the lines that separate three of the world's leading faiths.

Most of the story of this loftiest of all prophets is told in chapters 17 and 18 of the first book of Kings, though the final episode appears in Second Kings, chapter 2. Every Sunday School child knows how Elijah lived in the desert and was fed every morning and every evening by the ravens, who brought him both bread and meat, and how, when his source of drinking water dried up, he went to the home of a poor widow for a new supply, and there performed two famous miracles as a reward for her hospitality. One miracle was that throughout a severe famine the widow's meal and oil supply did not diminish, no matter how many cakes she made for Elijah, herself, and her son. The other was that when the son died, Elijah brought him back to life.

Elijah's biggest problem was the tendency of the Jews to worship the pagan fertility god Baal, without actually deserting Jahveh. The prophet would tolerate no such divided loyalty. The climax of his career came when he called the priests of Baal to the top of Mount Carmel and there challenged them to a contest that would prove which was the true God. They were to arrange a sacrifice to Baal; Elijah would arrange one to Jahveh. Each side would call on its deity to set fire to the sacrifice. The pagan priests, of course, failed completely, but in response to Elijah's prayer "the fire of the Lord fell" and consumed not only the sacrifice but the altar itself and the dust and the water around it.

According to II Kings, chapter 2, Elijah did not die but was taken up to heaven by a whirlwind, riding in a fiery chariot. Legend says that he is preserved alive to the end of time, to be entrusted with some glorious mission, but Jews and Christians have differing ideas about what that mission will be. Christians say it will be to convert the Jews. The rabbis say it will be to give explanations and answers that students of the Torah have not been able to find.

A Scarlet Woman

JULY 22ND

St. Mary Magdalen has become, in the mind of Protestant and Catholic alike, the symbol of the "scarlet woman" who has been forgiven and rehabilitated. It is not actually known that Mary was a bad woman, although everyone seems to have decided that she was. St. Luke says only that she had had "seven devils" cast out of her, (see Luke, chapter 8, verse 2), which might have meant that she had been unusually wicked, or that she had been unusually sick. Some scholars think her trouble was epilepsy.

Whatever she may have been before she met Jesus, she certainly became one of His most devoted followers. She was one of the small, loyal group that did not run away even at the Crucifixion, but stood at the foot of the Cross throughout the three horrible hours. She was also the first person to see the Lord after His Resurrection. When she came to the tomb early on Easter morning, He appeared and sent her to tell the Apostles what had happened: that He had risen. Mary is called Magdalen because she came from the little town of Magdala which was on the Sea of Galilee.

St. James the Great

JULY 25TH

July 25th is the day of St. James the Great, patron saint of Spain. It is a happy, lively holiday in that country, where they call him "Santiago." This James, who was one of the apostles, is known as "The Great" to distinguish him from the other Apostle James, who is called "The Less." What was greater about this one and lesser about the other is not quite clear. It may have to do with age, or it may mean that this James was the taller.

St. James was the brother of the beloved St. John. These two, with St. Peter, were obviously the Lord's favorite apostles. Several instances are recorded where He took these three with Him into some special situation in which the others did not participate. The most notable of these occasions was the Transfiguration.

The Spanish have a lovely legend about how St. James came to be their patron saint. They tell that when he died, in Palestine, his body was put into a boat and on the next day this little boat, without rudder or crew, arrived at Compostela on the Spanish coast. It had been guided and powered by angels.

St. James was buried, but his burial place was forgotten until about the year 800. A hermit who lived in the vicinity noted that strange heavenly lights constantly played about a certain spot. He investigated and found the body. A church was built there, around which the town of Santiago grew up. The place soon became a shrine with legends and miracles of its own. In the thirteenth century people began to call the Milky Way the Way of St. James because they believed it was put in the heavens to guide the pilgrims to St. James's grave.

Some Spanish stories about their patron are much like those the English told about St. George. In the tenth century, when Spanish troops were fighting the Moors, St. James appeared in their midst on a white charger and led them to victory, just as St. George led British soldiers during the Crusades.

The Motorists' Saint

July 25th

In these days of freeways, turnpikes, and six-lane highways, it is no wonder St. Christopher, patron of travelers and especially now of motorists, should be one of the most popular of all saints. Even Protestants carry St. Christopher medals or have them fastened to their cars. Very little is definitely known about this saint—so little, really, it is not possible even to be sure of his dates. A good guess is that he lived in the third century. Beyond the fact that there was a martyr named Christopher about that time, historians will not go.

But legend makes up for history's silence. The best place to read about Christopher is in William Caxton's *Golden Legend,* which starts out by saying, "Christopher before his baptism was named Reprobus, but afterwards he was named Christopher, which is as much as to say bearing Christ, for that he bare Him in four manners: he bare Him on his shoulders by conveying, in his body by making it lean, in mind by devotion, and in his mouth by confession and preaching."

Christopher Legends

Caxton goes on then to tell the stories that have made Christopher so famous and so widely beloved. As a soldier he made up his mind he would devote his life to the service of the strongest power in the world. At first he served a great king, but one day he saw that the king quaked at the mention of the Devil. So, Christopher reasoned, the Devil must be stronger than the king, whereupon he set out to find old Satan and serve him. But it was not long before he discovered his new master was afraid of a cross. And from then on he sought to serve Christ, who was mightier even than the Devil.

His service to Christ took the form of service to men, and thereby hangs the most famous of all tales about Christopher. The good man took up residence in a hut beside a river, where there was a ford used by pilgrims on their way to Jerusalem. The water, even at the ford, sometimes ran so deep many pilgrims lost their lives in it. So Christopher, who was of great stature and strength, lived by the river and carried across all the weak and small who came by, so that no more lives were lost there.

One night he was awakened by a child who asked to be taken over the ford. As they went across, the lad on Christopher's broad shoulders seemed to grow heavier and heavier, until finally Christopher said, "Thou weighest almost as I had all the world upon me." To which the boy replied, "Marvel not, for thou hast not only borne all the world upon thee, but thou hast borne Him that created all the world." Then Christopher knew his passenger was the Lord Himself, and his ambition to serve the mightiest power had been realized. This legend is, of course, the basis of St. Christopher's reputation as the patron of travelers and the protector of all against perils from water and storms.

St. Anne

JULY 26TH

July 26th is the anniversary of the death of the Virgin Mary's mother, St. Anne, whose famous church at Beaupré, in Quebec, is known to hundreds of thousands of Americans and Canadians. This shrine, known as the "Lourdes of the New World," attracts vast crowds of pilgrims from both countries, particularly at this time of the year.

In 1650, when the little French colony of Quebec was in its earliest beginnings, a group of Breton sailors built a tiny frame church in honor of St. Anne at the place where the town of Beaupre now stands. They did this because they had been caught in a vicious storm at sea and had vowed that if St. Anne would bring them safely to land they would build her a sanctuary at the spot where their feet should first touch the earth.

Only a few years later (in 1658) the people of the village began the construction of a new and larger church, and it was then that the first of St. Anne de Beaupre's miraculous cures took place. A local man, Louis Guimont, twisted and aching with rheumatism, came and painfully placed three stones in the foundation. He walked away in perfect health. Since that time there have been thousands of healings at this shrine.

According to early writings, which are not considered very trustworthy, the Blessed Virgin Mary came of a wealthy family. The story goes that her mother Hannah (Anne in English) and her father Joachim were greatly grieved and even embarrassed over the fact that for many years they were childless. Joachim once went to the Temple to make an offering and was turned away because men who had no children were not worthy to enter. He went off to a mountain to pray about it. His wife heard about his embarrassment and she, too, began to pray over the situation. She was soon visited by an angel who told her that she would have a child who would be blessed by the whole world. The main objection scholars make to the legend is that it is obviously a reworking of the Old Testament story of the birth of Samuel—see I Samuel, chapter 1.

The body of St. Anne is said to have been miraculously discovered in the ninth century at Apte, France, when a young boy who had never uttered a word in his life suddenly spoke and said, "Here lies the body of Anne, mother of the Blessed Virgin Mary." Behind this story lies the legend that St. Paul the Apostle had removed St. Anne's body from its original grave and carried it to Rome. Pope Clement shortly afterward entrusted the body to the Bishop of Apte, who buried it at the place where it was found eight hundred years later. However, a part of the body—a finger—is housed in the Beaupré Church, and is exposed there each year on St. Anne's Day.

Volunteers of America

JULY 28TH

July 28th is celebrated by the Volunteers of America as their Founder's Day. It is the birthday (1859) of Ballington Booth, second son of the famous William Booth, who established the Salvation Army. In the early days of the Salvation Army in England, young Ballington worked with his father so faithfully and well that in 1887 he was sent to America with his wife Maud, to be in charge of the Army in the United States and Canada. A disagreement over methods led the son to withdraw from the original organization in 1896 and to start his own group, which he named the Volunteers of America. The Volunteers grew rapidly and are now represented in nearly every state. The purposes of the Volunteers are essentially the same as those of the Salvation Army.

St. Martha

JULY 29TH

A good housekeeper never knows what outrageous interruption will turn up next. The patron saint of all housewives once had to stop her work and tie up a dragon because all the men of the community were too timid to deal with the monster. That saint was Martha, the sister of Mary, and of Lazarus, whom Jesus raised from the dead. Martha is best known from Luke's story (chapter 10, verses 38 to 42) about the Lord's visit to the house where Lazarus and his two sisters lived in Bethany. Mary sat in the parlor and listened to their guest, while Martha was "cumbered about much serving." When Martha complained, Jesus told her that what Mary was doing was much more important than housework. It was this episode that gave Martha her undying reputation as a painfully efficient housekeeper.

The place where Martha is said to have trussed up the dragon is in the south of France, near Marseilles. The dragon's name was Tarasque, and the town of Tarascon was built on the spot where Tarasque was killed after Martha had rendered him harmless. The whole story is an unlikely one, even if you believe in dragons, for Martha's presence in that part of the world depends on a legend that could hardly be true. Legend has it that Martha, Mary, and Lazarus, with two other women named Mary, fled from Palestine in a small boat that was without oars or sails. Eventually they were washed up on France's Mediterranean shores. But the people there hold tenaciously to the ancient story and say Martha lived there until her death on July 29th in the year 84.

The Society of Jesus
July 31st

One out of every seven Roman Catholic missionaries is a Jesuit, that is, a member of Rome's largest order, the Society of Jesus. In seventy-four countries there are 32,000 members of the society, operating more than 4,000 schools. The year 1956 marked the 400th anniversary of the death of their founder, St. Ignatius Loyola. They have come a long way since the stern, dynamic, and ambitious ex-soldier in 1524 gathered a half-dozen friends around him and began to devise the military type of spiritual discipline for which Jesuits are famous.

Loyola's prominence as a churchman probably surprised him as much as it surprised anyone. What he really wanted, or thought he wanted, was the glamorous life of a warrior, and it was for this that he trained himself. Born in Spain the year before Columbus discovered America, young Ignatius, the son of an impoverished noble family, grew up as a page in the court of Ferdinand and Isabella. He mingled with the knights and dreamed of the time when he could ride off to battle.

The military career he finally achieved was cut short when, in 1521, his leg was shattered in battle. The long period of recovery was a turning point in his life. Lying helpless, he could do nothing but read, and finding nothing else available, he read and reread the life of Christ and the lives of the saints. These books, and his reflections about them, made him resolve to give his life to the service of God.

Into the religious life Ignatius brought the habits and psychology of the soldier. He developed a sort of mental manual of arms known as Spiritual Exercises, a set of rules for posture, breathing, concentration, and contemplation. When perfected, these enabled him to say, "I can find God at all times, whenever I wish, and any man of good will can do the same." All Jesuits are still required to engage in the discipline of these same exercises eight days each year.

Soldiers in those days were men of meager education, and at thirty-three Ignatius had to start to college in Paris. It was here that he attracted his little group of six brilliant men (one of them was St. Francis Xavier). Out of this group grew the Society of Jesus, set up like a military body, with Ignatius as "general." By 1540 when Ignatius was forty-nine, the society had been formally approved and accepted by Pope Paul III. It had been assigned a special task—to combat the Protestant revolt that was sweeping Europe as a result of Luther's preaching in Germany. Wherever they were needed, Jesuits went to fight for the Catholic faith, disciplined soldiers in the spiritual wars.

A Day of Mourning

The ninth day of the Jewish month of Ab is a day of deep and complete mourning for devout Jews. The basic significance of this fast is its commemoration of the two occasions (seven centuries apart) on which the Temple and the city of Jerusalem were destroyed. Jews believe if Israel had not sinned it would not have lost its land and its identity as a nation. They fast on this day in expiation of their own individual sins and of their sins as a people. The Ninth of Ab is, then, a national memorial day, recalling the misfortunes of the past, pleading for the revival of Jewish national existence, and keeping alive the hope and courage of the Jewish people.

Various individual Jews keep the fast with varying degrees of severity. Among the pious it is a day of utter gloom and sorrow. Before the day begins at sunset, the evening meal must have been finished and no food or drink will be taken until the stars appear the next evening. At this last meal some will have sprinkled ashes on their food, symbolic of the ashes to which Temple and city were reduced. At night some will sleep without pillows, some will sleep on the floor, and some will go so far as to use a stone for a pillow. In the synagogues on this day they will chant in mournful tones the book of Lamentations, which was for many years credited to the prophet Jeremiah but is now known to be the work of many Jewish poets.

CHAPTER VIII

⇉⇉⇉⇉⇉⇉⇉⇉⇉⇉⇉⇉⇉ · ⇇⇇⇇⇇⇇⇇⇇⇇⇇⇇⇇⇇⇇

August

⇉⇉⇉⇉⇉⇉⇉⇉⇉⇉⇉⇉⇉ · ⇇⇇⇇⇇⇇⇇⇇⇇⇇⇇⇇⇇⇇

St. Peter's Chains

AUGUST 1ST

August 1st is the Feast of St. Peter's Chains, a day on which the Roman Catholic Church commemorates the miraculous release of the Apostle from prison, as recorded in the 12th chapter of Acts. Verses 6, 7, and 8 state that St. Peter, bound with two chains, was sleeping between two soldiers, when an angel came and wakened him and his chains fell off and he walked out a free man. Originally August 1st did not refer specifically to the incident of the chains. It started out only as the anniversary of the dedication of the fourth century church that was built on the Esquiline Hill in Rome in honor of St. Peter. Because this church was the repository of parts of the chains with which the Apostle had been bound, the emphasis on the anniversary gradually shifted to these relics and a new festival thus evolved.

Lammas Day
AUGUST 1ST

The British Lammas Day, no longer observed, is important as the ancestor of other special days that are still
very much alive. It was the grandfather of England's and
Canada's modern Harvest Festival and of America's
Thanksgiving. In medieval England August 1st was kept
as the day on which thank-offerings were made for the
grain crop that had just been harvested—that is, if any
worthwhile amount had been harvested. Hardheaded
Britishers saw no reason for thanksgiving if the harvest
had not been up to par. In good years, however, everyone
showed his gratitude by coming to church on August 1st
and bringing with him as an offering a loaf of bread
baked from the new wheat. This is how the day got its
name—lammas is a shortening of "loaf mass."

In modern times festivals of thanksgiving for the fruits
of the earth have sensibly been moved to a later time in
the year—September, October, and even, as in the United
States, November. By autumn all crops are in, not just
the early ones like grain. The timing of the festival thus
has a logic about it that it would not have if some items
were still to be gathered. In regard to both the loaves and
the timing, Lammas Day appears to have had a close relationship to the Jewish Feast of Weeks, or Pentecost.
This festival, too, came at the end of the grain harvest,
and the chief feature of its ceremonial was the offering
in the Temple of two loaves of bread made from the new
grain.

A Visitor by Night

AUGUST 3RD

The Gospel of St. John (chapter 3) tells of Nicodemus who came in the night to speak with Jesus and found himself involved in a conversation about the Holy Spirit that was completely beyond his ability to understand. It is not recorded that he became a follower of the Lord, but he turns up again in John, chapter 19, verse 39, bringing spices and helping with the burial after the Crucifixion. On this evidence the Church has accepted him as a Christian and a saint, and has set aside August 3rd in his honor.

Almost nothing is known about Nicodemus, and yet he has remained through the centuries one of the most fascinating characters of New Testament times. He must have been a prominent man in the community, for Jesus called him "a master in Israel." This would mean, too, that he was a learned man, for masters of Israel had to be students of the law. It is more than likely that he met the Lord under cover of darkness in order to avoid recognition by any passerby, and because well-known people always try to avoid crowds. If he was prominent, it is more than likely that he was wealthy, too, and the costly materials he brought for the embalming would seem to support this. Some scholars have also ventured a guess that he was old, because in his discussion with Jesus, he asked, "How can a man be born when he is old?" But all this is only conjecture. The mystery of the gentle, scholarly Nicodemus remains—a pleasant theme for poets, but an enigma never to be resolved in this world by any real factual data.

The Apostle to the Indians

AUGUST 5TH

On August 5th, in 1604, "the apostle to the Indians" was born. He was a man whose contribution to the spread of Christianity in America should have earned him much more fame than it did. The apostle's name was John Eliot. He grew up in England, studied for the ministry at Cambridge, and expected to lead the quiet life of an English parson. But the vindictive and shortsighted attitude of the Church of England in its dealings with the Puritans was more than he could stand, and in 1631 he came to Boston and entered the Congregational ministry.

It was not the proper Bostonians, however, but the Pequot Indians of the colony, who provided Eliot with his real lifework. Until he died in 1690, at the age of eighty-six, he continually made the rounds of the Indian villages of Massachusetts, preaching, organizing, teaching, and building churches. Two conspicuous "firsts" should be put down to Eliot's credit. His Catechism, published in England in 1653, was the first book ever printed in an Indian language. And his translation of the entire Bible into the Pequot tongue, completed in 1663, was the first book of any kind printed on the American continent.

The Feast of the Transfiguration

AUGUST 6TH

The Feast of the Transfiguration, a fairly late comer to the calendar of the western part of the Church, was dropped by most Protestants at the time of the Reformation and is now observed only by Roman Catholics, Lutherans, and Anglicans (Episcopalians). It commemorates the event recorded in Luke, chapter 9, verse 28, when Jesus took His three favorite apostles, Peter, James, and John, to the mountain top, and there, as they watched, His countenance became radiant, His garments glistened, and He began to hold a conversation with Moses and Elijah, who had miraculously appeared. A voice from a cloud said, "This is my beloved Son: hear him."

This tremendously significant incident came at a time when the Lord's ministry in Galilee had come to a close and was to all appearances a sad failure. The general populace was disappointed in Him because He had not turned out to be the nationalist, militarist kind of Messiah they had hoped would come and lead their little army to world supremacy, or more especially, to victory over the despised Roman occupation forces. Jewish leaders were beginning to plot ways of getting rid of Him. Even among His twelve close associates, Jesus could not actually count on any real understanding.

From a human standpoint, this was a time of decision. Either He should give up His mission as hopeless, or He should go on to inevitable suffering and humiliation. Selecting the three most sensitive of His Apostles, He made the journey to the mountaintop and there gave them this special insight into His role as the fulfillment of "The Law (symbolized by Moses) and the Prophets" (symbolized by Elijah). These three, at least, would remember this vision when the impending dark hours finally arrived.

Since as early as the fourth century the Transfiguration has been one of the major feasts of the Eastern Church. It was not officially observed in the West until 1497, when Pope Calixtus III proclaimed it in celebration of a great victory of the Western armies over the Turks at Belgrade.

The mountain on which the event took place is not

named in any of the Gospel accounts, but scholars are now pretty well agreed that it was Mt. Tabor.

The Holy Name
AUGUST 7TH

The name of Jesus has always had a special power of its own in the minds of Christians. The Lord often spoke to His followers about doing or asking something "in my name," and the Apostles, after the Ascension, immediately began to use the phrase "in the name of Jesus" almost as a formula. For example (Acts, chapter 3, verse 6) when St. Peter healed the lame man in the Temple, he said, "In the name of Jesus of Nazareth, rise up and walk."

Various churches have set apart different days to honor the Holy Name. Some observe January 1st, which is the Feast of the Circumcision, because, according to Jewish custom, Jesus was given his name when he was circumcized. The Roman Catholic Church observes the second Tuesday after the Epiphany (January 6th). At the time of the Reformation, August 7th was adopted by the Church of England (Episcopal in this country) as "the Holy Name of Jesus."

One of the most familiar, and yet least understood, symbols of the name of Jesus is the *IHS* design that is often seen carved in the furnishings or embroidered on the vestments of many churches. People give all sorts of explanations of this symbol. Some say the letters stand for Latin phrases meaning "In this Sign" or "Jesus Saviour of Mankind." Others say it means simply "In His Service." What confuses them is that these are Greek letters, and the middle one is not an H at all. It is a Greek *eta*, or "E."

The equivalent in English, therefore, would be JES, the first three letters of the name Jesus.

The Laziest Saint

AUGUST 10TH

"Lazy as Lawrence" used to be an expression in England. The origin of it was somewhat gruesome. It referred to the execution of St. Lawrence, who, while being roasted over a slow fire, would not bother to move himself but said to his torturers, "Turn me over now, this side is done."

There is not much recorded history about St. Lawrence, for whom the great North American river was named, but there is certainly plenty of legend. He was born in Aragon (Spain); he served Pope Sixtus II as a deacon; and he was martyred in the third century. That is as far as the facts go. Legend says that he was the Pope's treasurer, and that when Sixtus was led off to be killed, Lawrence begged to be taken along. Sixtus assured him that he would follow within three days, but instructed him that in the meantime he should give all the treasure to the poor. It was by carrying out this instruction that Lawrence brought about his own martyrdom. The authorities were so angered at this irretrievable distribution of the Church's wealth that they put Lawrence on a gridiron and roasted him to death.

Another story, which brought him the name of "the courteous Spaniard," tells that two hundred years after his death his tomb was opened to receive the bones of St. Stephen, the first of all Christian martyrs. When the time came to deposit Stephen's relics, the skeleton of St. Lawrence politely moved to the left, giving the place of honor on the right to the distinguished newcomer.

Lawrence is always represented in Christian art holding a gridiron. The gridiron on which St. Lawrence met his death is preserved in the church of San Lorenzo in Rome.

St. Clare

AUGUST 12TH

August 12th is the anniversary of the death of a great woman, St. Clare, founder of the Franciscan order of women known as Poor Clare Nuns. Part of Clare's glory is reflected from that of her famous friend and fellow townsman, St. Francis of Assisi, whose follower and co-worker she was. But it is more than likely that the world would have heard of her even if she had not had his influence and guidance.

They were much alike, these two young Italians who brought to religion a new note of happiness in an age when Christians tended to be somber about it. Francis was born of a noble family; so was Clare. But most of all, both had an unbounded, contagious joy that people found irresistible. Anyone who knew them both—and in the town of Assisi there must have been many who knew them—could have predicted that if Francis and Clare ever decided to work together they would be one of the happiest and most effective teams that ever served the Lord.

Clare ran away from home to become a follower of St. Francis when she was only seventeen or eighteen years old; the record is not clear as to whether she was born in 1193 or 1194. Francis received her profession as a nun, and on Palm Sunday, 1212, they founded the Order of Poor Ladies, which was later called by its present name, Poor Clares. Soon she was joined in the order by her two sisters and her widowed mother. Clothed in habits of coarse brown wool, these women went wherever

Francis and his monks went, practicing penance, rejoicing in God's wonderful world, and living on alms given to them by people along the way. Religious orders dependent on alms have many thousands of members today, but the idea was an entirely new one when St. Francis and St. Clare first dared to try it.

St. Clare is the patron saint of embroidery workers and washerwomen, for reasons now forgotten. She is also invoked for good weather, and it is easy to see why. To Clare all weather was good—everything in God's world was good. On her deathbed her last words were "Lord God, be blessed for having created me." The faithful nun, whom St. Francis called his "little spiritual plant" outlived her teacher by twenty-seven years. She died in 1253 and was canonized two years later.

The Assumption
AUGUST 15TH

Though it is only since 1950 that Roman Catholics have been required to believe in the Assumption of the Blessed Virgin Mary, many people have believed it and celebrated it since as early as the sixth century, and perhaps even before that. The dogma is simply that the body of the Lord's Mother, after her death, was not subjected to the usual disintegrating processes but was united with her soul in heaven. Tradition says that after the crucifixion Mary went and lived in the home of the Apostle John, in accordance with the arrangement made by Jesus Himself as He hung on the Cross. See St. John's Gospel, chapter 19, verses 26 and 27. John's home was in Jerusalem and it is said that Mary died there.

There is a charming legend in connection with Mary's death and assumption in the writings of another John:

St. John of Damascus. He tells that at the age of seventy-
three the Blessed Virgin was on her deathbed, and the
word went out miraculously to all the Apostles, most of
whom by that time were scattered all over the known
world. All of them hurried back to Jerusalem and gathered around the death-bed—all, that is, except one. St.
Thomas, as usual, was late. Arriving after the funeral,
Thomas, full of grief and self-condemnation, asked for
the special privilege of having the tomb reopened in
order that he might have one last look at the beloved
remains. The privilege was granted, but when the tomb
was opened it was found empty. The assumption had already taken place. Naturally the dogma is not based on
the legend. Rather, the point of the legend is that it
shows how early the idea of the assumption had taken
hold of people's minds and hearts.

In Armenia no one eats any of the new crop of grapes
until Assumption Day. A trayful of them is blessed at the
church on this day, and after the service everyone is free
to go ahead and enjoy the new fruit. The day therefore
has something of the tone of a harvest thanksgiving
among the Armenians, as it does also in Belgium, where
processions go from church to fields and the new fruits
and grains are blessed. Another pleasant Armenian custom is that every woman named Mary entertains her
friends on this day.

In Italy and Spain there are colorful processions
through the streets and in these countries displays of fireworks are a feature of the celebration. Italian-American
colonies in big American cities observe the day much the
same as they would back in their homeland—a spectacle
well worth seeing if you live in a city with a large Italian
population.

Strangest of all Assumption celebrations is perhaps the one at the monastery near Damascus, in Syria, where people come from far and near bringing offerings of new wheat to the Virgin. What makes it strange is that Mohammedans come, too, and join with the Christians in this festival that could not possibly be of religious significance to anyone but believers in the Divinity of Jesus.

The Father of American Lutheranism

AUGUST 15TH

The United Lutheran Church with its two million members is the largest body of Lutherans in America. It can trace its beginnings to August 15, 1748 when Henry Melchoir Muhlenberg, a German missionary, organized its first synod in what was then the colony of Pennsylvania. Eastern Pennsylvania in the early days had a great attraction for German immigrants, and there were many scattered Lutheran congregations in that part of the country when the thirty-one year old Muhlenberg came from Germany to minister to them. He soon saw, however, that something besides organization was needed.

This was new country, pioneer country, totally unlike the land and culture these people had left, and the greatest of all problems was to develop a Lutheranism adapted to the life of the New World rather than that of the Old. Muhlenberg did not limit his activities to eastern Pennsylvania. He ranged from New York to Georgia, building new congregations, training and ordaining pastors, and helping his people to make the transition that would change them from German Lutherans to American Lutherans. The energetic young missionary is still known as "the father of Lutheranism in America."

St. Roch and His Dog
AUGUST 16TH

In France if you want to indicate that two people are always seen together you say, "They are like St. Roch and his dog." The reference is to the great fourteenth century saint who according to legend was nursed through a long illness by his faithful dog. The story is that Roch was desperately ill and he was all alone in a forest. His dog disappeared every day, and after a while, always returned with a fresh loaf of bread. The man from whom the dog was stealing the bread finally discovered the theft. The regularity and apparent purposefulness of it interested the man, and he followed the dog and found the ailing saint. But by this time Roch was convalescent, entirely through the ministrations of the devoted animal, and the man's help was not needed.

In 1414, nearly a century after Roch's death when the great Council of Constance was meeting, a terrible plague broke out and threatened to wipe out not only the town of Constance, but also the hundreds of church dignitaries assembled there from all parts of the world. St. Roch, who up to that time had been quite obscure, was invoked for help and the plague immediately abated.

Roch's fame as a result of this miracle led the people of Venice to feel that they had need of this saint who had such power over contagious diseases. The Venetians at that time were the world's greatest traders, and their commercial contacts with the East constantly exposed them to pestilence. So, in 1485, they organized what appeared to be a band of pious pilgrims to visit the tomb of St. Roch, in Montpellier, France. Once at the tomb, however, the pilgrims turned out to be grave robbers.

They took the saint's bones back to Venice, where, to house the sacred relics, they built the great Church of St. Rocco. In extenuation of this act of theft, it should be said that the Venetians did establish in connection with the Church of St. Rocco, a community for the purpose of caring for persons with infectious diseases.

St. Roch has in all countries, of course, become the patron of all who suffer from contagion. His patronage has even been extended to sick animals. In art St. Roch is always represented with his dog.

From Rags to Riches
August 18th

The story of St. Helena outdoes any of Horatio Alger's rags-to-riches tales. Born the daughter of a poor tavern keeper, Helena ended her life as dowager empress of the Roman Empire. She also is known for her discovery of the cross on which the Lord had died. The rise from obscurity to such a peak of eminence was not always easy. It all began when a handsome young Roman officer, stopping at the little hotel in the province of Bithynia, fell in love with the innkeeper's beautiful daughter. The two were soon married. They had a son whom they named Constantine.

Everything was wonderful for a while, but there came a time when the husband's success began to affect their relationship. When he had risen to the point where he was one of three top men in the government, he felt that he had outgrown his wife. He divorced Helena and married a wealthy and prominent woman of Rome. And that is where he made his greatest mistake. The boy Constantine was even more brilliantly successful than his father. Constantine did not stop at being one of three running the empire—he became the emperor. And he brought his mother to the palace with him.

Constantine became a tentative sort of Christian in 318, although he was not baptized until he was on his deathbed, nearly twenty years later. Helena, though, accepted the faith wholeheartedly. In 326, at the age of eighty, she set off to make a pilgrimage to the Holy Land. There she supervised crews of men in many excavating operations and according to generally accepted tradition, succeeded in finding the true cross. She is also credited with having found the tomb in which Jesus was buried, and the house in which the Holy Family lived.

She died on August 18th in the year 328. It is likely that she died as she was returning from the Holy Land. She was buried in the Church of the Holy Apostles in Constantinople. The city of Constantinople, formerly called Byzantium, had been renamed in honor of her son.

The Emperor's Vision

AUGUST 19TH

It was supposedly on this day, in the year 312, that the Roman Emperor Constantine and his entire army saw their famous vision of a blazing cross in the sky surrounded by Latin words meaning "In this sign conquer." This happened just before an important battle, and the courage the heavenly sign gave to the emperor and his soldiers played no small part in the victory that followed. Constantine, though interested in Christianity and attracted by it, had not yet become a Christian, but within a year after this supernatural experience, he issued an order that put an end to the persecution of Christians which had been going on intermittently for nearly three hundred years. Thus this day's event was the turning point in the history of Christianity. From that time on, Christians were free to worship without fear of the legal authorities. Constantine himself waited twenty-five more years before becoming officially a Christian. He was baptized on his deathbed in 337.

The army had been encamped near the city of Treves when the Cross in the sky was seen. A chapel was built there, and still stands in commemoration of the vision.

The Saint Who Never Lived

AUGUST 19TH

For many years there appeared in the list of saints for August 19th the name of Magnus the Martyr. But there never really was such a person. It all came about because somebody did not read an earlier list properly. An early martyrology gave the name of *Andreas Tribunus, Magnus Martyr,* which meant Andrew the Tribune, Great Martyr. (A tribune was a high-ranking officer in Rome.) Some unknown copyist, either through absentmindedness or through eagerness to find all the saints he could, read it as if it meant two saints, Andrew and Magnus—and from then on there was a St. Magnus. In their enthusiasm, martyrologists even developed details about this invented saint, placing him fifty years before Andrew (who died in 303) and putting him in a different environment. Today, of course, the correction has been made and Magnus is recognized as an imaginary figure.

The Saint Who Burned Icicles

AUGUST 19TH

Even the most fanciful stories about the saints can usually be found to have a basis of truth if not a basis of fact.

For example, St. Sebaldus, who is commemorated on August 19th, is said to have built a fire out of icicles when a surly peasant to whom he had applied for shelter refused to put any more wood on the dying embers in his fireplace. It seems unlikely that a great and serious missionary, which Sebaldus was, would stoop to such a show of magic, or that a man with such magic powers would be dependent on a peasant for shelter.

But the legend is an allegory, not history. Sebaldus, the son of a petty chieftain of one of the semi-savage tribes along the Danube, went to Rome to be educated for the priesthood and then returned to his native territory to carry the Christian faith to that wild, cold land. And it was not only the climate that was cold; the people themselves received him with a frigid aloofness that would have discouraged anyone but a saint. The story of the burning of the icicles is really a picture, says one scholar, "of how Sebaldus quickened and made to flame with divine love the icy nature of the people with whom he was trying to work." That is what legends are for: to tell the truth, not the facts. Sebaldus lived in the eighth century. He is venerated now chiefly at Nuremburg, Germany, where there is a shrine of St. Sebaldus.

Love Me, Love My Dog
AUGUST 20TH

Bernard of Clairvaux, honored on this day in the Roman Catholic Church, was one of the all-time great men in Christian history. Born into a noble and wealthy French family, Bernard as a child and young man was one of those people for whom it is difficult to buy a present—the kind of person who "has everything." He had money, position, wit, charm, and good looks. In the light of what the Lord said about rich men and the trouble they have being interested in the Kingdom of Heaven, it is a wonder Bernard cared about the Church at all. There must have been something very special in the life of the home in which he grew up. Out of seven children in the family, this one became a saint and four others attained to that degree of religious distinction called "beatification," which is the next thing to being a saint.

When Bernard realized that he was called to the monastic life he never for one moment supposed the call applied only to him. He rounded up thirty-one of his friends and took them along when he showed up at the monastery door. And he did not stop there. Before he died he had founded and filled one hundred and sixty new monasteries. It was said that "mothers hid their sons and wives hid their husbands" when they heard Bernard was coming by, for they knew that anyone who listened to him would follow him.

Another thing they said about Bernard was that he "carried the twelfth century on his shoulder," by which they meant that he was a man of such wide horizons that he stood out above all other leaders of his time. He settled church problems; he admonished and guided kings; he wrote, preached, and taught; and he went up and down Europe organizing the Second Crusade (1146), the failure of which was the greatest disappointment of his life. No one else had anything like the influence or effect he had on the century in which he lived. Pope Pius VIII, in 1830, recognized his importance by naming him one of the "Doctors of the Church," of whom to this day there have been only twenty-nine. This puts him officially in the company of such men as St. Augustine of Hippo and St. Thomas Aquinas.

Of Bernard's voluminous writings there still remain

eleven treaties, three hundred sermons, and more than five hundred letters. In one of his sermons—the first one, in fact—you will find that famous injunction: "Love me, love my dog." Bernard was the first person who ever said that. He said it in Latin, of course, but in that time and that language it meant exactly what it means in English today: that you do not really accept a man unless you accept his peculiarities and secondary attachments.

First Methodist Bishop
AUGUST 20TH

This date was the birthday in 1745 of Francis Asbury, the harnessmaker's apprentice who became a Methodist preacher at eighteen and was head of all Methodists in America when he was thirty-nine. Asbury, an English boy of great promise, was sent to America by John Wesley in 1771. At this time the American Methodists still considered themselves a society within the Church of England. Their leaders were not Church of England ministers and therefore did not claim to be clergymen at all.

The War of Independence changed this, and Asbury was glad to lead in the change. Wesley had said, "Who leaves the Church of England leaves us." But when Asbury was elected general superintendent of all American Methodist groups in 1784, he began at once to call himself a bishop and to ordain ministers. The people were in the mood for independence of everything English, and the Methodist Church as a separate entity quickly became a fact.

Asbury was perhaps the most tireless missionary traveler since St. Paul. He was a great believer in the itinerant preaching for which Methodism was famous in pioneer America. On horseback he ranged many times from New

Hampshire to Georgia, preaching, organizing, and ordaining, until his death in 1816. It has been estimated that over his lifetime of seventy-one years he covered a total of 270,000 miles.

The Heart of Mary

AUGUST 22ND

The poets have so successfully spoken of the heart as the seat of our feelings and our virtues (or shortcomings) that the idea is by now a part of our everyday language. A man is good-hearted, big-hearted, broken-hearted, black-hearted, chicken-hearted, and so on. Such expressions are universally in use. As long ago as New Testament times, people spoke in similar terms. In St. Luke's Gospel there are three references to the heart of the Blessed Virgin Mary. A wise old man predicted her sorrow, saying "A sword shall pierce thine own heart also" (chapter 2, verse 35) and twice, when flashes of her Son's divine nature were unmistakably apparent, Luke tells that "she kept these things in her heart," meaning that she thought about them privately (chapter 2, verses 19 and 51).

At this time of year many orders in the Roman Catholic Church keep the festival of the Immaculate Heart of Mary, commemorating the joys and sorrows her heart held, her virtues, and her love—for God, for her divine Son, and for mankind.

The Negroes' Great Benefactor

AUGUST 24TH

William Wilberforce, who was born in England on August 24th, in 1759, could legitimately be called a Protestant saint, and is certainly so regarded by Negroes throughout the world. He, more than any other one man, awakened the world to the evils of the slave trade, and began the movement toward its abolition. Wilberforce started life as a wealthy boy whose worst fault was aimlessness. There was nothing especially bad about him. He just didn't amount to much, or care to.

In 1784, at the age of twenty-five, he was suddenly converted to what was called "evangelical" Christianity— a real and active dedication to Christ rather than the formal religion of the Church of England of those times. From that time on he gave his life and most of his fortune in a steady campaign to help the underdog—any underdog. He crusaded against all kinds of oppression.

The most obvious and pathetic of all persecuted people at that point in history were the poor Africans who were being carried off from their native land and sold into slavery. Wilberforce took up their cause in the British House of Commons, of which he was a member. He made slow progress—so slow that it was 1823 before he was able even to organize an antislavery society. But his efforts in the Negro's behalf finally bore fruit, and in 1833 the emancipation bill was passed and slavery was at an end in the British empire, some thirty years before the same action was taken in America. Wilberforce, however, did not live to see his final victory—he died a month earlier. American Negroes have a Wilberforce College, located in Ohio, in honor of this man whose Christian concern about their plight was so largely responsible for their present freedom.

The St. Bartholomew's Massacre
AUGUST 24TH

August 24th is St. Bartholomew's Day, honoring one of the Twelve Apostles. Almost nothing is known about St.

Bartholomew—even his name is in doubt. *Bar* in Hebrew means "son"; Bar-thol-omew means Tholmai's son. Some scholars think this man was the Apostle Nathaniel, because the lists of the Apostles that include Nathaniel do not include Bartholomew, and vice versa.

St. Bartholomew's Day is famous—or infamous—in history for the horrible massacre that began in Paris on that day in 1572 and spread over all France, until 50,000 Huguenots had been killed. It was a senseless thing, engineered by Catherine de Medici, who was disturbed by the growing influence of the Protestant Admiral Coligny. She tried to have him assassinated and when the attempt failed, she took her rage out on all French Protestants.

St. Bartholomew, for some obscure reason, is the patron saint of plasterers.

Not much happens on St. Bartholomew's Day in these times, but for more than seven hundred years the whole routine of English life was upset by it every year. From 1133 to 1855 Bartholomew's Fair was a tremendous national event. It all started when a man named Rahere, who was Court Jester to King Henry I, decided to become a monk. His motives, one might guess, were more materialistic than spiritual. He drained a swamp at Smithfield on the outskirts of London, built a monastery, and piously cared for a nearby shrine of St. Bartholomew. Then, shrewd business man that he was, he started an annual fair on the good saint's day.

The fair was actually a public service; in twelfth century England the exchange of goods was not easy. Traders were afraid to travel about with their goods, for the country was full of bandits. So Rahere got royal protection for all travelers to and from Smithfield and invited all who wished to buy or sell to come to his Bartholomew Fair. And they came from every part of England. At first the fair was mainly for buying and selling of cloth, but it was not long before every kind of commodity was for sale there. The qualities that had made Rahere a court jester soon showed up, too. Sideshows and all kinds of rowdy entertainment became an essential part of the annual occasion. Bartholomew Fair has been called the "Coney Island of medieval England."

After a time, of course, the commercial life of the country became more settled and the fair was no longer needed as a marketing facility. But by then it was so much a part of English tradition that it was continued for pleasure alone, until by the nineteenth century, the entertainment had become so vulgar and debased that a movement was started to close it up. The closing, however, was not easily accomplished. In 1822 thousands of people rioted in protest against the threat that the Fair would not be held. Finally, in 1855, it was permanently abolished. The licentious merrymaking of Bartholomew Fair was a strange memorial to the gentle saint, whom Jesus Himself had called "a man in whom there is no guile." (John, chapter 1, verse 47).

Good King Louis
AUGUST 25TH

All towns called St. Louis, and there are a good many of them, are named for the good King Louis IX of France, whose piety was so widely known that he was proclaimed a saint less than thirty years after his death. Louis IX, who came to the throne in 1226 at the age of twelve, was not a great statesman, but he was a great Christian, and that is even rarer. He fed beggars from his own table, and washed their feet. He went among lepers and ministered to them. He cared about his people, and his people loved him devotedly. In 1224 Louis fell gravely ill, and made a vow that if he came through this sickness he would lead a Crusade to Palestine, to recover the holy places in the hands of the Turks. He did get well, and he became the leader of two Crusades, one in 1248 and one in 1270. Neither was greatly successful. Louis was stricken with a plague and died on August 20, 1270.

The Baby Saint

August 28th

August 28th commemorates the most precocious and shortest-lived saint on record—St. Rumbald of Kent, who at his birth cried three times, "I am a Christian," and immediately demanded baptism. For the ceremony he chose his own name and selected and instructed his god-parents. After being baptized, he walked to a well nearby and took up a stand where he preached without inter-ruption for three days and then died.

This is, of course, a most incredible story, but what-ever actually did happen occurred so long ago that it is impossible to say now what was the basis of the absurd legend. Certainly there must have been some saintly boy-wonder in Kent named Rumbald, whose piety greatly im-pressed his elders.

For several centuries Kentish fishermen invoked the blessing and protection of St. Rumbald on their labors. They saved the eight largest fish from every catch and sold them, putting the proceeds into a special fund which they allowed to accumulate for a whole year. Then, on Christmas Eve they spent the entire year's savings on one great, uproarious feast, which they called a "Rumbald," in their patron's honor. The custom died out long ago,

but even now in Kent it is still not uncommon to hear
Christmas Eve called "Rumbald Night."

"Make Me Pure—But Not Yet"
AUGUST 28TH

On August 28th, in 1565, a company of Spanish soldiers
landed on the Florida coast and began to establish what
is now the town of St. Augustine, America's oldest community. The settlement was named in honor of St. Augustine of Hippo (Hippo is in North Africa) on whose feast
day the landing was made. Augustine is one of the towering figures of Christian history. When people speak of
him they always use the word "greatest"—the greatest
teacher since St. Paul, the greatest of the Church Fathers,
the greatest influence on Christian doctrine, etc. And indeed he was the greatest.

But for many years he was anything but a saint. Born
in the middle of the fourth century, Augustine was for
thirty years the despair of his Christian mother, St.
Monica. To say he was wild is a real understatement.
Through all the years of dissipation, however, the Holy
Spirit and his mother's prayers apparently were working
on him. By the time he was thirty-two he was being
pulled so hard in two directions that he was praying, but
hoping his prayers would not be answered. "O God," he
prayed, "make me pure—but not yet." When he was
thirty-three he was baptized, and thereafter his story is
the story of one of the giants of the Church. Within four
years he was Bishop of Hippo, and for the next forty
years, as teacher, writer, preacher, and theologian, he
carved out for himself one of the really big niches in
Christianity's hall of fame.

St. Augustine tells the following story in his famous

autobiography, *Confessions,* which scholars say is the first completely honest book of self-analysis in the history of literature. One day in the year 372, when he was thirty-one years old, Augustine who was at that time a dissipated young rake, was lying under a fig tree when he heard a voice saying, "Take and read, take and read." He looked all around, but there was no one there—so Augustine thought he had better obey the voice. He went at once to his library, which was a large one, and opened the first scroll he picked up. And the first words he read were the thirteenth verse of the thirteenth chapter of St. Paul's Epistle to the Romans: "Let us walk honestly, as in the day; not in rioting and drunkenness, not in chambering and wantonness." This was enough for Augustine. The passage applied to him perfectly. He became a Christian.

No one can say, however, that he did not put up a good fight. He had an answer for everything. When, as a child, he had been persuaded to read the Bible, he resisted its influence by saying that he was "repelled by its vulgar style." St. Peter, St. Paul, and many others since have found out that the Lord has a way of winning His man, and in the end He won Augustine. Once the struggle was over, the former playboy turned out to be the greatest of the selected group known as the Fathers of the Church. No one else, not even Thomas Aquinas, ever exerted so profound an influence on the development of Christian doctrine. Saint Augustine is the patron saint of theologians.

St. John the Baptist
AUGUST 29TH

Way back in the fourth century Christians began to commemorate the beheading of John the Baptist. The ob-

servance started at Sebaste, where the Baptist was supposed to have been buried. Anyone can read the grim
account in Mark, chapter 6, verses 17-28, of how the
queen's daughter (by a former marriage) so greatly
pleased her stepfather, King Herod, with her dancing at
his birthday party that he offered to give her whatever
she asked, even half his kingdom, and how the girl, at
her mother's urging, asked for the head of John the Baptist on a platter.

It has come to be taken for granted that the dancer's
name was Salome, but this name is not mentioned in the
Bible. She is called only "the damsel." The Jewish historian Josephus says that the queen did have a daughter
named Salome, but there is nothing definite to indicate
that it was she who danced. Nevertheless, writers like
Oscar Wilde and composers like Richard Strauss have
clung to Salome, and Salome it is and probably always
will be in the popular mind.

There was a medieval legend that said the queen—
Herodias was her name—was in love with the Baptist.
Wilde in his play and Strauss in his opera made "the
damsel" in love with him, too. According to another old
legend, Herod, in grief over having let himself be ma-
neuvered into a position where he had to kill an innocent
and good man, had the head concealed and buried within
the palace walls. The disciples, according to Mark, chapter 6, verse 29, took the headless body "and laid it in a
tomb."

According to superstition, red spots appear (on August
29th only) on the herb known as St. Johnswort. This is
how the plant honors St. John Baptist. Apparently the little
perennial grows almost everywhere, and has been valued
by many peoples, sometimes for supposed magic prop-

erties and sometimes for its actual medicinal qualities. American Indians used it effectively for everything from snake bite to tuberculosis. It was especially good for chest ailments and for drawing poisons from infected wounds. On the Isle of Wight they have less practical and more romantic ideas about St. Johnswort. If you were on the island on the night of August 29th and should unhappily chance to step on this plant, a fairy horse would rise up under you and take you for the ride of your life.

The little yellow-flowered herb became connected with the name of St. John Baptist in an accidental but interesting way. Crusaders in the Holy Land found that the inhabitants hung bunches of it over their doors to frighten away demons. They called it "Devil's Flight," and under this name brought it back to Europe, where it flourished in especial profusion around the end of June. It was used to festoon doors and windows at the time of the summer solstice, when the air was thought to be especially full of evil spirits. The anniversary of St. John Baptist's birth falls on July 24th right in the midst of the midsummer celebration, so it was quite natural that his name should be attached, in Christian minds, to the flower most in evidence at this time. And after that it was also quite natural that it should be connected with this second day on which the Baptist is remembered while the herb is still in bloom.

The Patron Saint of Cab Drivers

AUGUST 30TH

St. Fiacre was a hermit back in the seventh century. He was also a hotheaded Irishman. One time when he went to see a French bishop his reputation for impatience had preceded him, and the bishop thought he would teach the terrible tempered Irishman a lesson. So the bishop kept him sitting all day on a rock in the garden for an appointment. The story does not tell how Fiacre took this discipline, but one may judge from what followed that he did not spend the entire time expressing anger. Apparently some of the waiting time was given to devotions. Or maybe some of the old hermit's goodness just rubbed off on the rock. At any rate the rock was soon discovered to have miraculous powers. Not long afterward the king, sitting in the place where Fiacre had waited for the bishop, was cured of an illness.

The news spread quickly, of course, and the place became a shrine, to which many pilgrims went to be cured of all kinds of ailments. Then, because of the great numbers of pilgrims who were passing through Paris on their way to the shrine of St. Fiacre, some alert Parisian put up a tavern along the route through the city and called it Hotel de St. Fiacre. From that time it was not long before there was a thriving cab business going between hotel and shrine, and the cabs that carried the pilgrims back and forth were called "fiacres." And that is why to this day the French word for cab is "fiacre," and St. Fiacre is the patron saint of all cab drivers.

The Banishment of Anne Hutchinson

AUGUST 30TH

Those who fight tyranny often turn out to be tyrants themselves, when their chance comes. Something like that was the case in the Massachusetts Colony where the Puritans, who had left Europe in order to be free, soon developed the most strait-laced dictatorship this country has ever seen. August 30th is the anniversary of the banishment from Massachusetts of Anne Hutchinson, a woman who had the reckless courage to speak out against the despotic authority of the Boston clergy.

At the age of thirty-four Anne had come from England to the new colony, and she did not like what she found there. Not being able to get a hearing from the church leaders, she organized weekly meetings of the women of the town of Boston. At these meetings she held the floor, commenting with intelligence and insight on the previous Sunday's sermons and never missing a chance to point out that the clergy were autocrats. She was by no means just a troublemaker. She was a brilliant woman, with a mind that perceived the difference between real Christianity and the petty legalistic regulations of the Puritans.

It was not the way to make herself popular with the men who ruled the colony. Although her campaign divided the populace into factions, the clerical party won out easily. In 1637, Anne was tried—by the opposition of course—and expelled from Massachusetts. The charge against her was "traducing the clergy." (To *traduce* means to slander or hold up to contempt.) She went from Boston to the wilds of Long Island where, in 1643 she was killed by Indians—a proper fate, said the stern Massachusetts preachers, for one who had traduced them.

VARIABLE HOLIDAYS AND OBSERVANCES

The Festival of Christ the King

Both Protestant and Roman Catholic Churches have a Festival of Christ the King. The Catholics hold theirs in October. Protestants since 1937 have held theirs on the last Sunday in August. In the early 1930's the Federal Council of Churches appointed a committee to work out a calendar that would be acceptable to all its member

denominations. Included in the proposed calendar was a
new season, Kingdomtide, to begin on the last Sunday in
August and continue until Advent (four Sundays before
Christmas). The emphasis is upon Christ as King in the
affairs of this world—political, economic, and social.
Services of worship throughout this season are built
around the hope of the coming of the Kingdom of Heaven
on earth. The general text suggested for Kingdomtide is
Mark, chapter 1, verse 14: "Jesus came into Galilee
preaching the Gospel of God, saying, 'The time is fulfilled and the Kingdom of God is at hand.'"

The committee's recommended calendar was officially
accepted by the National Council of Churches when it
replaced the Federal Council. It was soon obvious, however, that the makers of the new calendar had unfortunately overlooked one fact in planning an important
festival for the end of August: church attendance at this
time of year reaches its lowest point. For this reason the
Festival of Christ the King has not achieved the prominence it deserves in Protestant life.

The Month of Elul

The first two days of the month Elul are observed among
the Jews as the beginning of the last month of the civil
year. The entire month is devoted to preparation for the
New Year and the solemn "high holidays" with which
each Jewish year begins. Originally, the Jewish people
had no names for either their months or for the days of
the week. Both months and days were simply numbered.
The name Elul, like the names of most of the other
months, was borrowed from the Babylonians, in whose
country the Jews spent seventy weary years as captives,
some twenty-five centuries ago.

Although the name *Elul* originally was probably the name of some Babylonian god, certain rabbis, with their happy inventiveness, have adapted it to Judaism by pointing out that the letters, E,L,U, and L stand for the Hebrew words of the sixteenth verse of the second chapter of the Song of Songs: "I am for my Beloved and my Beloved is for me." It is explained that this verse dramatizes the relationship between God and man, a relationship of love not dependent upon any intermediary. The emphasis on such a relationship is obviously appropriate in a month of preparation for the climax of the annual religious cycle. During the month of Elul the Shofar (ceremonial horn) is blown each day except on the Sabbaths, the 27th Psalm is read both morning and evening, and all letters written are customarily concluded with good wishes for the coming New Year.

CHAPTER IX

September

The Cripples' Best Friend

SEPTEMBER 1ST

In the eastern section of London there is a church called St. Giles Cripplesgate. When it was built it was at the edge of town, beside a city-gate, where it would be especially handy for cripples, for it was the custom in those days to build any church dedicated to St. Giles in a place where lame people from all the countryside might reach it easily without having to struggle through the congested streets. St. Giles is the patron saint of cripples, and in the Middle Ages there were many churches built to honor him and to provide shrines for the afflicted people who wished to invoke his help.

There is a legend that tells how St. Giles came to have this relationship with the physically handicapped. The good man lived alone in a cave in France, entirely withdrawn from the world. His one companion was a doe, which came daily to the cave and allowed the hermit to milk her. This milk was his only food. One day the doe came dashing frantically into the cave, hotly pursued by a hunter. An arrow, intended for the animal, struck Giles in the thigh. Right on the trail of the arrow came the hunter who turned out to be, of all people, the king himself! When he saw what he had done, the distraught ruler offered the hermit the best of medical attention, but Giles declined to be healed because, he said, his lameness would keep down his pride and would help him to understand others who were afflicted. Paintings of St. Giles always show him with his friend, the doe.

The Newest Saint

SEPTEMBER 3RD

Newest of saints in the Roman Catholic calendar is St. Pius X, a Pope who died less than half a century ago and was canonized in 1954. Christianity is still producing saints. Pius was born Giuseppe Sarto (in English that would be Joseph Tailor) in 1835, in the Italian village of Riese. His father was a postman. Many people still living knew Pius X, so it is possible to know what this saint was really like without having to pick one's way through a maze of legend. Men who have been face to face with him say that he was of irresistible personality and that what made him irresistible was a forth-right simplicity and an angelic kindness. "Everyone with him," says one writer, "had a deep conviction of being with a saint."

There are people still living who were eyewitnesses to miracles of healing performed by Pius. Their stories do not tell of spectacular exhibitions by a dramatic faith healer, but rather of a kind man who was tremendously

concerned about others. For example, a man with a paralyzed arm said to him, "Cure me, holy Father," and Pius,
stroking the man's arm, simply said, "Yes, yes, yes," and
the arm became well.

Pius became Pope in 1903. World War I broke out on
the eleventh anniversary of his election—August 4th—and
three weeks later he died. Until his canonization several
years ago, no Pope had been raised to sainthood since
1712.

Old Testament Saint

SEPTEMBER 6TH

Many Old Testament figures are carried as saints in the
Christian calendar, among them the prophet Zachariah,
who is commemorated on September 6th. He lived nearly
six centuries before Christianity began, and it is only fair
to wonder whether he would accept the honor of Christian sainthood if he had any choice in the matter. Among
the people of his own time Zachariah was important because of his untiring promotion of the rebuilding of the
Temple, which had been destroyed when the Syrian King
Nebuchadnezzar defeated the Jews, leveled the city of
Jerusalem, and carried off most of the nation into seventy
years of captivity. When the seventy sad years were
ended and the people returned to their own land, Zachariah kept insisting that they could not honestly say
that their exile was over until the Temple again stood in
its traditional place as the center of Jewish life and worship. His efforts were successful—the Temple was rebuilt.

From the Christian point of view, Zachariah deserves
to be included as one of the key persons in the story of
man's redemption because of his prophecies about the
Messiah, which Christians interpret as predictions having
to do with Jesus. Both Matthew and John in writing their

Gospels saw some of Zachariah's prophecies fulfilled in actual events in Jesus' earthly life. For example, Zachariah (chapter 9, verse 9) wrote of the king coming into Jerusalem riding upon an ass. Matthew finds here a prediction of the Palm Sunday procession. The bargain between Judas Iscariot and the chief priests is foretold, Matthew says, in Zachariah's chapter 11, verse 12. And when the prophet, chapter 12, verse 10, says "they shall look upon me whom they have pierced," John sees in these words a reference to the Crucifixion.

Zachariah's name, sometimes rendered *Zechariah*, sometimes *Zacharias*, means "Yahweh remembers." He was one of the twelve "minor prophets" of the Old Testament.

The Saint with Twelve Birthdays

SEPTEMBER 8TH

Naturally, it is not mathematically possible for anyone to have twelve birthdays in one year, but in the Coptic and Abyssinian Churches the first day of every month is celebrated as the birthday of the Virgin Mary. In addition to these twelve days they also devote the entire month of May to special honors for Mary. It is their way of showing how important they consider her. The rest of the ancient Church observes only one birthday of the Lord's mother, but it has many other festivals in her honor—more than are accorded to any other saint. The Immaculate Conception, the Annunciation, the Purification, the Visitation, and the Assumption are the chief ones, and there are several minor ones, too.

September 8th is called the Nativity of the Blessed Virgin Mary. There are only three birthdays in the whole Christian calendar: this one, John the Baptist's, and Christmas. Stories of John's birth and the Lord's are told in detail in the New Testament, but nothing appears there about Mary's. But by the end of the seventh century, Christians, anxious to find more ways of honoring this greatest of all saints, had established September 8th as her birthday and were keeping it as a feast. Their reason for selecting September 8th as the proper day is not known.

In Mexico they lead up to this day with a week-long festival in honor of the "Virgin of the Remedies," a crude and primitive little statue with a most interesting history. When Cortez conquered the Aztecs and took Mexico he ordered all the natives' religious images destroyed, and then he found that in his entire army there was only one Christian image with which to replace the heathen idols. And that one was a little wooden Virgin-and-Child that was obviously a homemade peasant work, with simple round holes for eyes and mouth.

Even this one was soon lost, and it stayed lost for twenty years, until it was discovered on a hillside by an old man who took it home with him. Next morning the statue had disappeared, and was found back on the hillside again. This went on for days—the old man taking it home each night and finding it back in the same place on the hill next day. The priests concluded that the Virgin wanted to be in that particular place, and they built her a church there, which in time became the wealthiest shrine in all Mexico because of the jewels and gold that were showered on the statue by pilgrims.

Unfortunately, this Virgin was adopted as their patron by the loyalist party in the Mexican revolution of 1810. She was on the wrong side. When the revolutionists were victorious they appropriated the shrine's treasure and despoiled the church. The little wooden Virgin of the Remedies, however, still has a devoted following, and during the week before the birthday of the Lady she represents they honor her with a great fiesta.

In Honor of the Cross
SEPTEMBER 14TH

September 14th is the Exaltation of the Holy Cross, a day with a history almost as long as the history of Christianity itself. It goes back to 334, when, on September 14th, two churches were dedicated in Jerusalem—one over the tomb of Jesus, and one on Calvary on the site of the Crucifixion. On that occasion the True Cross, discovered only a few years earlier, was for the first time displayed to the people and housed in a fitting place of its own. For many years thereafter, September 14th was known as the Feast of the Dedication, and was one of the high ranking days in the Christian calendar. Every devout Christian who could make the pilgrimage was in Jerusalem for the elaborate ceremonies on this day.

The Founder of Sunday Schools
SEPTEMBER 14TH

There has hardly been a child in the western world in the last one hundred and fifty years who has not come under the influence of Robert Raikes, an English newspaper publisher who was born on this day in 1735. In those days most children received constant religious instruction as a normal part of family home life, but Raikes was worried about the children in an orphanage in his town of Gloucester. Concentrating on children aged six to twelve, Raikes organized a special class on Sundays for the orphanage youngsters. Today's Sunday School children would shudder to think that Raikes' school lasted from five to eight hours, and today's educators would shudder to think that there was no attempt to grade the material to suit the age of the child. Six-year-olds and twelve-year-olds all had same lessons in the same form. The main text was a Catechism, and the only plan of instruction was to make everyone memorize the answers. The Bible was used in an entirely secondary sort of way—to illustrate points in the Catechism.

Although there had been Sunday instructions for children here and there (Roxbury, Massachusetts had a Sunday School as early as 1674) it was Raikes' school that first attracted general attention, and Raikes is considered the founder of the Sunday School movement. It is worth noting that Raikes intended only to supplement (never to replace) the home as the principal teacher of religion.

A Far-Reaching Bequest
SEPTEMBER 14TH

September 14th in 1607 was the birthday of John Harvard, a Congregationalist preacher who lived only to the age of thirty-one and was in no way remarkable, but whose name is known wherever Harvard University is heard of, which takes in pretty much the whole world. John Harvard did not even take any active part in the founding of the university. In fact, he was already dead when it finally got under way. All that happened was that the young minister, dying in Charlestown, Massachusetts, left 260 books and half his $4,000 cash estate to a proposed school that some of the colonists were trying to start. The bequest supplied the necessary stimulation. The college began in 1689 and was named in Harvard's honor. Also, the town in which it was established was named Cambridge, in honor of Harvard's own university back in England.

Brittany's Martyr-Pope

SEPTEMBER 14TH

Although he did not actually die at the hands of an executioner, St. Cornelius, whose memory is honored on September 14th, is listed as a martyr for the faith. He became Pope in 251, and within a year had endured sufferings that brought about his death and earned him the martyr's title. In the pleasant land of Brittany they make much of this day, which they call St. Cornely's Day. The festival centers around St. Cornely's Church in the seaside town of Carnac, and a feature of the day is the blessing of all horned animals, particularly the cattle.

There is a legend about the saint's special interest in these beasts. It is said that once when he was fleeing from a band of soldiers who were under orders to kill him, he reached the sea at Carnac and was unable to continue any farther. In a last desperate plea for divine help he stretched his arms to heaven, and the kindly oxen in a nearby meadow fell to their knees and joined their prayers to his. So effective was the appeal that the soldiers were stopped in their pursuit and turned to stone. It was by this legend that the devout people of Carnac accounted for a great number of oddly shaped rocks, some resembling human forms, in the fields near the town.

The Stigmata

SEPTEMBER 17TH

On September 17th the Roman Catholic Church commemorates the well-authenticated fact that St. Francis of Assisi bore on his hands, feet, and side the marks of the Lord's five wounds of the Crucifixion. These marks, which have spontaneously appeared on the bodies of more than three hundred of the saints, are called the "stigmata." September 17th is set apart in honor of the "Stigmata of St. Francis." No case of the stigmata is known to have existed before the time of St. Francis (early thirteenth century), but three hundred and twenty have been counted since. There were twenty-nine in the nineteenth century.

What happens is that actual open wounds like those made by the nails and the spear appear on the bodies of certain holy people, reproducing the wounds of Jesus. In some cases the wounds bleed from time to time. Science has no explanation, beyond the inadequate one that the marks could be of psychological origin. But there can be no doubt that this amazing thing does really happen. There have been many eyewitnesses to all the stigmata on record. Those of St. Francis were looked upon with wonder and described in detail by his companions. Scientific studies of the stigmata of many saints have been made by impartial medical examiners, and the strange phenomenon has been verified beyond any question.

The Patron Saint of Aviators

SEPTEMBER 18TH

St. Joseph of Cupertina must have been an alarming fellow. He could almost fly. You might be walking along with him, quietly talking, and all of a sudden he wouldn't be there—he had taken a notion to jump up into a tree. Naturally, St. Joseph is the patron saint of aviators. The saint, however, needed no airplanes for his flights. There are many stories of his extraordinary leaps. Once, on Christmas Eve, he was so moved by the carols that, vestments and all, he bounded with a shout from the choir to the high altar and landed there so lightly that the candles did not even shake. From the altar he leapt effortlessly to the pulpit—a distance of fifteen feet.

People were always eager to be around St. Joseph and see his remarkable demonstrations of agility. To his actual powers legend was sure to add even greater ones. It was said that once while saying Mass he converted a heretic by floating in the air a few inches off the floor in front of the altar for six or seven minutes.

Of course, no one ever got to be a saint just because he was an expert jumper, and certainly it was not this sort of thing that brought canonization to St. Joseph. He was no freak and no buffoon, even if he was a little eccentric in this one respect. He was a strange, humble man who won the hearts of all who met him. His penetrating insights into the depths of men's minds and motivations encouraged princes and cardinals to come to him for advice, while his simple affectionate manner brought many sick people to him for the healing that was in his touch. Joseph died September 18, 1663.

The Miracle of Liquefaction

SEPTEMBER 19TH

For three days they heated a furnace, and then they put St. Januarius, bishop of Benevento, into it—but nothing happened at all. He was perfectly comfortable. So then they threw him into the arena with the wild animals, but the beasts just stood around and ignored him. All this was in Naples, in A.D. 305. The people watched these incredible events with astonishment, and 5,000 of them were converted to the God whose power was in the heart of Januarius. But the judge, who hated Christians himself, obeyed the orders of the Emperor Diocletian by claiming the power was black magic and ordering the bishop to be beheaded. The judge was struck blind when he pronounced the sentence, and the execution was delayed long enough to allow Januarius to restore his sight.

No wonder Naples took this native son as its patron and preserved his relics in the cathedral there. His skull is kept in a silver bust, but the chief and most famous relics of St. Januarius are two small vials of his blood, which, according to legend, were collected by a devout woman bystander at the time of the execution. Eighteen times during the year—in May, September, and on December 16th—these vials are exhibited. And when the vials are placed close to the silver bust, the miracle occurs: the blood, which is ordinarily congealed, becomes liquid. There is no adequate scientific explanation of this, but neither is there any doubt about it. Thousands of people over hundreds of years have seen it happen. The May exhibitions of the vials are made in connection with the anniversary of the translation of the saint's relics from another burial place to the present one. The exhibitions in September are connected with his feast-day in the calendar of saints. The one on December 16th is in commemoration of the time, December 16, 1631, when in answer to the frantic prayers of the people of Naples, St. Januarius saved the city from destruction by the nearby volcano, Mt. Vesuvius.

From Tax Collector to Saint

SEPTEMBER 21ST

In any age people dislike taxes, but 2,000 years ago in Palestine the system really gave the taxpayers cause to complain. The government did not set up its own collection machinery; it "farmed out" the collecting of tolls, duties, and taxes to private individuals called "publicans."

The publican gouged what he could out of the people, paid the government its share and kept the rest. Naturally, most publicans got rich. But they won no popularity contests, and they established no reputation for honesty. The last place you would look for a saint would be among the publicans.

But St. Matthew, Apostle, and writer of the first book of the New Testament, was a publican. When Jesus found him he was, the story says, "sitting at receipt of customs." (Matthew, chapter 9, verse 9) His special job was to collect the tolls on goods that were being shipped across the Sea of Galilee, and it is safe to assume that he was lining his own pockets well, after the manner of publicans. But the Lord called him and Matthew answered, and all Christian history has been enriched by this unlikely candidate for sainthood. His name at the time was Levi. Along with the change in his life and his personality, he changed his name to Matthew, which means "Gift of God."

Very little is known about this reformed publican. It may be taken for granted that he had money, and it is certain that he was not socially acceptable among the elite of Palestine. When he gave a dinner party to celebrate his new friendship with Jesus, the Pharisees condemned Jesus for associating with the sort of people Matthew invited. (Matthew, chapter 9, verses 10 and 11). Though his book is placed first in the New Testament, it is not as old as Mark's Gospel. There is at least ten years difference. Scholars say Matthew used the book of Mark as his source. Matthew's chief reason for writing his Gospel, according to legend, was that he wanted to leave his version with his friends while he himself went to other countries to preach. He is said to have carried

Christianity to both Persia and Ethiopia. It is not known
how or when he died.

Schwenkenfelder Thanksgiving

SEPTEMBER 24TH

In the quiet Pennsylvania Dutch country, September
24th is observed by members of the Schwenkenfelder Society, as it has been observed by them and their ancestors
for two hundred and twenty years. This little group,
transplanted from Germany to America in the early eighteenth century, was one of innumerable little Protestant
sects that sprang up on the European continent at the
time of the Reformation. Their leader, Caspar von
Schwenkenfelder, attracted by Martin Luther's new doctrines, gave up a prominent position in the Roman Catholic church and set out by himself on a career of evangelistic preachings.

After Schwenkenfelder's death in 1562 the little band
endured hardship and persecution for more than a century. In 1733 a handful of them arrived in Philadelphia,
and finding it to their liking, immediately sent for the
rest of the Society. The second group—184 of them—arrived on September 22nd, 1734. On the 24th, the second
day after their arrival, they went to the state house in a
body, swore allegiance to the British king, and spent the
remainder of the day expressing their gratitude to God
for having delivered them from persecution and having
led them to a land of freedom. They set September 24th
as a day of thanksgiving to be observed by them and their
descendants forever, and in the Pennsylvania Dutch
counties where the Schwenkenfelders live, this day is still
Thanksgiving Day.

The North American Martyrs

SEPTEMBER 26TH

When people think about the early beginnings of Christianity on this continent, the chances are they have in mind the Puritan settlement in Massachusetts or the Church of Englanders at Jamestown, Virginia. Both of these groups appeared in North America during the early 1600's. But at exactly the same time there was a great amount of missionary activity being carried on by Jesuit and Franciscan priests in the inland regions of Canada and what is now upstate New York. In Roman Catholic Churches in the United States and Canada September 26th is set apart as the Feast of Martyrs of North America, honoring eight priests who lost their lives trying to bring the Christian faith to the Indians.

From 1608 on, from Nova Scotia to the Great Lakes, devoted missionaries ranged over the unexplored forest. They not only underwent the normal hardships of life in an untamed wilderness but suffered discouragement, torture, and in some cases cruel death at the hands of the savages to whom they were trying to minister. Eight at least were killed by the Indians and it is these eight who are commemorated on this day. All of them were canonized together in 1930. A shrine has been built at Auriesville, New York, in honor of three of the eight priests who lost their lives there.

Poisoned Blackberries

SEPTEMBER 29TH

Better pass up the blackberries on September 29th. The devil put his foot on them the night before and every blackberry in the world is poisoned. Why this superstition should have grown up in connection with St. Michael's Day is not known. Probably because people ate and drank too much on this festive occasion and had to blame something for the way they felt the next morning. St. Michael's Day, coming at the end of the harvest season, was a "natural" for over-indulgence. Crops were in and the season of hard work was over, new wine was readily available, barnyard fowls were fat and sleek, the weather was still nice, and everyone had a little extra money in his pocket. It is easy to imagine that on the morning after, many a chastened reveller, piously pretending that he had not misbehaved, would say "I never should have eaten those blackberries."

St. Michael the Archangel was—and is—"the Angel of the Lord." He is the chief of the archangels and the generalissimo of the army of Heaven. It was Michael who led the heavenly host when Lucifer, another archangel, rebelled and "there was war in heaven" (Revelation, chapter 12, verse 7). Michael was victorious. Lucifer was cast out and became the lord of the lower regions. In religious paintings Michael is usually shown with the devil under his foot. The name Michael means "Who is like God?"

The Vulgate Bible
SEPTEMBER 30TH

The greatest debt the world owes to St. Jerome, who is honored in the Christian calendar on this day, is for his translation of the Bible into Latin. His translation is known as the Vulgate, which is the official, authorized version used throughout the world by the Roman Catholic Church. There had been an earlier Latin Bible, and what Pope Damasus I wanted when he called Jerome in was only a revision of this one. But Jerome was too much of a scholar to stop there. Using the old Bible, plus one in Greek and all available manuscripts—some in Hebrew—he produced a completely new work. It was finished in A.D. 385. The term Vulgate means simply that this new Bible was in the language of the people. It comes from the word *vulgus*—the common people. Classical Latin was at that time the spoken language of most of Europe.

VARIABLE HOLIDAYS AND OBSERVANCES

The Jews' Most Solemn Season

The High Holy Days are the first ten days of the new Jewish civil year. Opening with Rosh Hashonoh and ending ten days later with Yom Kippur, this is the Jews' most solemn season, a time of deep penitence and prayer. For in these ten days each man's fate is sealed in heaven for another year. Ancient tradition says that on Rosh Hashonoh God opens three books: one for the wicked, one for the righteous, and a third for those in between. The righteous are immediately inscribed and sealed in the book of life; the wicked are inscribed for death. But judgment on the third, or middle group, is suspended until Yom Kippur, giving them ten days in which to attain merit. This period is therefore a profoundly serious one, "a time of the soul." The New Year's greeting, exchanged verbally, and in America on the increasingly popular New Year cards, is "May you be inscribed and sealed for a good year."

The holidays are not, for all their seriousness, a time of sadness. In Jewish homes after the evening service at the synagogue, the table is festive and the spirit around it is far from unhappy. The menu varies from home to home according to taste, but on every table two items are sure to be found: honey and fresh fruit. The honey is an omen "for a sweet year." The presence of the fruit perhaps goes back to an ancient time when Rosh Hashonoh had in it something of the character of a harvest festival.

It is at the High Holy Days that the essential unity of all Israel is most in evidence. Nearly every Jew in the world, no matter how casual or negligent he may be about his religion during the rest of the year, feels the pull of his heritage upon him at this time. Synagogue and temple will be crowded as at no other time of the year.

Rosh Hashonoh means literally "the head of the year." The day has many other names, each of which emphasizes some one aspect of the occasion. It is called the Day of Remembrance, because each person is to recall and repent his sins of the past year; the Day of the Blowing (of the trumpets) because all are to hear the sound of the Shofar, the ceremonial horn, and return to the blessings of religion; and the Day of Judgment, because this is the day on which God judges each man's life over the course of the past year.

The new year always starts, as Jews believe the world itself did, on this first day of the month of Tishri. Jewish days all begin at sundown, and in the evening as Tishri 1 begins, the Shofar is blown and all Jews—Orthodox, Conservative and Reformed—welcome in another year.

Fast of Gedaliah

The first day following Rosh Hashonoh, is the Jews's Fast of Gedaliah, named for a man who was assassinated at a time when it was very important that he remain alive. When the Babylonian king, Nebuchadnezzar, destroyed Jerusalem and carried away most of the nation into slavery (586 B.C.), he left behind a few farmers and their families, under the supervision of Gedaliah, son of Ahikam. This was done with the idea that they might clean up the ruins left by the army and begin to reclaim the devastated land. Including wives and children, there were at first only 1000 of these workers, but once the army was gone it was not long before others began to show up. They had managed to hide out in the hills and the back country, and now, with the danger gone, they began to emerge, ready to join in the work.

Things were progressing well under Gedaliah's leadership. Farms were being brought back into shape, and there was even some rebuilding going on in some of the towns. But everything was wrecked when a few hot-headed traitors, who considered Gedaliah a collaborationist, murdered him and the small garrison of soldiers Nebuchadnezzar had stationed there. Many of the farmers took their families and fled in terror to Egypt. The rest, 745 in number, were either killed or taken to Babylon, and the country was left desolate, populated only by wild beasts.

Day of Atonement

Yom Kippur, the Day of Atonement set by Moses nearly thirty centuries ago, brings to an end the Jews' High Holidays. On Rosh Hashonoh (New Year), the Book of Life was opened in heaven and God prepared to write in it the names of those who were worthy of a good year. But in His mercy He did not make the final decision then, but allowed ten more days in which those who fell short might repent and attain merit. On Yom Kippur that extension comes to an end and every man's fate is finally sealed. No wonder, then, that this day is the holiest, most solemn day of the Jewish year.

It is a day of penitence and prayer, to be spent in the synagogue, where services will be continuous. It is a day of rest. No Jew will work or transact business on Yom Kippur. It is a day of absolute fast. Not even water may be taken from sundown to sundown. The only persons excused from this severe fasting are the sick (and only if they ask to be excused) and children less than nine years old. The child of nine will not fast for the entire twenty-four hours, but he will begin on Yom Kippur to learn to fast, by going without food a few hours beyond his regular eating time. It is a day of reconciliation, between those who during the past year have done injury to each other, for no man can expect forgiveness from God if he hardens his heart against his fellow man. And it is a day of charity, of giving to the needs of those less fortunate. Traditionally, Yom Kippur is the time of appeals for funds for the synagogue, for Jewish institutions and for organized charities. Memorial services are a feature of the day—partly because the dead need atonement, too, and partly because the remembrance of death breaks the pride and humbles the heart of man.

Labor Sunday

Ever since 1910 the day before Labor Day has been known as "Labor Sunday." It became so at the specific request of the American Federation of Labor, which in 1909 had sent a resolution to the Federal Council of Churches asking that the churches "devote some part of the day to a presentation of the labor question." Beginning in 1917, the Federal Council prepared each year a Labor Sunday message to be read in the churches, and the Federal Council's successor, the National Council, has continued the custom.

Labor Day

Workingmen's holidays are by no means a new thing. In ancient Greece artisans had a day on which they paraded through the streets carrying torches. In medieval Europe each trade had its guild (a sort of union) and each guild had its patron saint, on whose feast day all the guild members laid off work and celebrated. Thus there were as many Labor Days as there were guilds.

But the United States had no Labor Day—the right name is Labor's Holiday—until 1882, when Peter McGuire, president of the Carpenter's brotherhood, proposed to the Central Labor union of New York that a special day be proclaimed "to show the strength and esprit de corps" of American workers. He suggested that the first Monday in September would be a good time for the holiday, since it is about halfway between Independence Day and Thanksgiving. The idea caught on at once. Local observances began to be held almost everywhere in the country in the next few years, and by 1894 Labor Day had been officially established by Congress as a national holiday.

CHAPTER X

October

Guardian Angels
OCTOBER 2ND

Although no church requires it, Christians of many communions believe in guardian angels. In the Roman Catholic Church October 2nd is Guardian Angels Day. Theologians have long taught that angels are pure spirits, persons but bodiless, created by God, and having more power and intelligence than mankind. Their functions are threefold; to praise God, to be His messengers (angel means messenger), and to watch over man. The idea that a particular angel is assigned to watch over a particular human being is easily inferred from many passages in Scripture, as for example, Psalm 91, verse 11: "He shall give His angels charge over thee, to keep thee in all thy ways."

From as early as the ninth century, honor was paid to

the angels along with the archangel Michael on September 29th (St. Michael and *All Angels* day). But devout people were not quite satisfied with such anonymous homage—they wanted to thank their own personal protectors. In various countries and on varying dates the custom grew up of honoring guardian angels, not only those of individuals but also those of cities and provinces. In 1672 Pope Clement X set October 2nd as the universal day for such a festival.

The Little Flower

OCTOBER 3RD

Even when it comes to saints mankind is likely to be impressed by the spectacular—the visionaries, the martyrs, the spectacular dragon-slayers. But St. Therese of the child Jesus, the world's beloved "Little Flower," was exactly the opposite kind of saint. Her sainthood was in the holiness she brought into the little obscure things of everyday life. The Saint Pauls with their dramatic visions, the Saint Thomases with their keen intellects, the Saint Francises with their winning personalities—these are the rare and gifted ones, set apart from the ordinary run of humanity.

Most people live little lives, and therefore the "Little Way" of St. Therese makes its appeal to the millions of average folks who form the majority of the human race. Therese, a French girl who died in 1897 at the age of twenty-four wanted only obscurity. She said her hope was that "I may be forgotten and trodden under foot like a grain of salt." Once, at the Convent of Lisieux where she spent the last nine years of her short life, she heard some of the novices talking outside her window. One of them said, "I wonder what the Mother Prioress will find to say about Sister Therese when she dies. She has never done anything worth speaking of." Nothing could have pleased Therese more.

Her central idea was that one should use the small events and situations of routine daily life as the material out of which holiness is developed. Everyone has his chance to do this—in child-like trust and in obscurity. Therese once said "To pick up a pin for love can convert a soul." Another famous Christian, Brother Lawrence, had found the same secret some centuries before, when he learned that in his simple monastic cell he could "pick up pieces of string to the glory of God."

"The Little Way" is no pious variation on Christianity. The Lord Himself made it the heart of the matter: "He who is least among you is the one who is great." (Luke, chapter 9, verse 48). But it takes a Brother Lawrence or a St. Therese to see clearly what this means and to translate it into living terms for the countless anonymous Christians who tend to think small things are necessarily insignificant things, and that their little lives therefore could not matter much. St. Therese's special devotion was to the Child Jesus, before whose statue in the Convent chapel she kept always a fresh bouquet of flowers.

The Most Happy Saint

OCTOBER 4TH

St. Francis of Assisi is said to be the most popular of all saints, and it is not difficult to see why. There is nothing so attractive as a happy person, and probably no one happier than St. Francis ever lived. Up to his nineteenth year Francis was one of the rich playboys of the Italian city of Assisi. Then a severe illness took him out of circulation for a while and gave him time to think. He came out of the illness with much more serious things on his mind, and he immediately gave up all claim to his family's wealth and went to live in a shack. He began to spend his time among the poor and sick. But to his new status he carried the same rollicking personality that had endeared him to everyone when he was a wealthy young man-about-town. People flocked to him—to hear him preach, or just to be within range of his immense gaiety. Eleven of his boyhood friends left home and joined him in his poverty.

What had happened to Francis was very simple. He had discovered what almost everyone believes and few people act upon: that all creation belongs to God. Knowing this wholeheartedly made him brother to almost every other creature—people, animals, and birds. The world was one big family to Francis. He had found the key to communicating with the universe, and it gave him a zestful excitement and a gentle courtesy that captured every heart. In 1210 Francis and his friends went to Rome to get the blessing and recognition of Pope Innocent III. That was the beginning of the Franciscan order, which spread rapidly over the world.

In 1224, two years before he died, Francis had a vision in which he saw a cherub crucified and burning. It was at this time that he received the "stigmata"—actual wounds on his hands, feet and side, reproducing the wounds of Jesus. He died in Assisi in 1226 at the age of forty-four and was canonized two years later.

Christian Courtesan

OCTOBER 8TH

The legend of Thais, the beautiful courtesan, has produced both a great novel and a great opera. The story is that in the fourth century in Egypt there was a most attractive woman named Thais, who, though she had been brought up a Christian, drifted away from the faith and engaged in a life of prostitution, an occupation that brought her both wealth and renown. An aged hermit by the name of Paphnutius, having heard of the wayward lady, went to talk with her. So effective were his admonitions that Thais burst into tears of repentance and asked for three hours in which to settle her affairs. After this, she said, she would be willing to obey whatever orders the old man might have for her.

She then spent the three hours piling all her wealth, clothing, and jewelry in the street and burning it up, all the while inviting the crowd that gathered around (many of whom were clients of hers) to join her in penitence. Paphnutius took her to a convent and sealed her in a cell never to be opened, where she existed for three years on bread and water. After three years Paphnutius deemed that her penance was sufficient and he allowed her to come out and mingle with the nuns. She died, however, within fifteen days.

This legend has satisfied the Greek Church, which honors Thais in its calendar on this day, but the Roman Church has never canonized her. In the novel *Thais,* by Anatole France, Paphnutius is represented as a young man who converts Thais and sends her to the convent, but at the same time falls in love with her and is miserable without her. The opera, by Massenet, follows much the same line.

He Carried His Head in His Hands

OCTOBER 9TH

The truth about St. Denis, one of the early patrons of France, is interesting enough, but the confusion about him is fascinating. The simple story is that he heard St. Paul preaching to the men of Athens, on Mars Hill in that wonderful city, and was converted to Christianity. This was, of course, very early in the Christian era—almost at the beginning. Going on to Rome, Denis was singled out by Clement, the first pope after St. Peter himself, and sent to what is now France to establish the Church there. The pagans in the new country did not treat Denis well. When he came to Paris as their first bishop they threw him to the wild beasts—but the beasts licked his feet. They put him in a fiery furnace, and he emerged unharmed. They beheaded him on Martyr's Hill, the spot in Paris now known as Montmartre, and from that final indignity he arose, took his head in his hands, and with an angel choir singing above him proceeded to the place where the Church of St. Denis now stands.

But there is still more to the story. The name of St. Denis is so mixed up with that of another saint—called Dionysius—that history can never quite separate the two. And this leads to the possibility of an allegory. It is especially significant that St. Denis' day should fall on October 9th, which was exactly the time when the pagans were having their great festival of a Dionysius who was no saint at all, but was the old, disreputable Roman god of wine. And the part of the story that may be allegory is that during this festival it was almost a general rule that men "lost their heads." So what we have here in the account of Denis, first Bishop of Paris, may be a garbled fusion of the story of an early Christian hero and the usual pagan excesses during the festival in honor of Dionysius, the wine-god.

Semi-Religious Holiday

OCTOBER 12TH

In 1492 Christopher Columbus first set foot on the soil of the new world. That in itself was, of course, not a religious event. Columbus Day cannot be considered a Christian holiday. Nevertheless, a distinctly religious flavor has been brought into the day's observances, because its most active celebrants are people whose lives are closely tied to the Roman Catholic Church. In large American cities Italian Americans honor their fellow countryman whose voyage opened this continent to them as to all other nations. The Knights of Columbus, a Roman Catholic men's organization, also has a program of special festivities. And it is natural that these groups should make church services the center of their commemoration.

Jews will be interested in the speculation among some modern scholars that Christopher Columbus was a Spanish Jew. If true, this would provide one of history's most ironical pranks, since Queen Isabella, who financed Columbus' voyage with her crown jewels was notoriously anti-Semitic. In 1491, the same year in which she sponsored Columbus, she and her husband, King Ferdinand, expelled all Jews from Spain.

Whatever may have been the ancestral background of Columbus, it is certain that he had a Jew with him on his trip—one Luis de Torres, a physician. We are indebted to de Torres for naming our Thanksgiving bird for us. When the doctor saw the strange big fowl for the first time, he said *Tukki*, which is the Hebrew word for "big bird." His exclamation was mistaken for a name by his non-Jewish companions, and the bird has been called a "turkey" ever since.

During the next three hundred years little notice was taken of the 12th of October, but in 1892 the Columbian Exposition was planned by the city of Chicago as a national celebration of the 400th anniversary. Unfortunately, Chicago could not get everything ready in time and the Exposition was not held until 1893, but the Exposition and its accompanying publicity brought the anniversary into the minds of the American people, and Columbus Day has been a semi-holiday in the United States ever since.

The Builder of the Abbey
OCTOBER 13TH

All through the coronation of Elizabeth II reference was continually made to St. Edward or King Edward. The new queen sat in King Edward's chair. She wore St. Edward's crown and held St. Edward's staff. And part of the ceremony took place in St. Edward's Chapel of Westminster Abbey. October 13th is St. Edward's Day, in honor of the beloved English king who built the great abbey at Westminster and whose name still figures so prominently in British tradition. Successor to Canute, the king who is supposed to have commanded the sea to roll back, Edward was the last of the Saxon kings of England. He died only a few months before William the Conqueror and his French army took over the country in 1066.

It is hard to account for Edward's reputation as a saint or for his vast popularity in the memory of the English people. He was not even a very good king. The best explanation is that the people hated their French invaders so much that they looked back to Edward's somewhat feeble reign as "the good old days" and glorified him with many legends that were really not consistent with fact. At any rate, Edward became so much the symbol of old England that for a century and a half he was the country's hero and patron saint, until the glamorous St. George replaced him.

Until he was nearly forty years old Edward was exiled from his native country by King Canute, who had taken the throne away from him, and the story goes that during the exile he made a vow that if he were ever permitted to return to England and assume his rightful place on the throne, he would make a pilgrimage to the tombs of all the Apostles. Later, when in 1042 he did become king, he was released from his vow by Pope Leo IX on condition that he would build an abbey church in honor of the Apostle Peter. The church he built was Westminster Abbey, which few people realize is dedicated to St. Peter. Edward lived just long enough to see his abbey dedicated on December 28, 1065. He died on January 1, 1066.

William Penn
OCTOBER 14TH

October 14th is the birthday of William Penn, the great Quaker who founded the colony of Pennsylvania. The colony was not named for Penn himself, however, but for his father, Admiral Sir William Penn. Penn's idea was to name the new settlement simply "Sylvania," which means "woods." The king, Charles II of England, forced the addition of the name Penn in honor of the colonizer's illustrious father.

William Penn came to maturity at a time in English history when religious tolerance was at its lowest. The Protestant rebellion of Oliver Cromwell, which had taken over the government for twenty years, had finally been overcome and the Stuart family was back on the throne. But everyone was jittery, and wanted to be sure that nothing like Cromwell's uprising could happen again. On the other side, the new king's son was frankly a Roman Catholic, and people were worried about danger from that direction, too.

As a college student at Oxford young Penn and other students resisted the vigorous campaign to make everyone "conform," that is, belong to the Church of England. While at college Penn joined a new group called the Friends, or "Quakers," and his zeal as a member of this non-conformist society soon led to his expulsion from Oxford. When in 1672 he had an opportunity to help draft a constitution for the New Jersey colony in America, the first provision he insisted upon was that complete toleration be granted to people of any and all religions.

His biggest chance came in 1681, when the king deeded to him a huge tract of land west of the Delaware River and north of the Maryland colony. Penn had inherited from his famous father a claim of about $80,000 against the government, which the Crown paid off in this way. He immediately set up on this immense estate a new settlement based on the principle he had found so sadly lacking in England: absolute religious toleration. Many harassed people from Europe, particularly Penn's own fellow-Quakers, were attracted to the new colony by this promise of religious freedom.

The Mothers' Saint

OCTOBER 15TH

One would naturally expect the patron saint of mothers to be a woman, one who had herself experienced motherhood. Certainly one would not expect to find a man, and a lay monk at that, to be the mothers' saint. But the fact is that millions of women pray to St. Gerard Majekla, both for the blessings of motherhood itself and for help in the difficulties all mothers have in the rearing of their families.

St. Gerard, born in eighteenth century Italy, was renowned during his life time for his miracles, none of which, however, seems related to his present position as the mothers' saint. He was often seen to float several inches off the floor during his prayers. He once restored to life a child who had been killed in a fall from a precipice. There are authentic records of his having been seen and heard in two separate places at the same time. There was one occasion on which he blessed a poor family's scanty wheat supply and it miraculously lasted until the next harvest. And once he walked across the water to rescue a stricken boatload of fishermen. He was called in his time "the wonder worker of our day." And after his death on October 15, 1755, his wonders continued to be showered on those who asked for them.

It was the mothers of Italy who, for reasons not now discoverable, first took him as their patron, calling him "the saint of happy childbirth." His popularity spread and still continues. Thousands of women in the United States and Canada wear his medal as their confinement approaches, and many Roman Catholic hospitals dedicate their maternity wards to him.

A Woman Reformer
OCTOBER 15TH

What St. Teresa of Avila (in Spain) did may seem remote and not very important now, four centuries later, but her contribution to the life of her church was one of immeasurable value. She came along at a time when the discipline in monastic orders, both men's and women's, had relaxed to a point where some convents were little more than social clubs. Teresa was a Carmelite nun, in a house of 140 members. Nuns came and went as they pleased, received guests even in their cells, and neglected their devotions. The convent parlor was one continuous salon. It was a fine place for any woman who wanted security and a pleasant life with no responsibility. And there were many other houses exactly like it. It is, of course, more than likely that if Teresa had not done something about it someone else would have. The situation cried out for reform. But the point is that Teresa was the one who did do something.

For a while she tried to live the life of a religious in this strongly secular atmosphere, but in the end she found it utterly impossible. In 1562, amid intense opposition, she withdrew from the big convent ("too many women," she said) and established a small house with only thirteen members, all of them bound to a rigorous way of life. Teresa's nuns could not leave the convent; they maintained almost perpetual silence; they lived in austere poverty; and as a badge of their complete humility they wore sandals instead of shoes. The sandals brought them the designation of "discalced" which literally means barefoot.

Naturally, the resentment and resistance were terrific. Nobody wants the status quo changed, particularly when that status means they "never had it so good." But Teresa had the right on her side. The time had come when monasticism must reform or perish. And before she died she had established seventeen of her new kind of communities and had set the Carmelites once more on the proper path.

St. Teresa's versatility is shown by the fact that she also gained equal fame in an entirely different area. Although she was a relatively uneducated woman, her autobiography is so beautifully written and the doctrine set forth in it so pure that she has been popularly (though, of course, not officially) called one of the Doctors of the Church. In the autobiography she tells of the many visions for which she was renowned and at the same time ridiculed during her lifetime. Perhaps the best known of her visions is the one in which an angel pierced her heart with a fiery sword. After her death her heart was examined and a long scar was found upon it.

The Lion Sermon

OCTOBER 16TH

On every October 16th since 1647 the people of the Church of St. Katherine Cree, London, have heard the "Lion Sermon" preached in commemoration of the miraculous deliverance of Sir John Gayer from the wild and hungry beasts of the desert. Sir John was a London merchant with a yen for adventure. He traveled from London to the Near East, and there joined a caravan and set out to cross the desert. One night he found himself in a terrifying position, separated from the caravan and surrounded by snarling lions. Even in his fright his memory still served him, and he prayed the prayer of Daniel. The lions did not touch him. (It is not recorded that Daniel prayed while he was actually in the lion's den— at least, his words are not given. Probably the prayer Sir John remembered and said was the one to be found in Daniel, chapter 9, verses 4 to 19.) Gayer's experience happened on the night of October 16th. In his will he left money to provide a fee for a preacher to deliver a sermon on this date every year. The sermon deals with Sir John's life history and with his providential escape from the lions.

The Beloved Physician

OCTOBER 18TH

St. Luke is the patron saint of artists because of a legend that says he painted a portrait of the Virgin Mary. Of all the portraits of her, this one was the only one painted from life. The painting, known as "The Black Madonna of Poland," is still preserved in a Polish shrine. The authenticity of this picture as the work of St. Luke would, of course, be very difficult to establish, but it has been a prized national possession ever since the seventh century, when the great Emperor Charlemagne presented it to Poland's ruling prince. The picture, showing both Mother and Child, is painted on a piece of cypress wood, which according to tradition, was the top of a table owned by the Holy family and was part of the furniture of their home in Nazareth. Since 1326 the picture has been in the Polish shrine in Czestochowa. The faces of both figures are darkened by age. The face of the Virgin shows two deep scars, made by the swords of vandals in 1430 when they raided and desecrated the shrine.

St. Luke was a doctor and a writer, as well as a painter. St. Paul called him "the beloved physician." He wrote both the Gospel According to St. Luke and the Acts of the Apostles. He was a Gentile who "came lately" into the early Christian group, but hardly any member of the original company made as large a contribution as he did. Without St. Luke's Gospel we should have missed many of the loveliest elements in Christian literature. He is, for example, the only writer who tells the stories of the

Prodigal Son and the Good Samaritan. Without his book of the Acts of the Apostles we would know very little of what happened in the days immediately following the Resurrection.

Both of Luke's books, incidentally, are addressed to someone named Theophilus, and there have been many conjectures about who this Theophilus was. It is possible that there was no such person. The name Theophilus mean "beloved of God," and it may be that Luke was writing to some Christian convert whose real name he thought he had better not use. He calls him "most excellent" Theophilus, indicating that this must have been someone of high rank. Perhaps it was better to protect him by keeping him anonymous and just call him "beloved of God." Christians were not too popular in those days. The recipient of Luke's writings could have been risking his high position, or even his life.

There is a dim tradition about Luke's having written a third book, which is supposed to have been about the activities of St. Paul in Rome. Such a book, and especially one in the beautiful literary style of St. Luke, would have been a tremendous addition to Christian historical material, and the loss of the book, if it ever existed, is a great tragedy.

St. Ursula

OCTOBER 21ST

St. Ursula was a princess in Cornwall late in the fourth century. All princesses, of course, are beautiful, intelligent, and virtuous, and Ursula was no exception. Her fame spread far beyond Cornwall, far enough to reach a Scottish prince named Conan, who sent for her to come and marry him. With his own proposal of marriage Conan requested that Ursula bring other girls to marry

Christian soldiers who were with him. Here legend takes over on a large scale. It says that Ursula set sail in three boats with 11,000 eligible young ladies. Caught in a storm, they were driven off their course and up the Rhine river, where they were all killed by the barbarian Huns, against whom they defended their virtue. This was in 383 A.D., at Cologne.

It is far more likely that Ursula was accompanied by eleven maidens. They may have come to a violent end at Cologne, and it may have been under the circumstances set forth in the legend. But the extravagant number of girls purportedly involved is, scholars say, connected with the twelfth century discovery of a vast quantity of human bones at Cologne. What was found was probably an old Roman cemetery, but popular opinion immediately proclaimed the bones to be the remains of the ill-fated bridal party.

In the early history of our country there is an interesting sequel to this ancient story. It has a happier ending, however. Louisiana settlers in the eighteenth century found themselves in much the same situation as the bachelors in Prince Conan's army, and the king of France did what Ursula had done about it. Louisiana at that time belonged to France. The king sent boatloads of girls to marry the lonely settlers. Each girl was given the "King's dowry": a small chest, called a casket, containing one blanket, four sheets, two pairs of stockings, six headdresses and a "pelisse"—an outer garment. They were called "casket girls" because of the chests of gifts they carried. Appropriately, the arrival of the casket girls in New Orleans was celebrated with a procession in honor of St. Ursula, and they were housed in the Ursuline Convent while waiting for the young men to make their choices.

Mother of Apostles

St. Mary Salome, who is commemorated October 22nd in the Christian calendar, was the wife of Zebedee and the mother of the Apostles James and John. There has been some speculation that she was the sister of the Blessed Virgin Mary, but that is doubtful, for it is improbable that two daughters in the same household would be named Mary. But her two sons are referred to as cousins of Jesus, so it is clear that in some way she was related to the Holy Family. One theory is that she was the niece of St. Joseph, in which case her sons' relationship to the Lord would have been that of first cousins once removed.

Mary is mentioned three times in the New Testament: in Matthew, chapter 20, verse 21, when she asked Jesus to give her sons the seats of honor in His kingdom; in Mark, chapter 15, verse 40, when she is listed among the women who watched the Crucifixion from a distance; and in Mark, chapter 16, verse 1, when she visited the Lord's tomb.

Her ambition for her sons brought her one of the stiffest rebukes anyone ever received from Jesus. St. Matthew tells the story of how she tried to make a special deal with the Master which would guarantee James and John the two top positions when Jesus became king. This not only angered Jesus but also stirred up jealousy among the other ten Apostles. Jesus lost no time and minced no words in putting her in her place. Read in Matthew, chapter 20, verses 20 to 28, how He told them all how mistaken they were about what His kingdom really was to be.

There is a legend that she moved, after the Resurrection, to the Italian town of Veroli, and that her body was discovered there in 1209.

Huguenot History
OCTOBER 22ND

October 22nd is a black day in the history of the Huguenots (early French Protestants). After long and violent persecution, in which thousands were massacred and thousands fled the country, the Huguenots were granted religious liberty by Henry IV's Edict of Nantes in 1598. But on October 22, 1685, the edict was revoked by Louis XIV, and the Protestants were again deprived of their freedom of belief and worship. The result was a great wave of Huguenot emigration to Holland and England, and a gain of many thrifty Gallic families for those two countries, and ultimately for America, for many of them eventually came here.

Raphael the Healer
OCTOBER 24TH

October 24th honors the Archangel Raphael, whose name, though generally known, does not appear in any of the Old or New Testament books accepted by Protestant churches. He does, however, figure prominently in the apocryphal book of Tobit. This book is largely devoted to the story of a journey taken by a young man named Tobias. Raphael, disguised in human form under the name of Azarias, went with young Tobias to protect and guide the young man. The story is in Tobit, chapter 5 through 12. When the journey was over, Raphael healed the blindness of the elder Tobias, father of his traveling companion. Not until then did he reveal his identity. In chapter 12, verse 15, he told them, "I am Raphael, one of the seven holy angels, which present the prayers of the saints, and which go in and out before the glory of the Holy One."

The name Raphael means "God has healed." This, together with the archangel's healing power as recorded in Tobit, has led to the belief that Raphael's special function is healing the sick. An unsupported legend says that Raphael is the angel referred to in John (chapter 5, verse 4), who stirred up the waters of the pool called Bethesda, and infused them with healing properties.

Raphael indicated that he is one of a group of seven archangels. Of the other six, only Michael and Gabriel are mentioned by name in the Bible. Although the names of the remaining four are not given, they are said to be Uriel, Raquel, Sabriel and Jerahmee. However, there are in existence lists giving other names for them.

Shoe Leather from Angels
OCTOBER 25TH

Saints Crispin and Crispinian were twin brothers who came from Rome, late in the third century, to the French town of Soissons, and there set up shop as shoemakers, to support themselves while they went about their real work of preaching the Christian Gospel. It is said that they made shoes for the poor, and that these free shoes were made from leather the angels brought to the brothers' shop by night and left there as their contribution toward this worthy charity.

In those times the persecution of Christians had reached its greatest heights. It was that period of most intense darkness that comes just before the dawn, for only a few years later, in 325, the Emperor Constantine put an end to all persecution, and Christianity was officially permitted by the state. But this approaching freedom did Crispin and Crispinian no good. They were caught in the last wave of atrocities.

There is a long story of how their tormentors tried to put them to death—always unsuccessfully. It is said that first they tied millstones around the twins' necks and dropped them into the river. The saints casually swam across and climbed out on the opposite bank. Then, boiling lead was poured over the two holy men, but that had about the same effect as a refreshing shower bath. Finally, when it was clear that they were under a supernatural protection against which the executioners could not hope to prevail, Crispin and Crispinian, having made their point, quietly knelt and allowed themselves to be beheaded. October 25th in medieval times was the biggest day of the year for the shoemaker's union, or guild, as labor organizations were then called.

Pilate's Wife—A Saint

OCTOBER 27TH

In all the New Testament there is only one reference to the wife of Pontius Pilate (Matthew, chapter 27, verse 19) and that brief passage does not reveal her name. Tradition, however, calls her Claudia and has a good deal to say about her. The story is that while she was with her husband in Judea, she showed considerable interest in the Jewish religion and then, when Jesus appeared and began to preach, she was so captivated by His life and teaching that she risked everything by becoming a secret follower of His. Although Claudia is not a saint in the western calendar, there are parts of the Eastern Church in which she has been canonized and is honored on October 27th.

Two Apostles

OCTOBER 28TH

October 28th is a day dedicated to the honor of two Apostles, Simon and Jude, about whom almost nothing is known beyond the fact that they *were* Apostles. St. Simon is called Simon Zelotes in the New Testament, which means that he was a member of the Zealots, a fanatical little band of Jewish patriots who resisted the Roman occupation of their country. They would have liked to attack the Roman army frontally and drive it out of their beloved land, and they believed that when the Messiah came He would lead their tiny forces to glorious victory over the mighty intruder. It may have been that Simon joined with Jesus in the hope that the gentle Nazarene would turn out to be the long-awaited military leader from heaven.

While they were waiting for the Messiah the Zealots harassed the Romans in guerilla fashion, much as European patriots during World War II made things uncomfortable for the German army of occupation. It is easy to see how the word "zealot" found a place in our language to describe a person of intense devotion to a cause.

The only thing the New Testament really says about Jude is that he was not Judas Iscariot. Whenever in the Gospels you read, "Judas, not Iscariot" that means St. Jude. Tradition has it that Simon and Jude both went to Persia to preach Christianity, and that they were martyred there together. That is why they are honored on the same day.

The Festival of Booths

An important holiday to the Jews is the festival of *Sukkoth,* the translation of which is "booths" or "tabernacles." It is a festival featuring the memory of the tent-like structures in which the primitive Israelites lived during their forty years of wandering in the wilderness under the leadership of Moses, after their dramatic escape from slavery in Egypt. Every year for nine days, beginning on the 15th day of Tishri, modern Jews keep this feast in various ways. Strictly, they are expected to live in booths of their own building during the entire period, but in these days of urban life when many Jews are city apartment dwellers, the observance is necessarily modified.

The traditional way of observing the festival was for the father of the family, with the help of wife and children, to build a small tabernacle of wood or cloth which was covered with branches in such a way as to leave the sky and stars visible, because man must look to the heavens rather than to a roof for his protection. The interior of the booth was decorated with flowers, and since this is also the time of the harvest thanksgiving, fruit was sometimes used. This pleasant bower then became the family's temporary home during the nine-day festival. Nowadays Orthodox congregations build one booth in the synagogue, while the Reformed make miniature models of the ancient tents and use them as centerpieces on the family table.

In the newly resettled country of Israel the festival of Sukkoth has a special significance. In that overcrowded land many Jews are again living in temporary dwellings not unlike the desert booths of their ancient ancestors.

An interesting symbolism is connected with the four plants that were chiefly used in the building of the booths.

First, the *Aravan*—two willow branches, which have neither beauty nor fragrance. They stand for the man who neither knows the Law nor does any good deeds.

Second, the *Hadassah*—three twigs of myrtle, having fragrance but without any beauty to the eye. These represent the man who does good works without any knowledge of the Law.

Third, there is the *Lulab*—a palm shoot. It is the man who knows the Law but fails to apply its precepts to his living.

And last, there is the *Ethrog*—a citron fruit that is both fragrant and lovely. It is the man who knows the Law of God and keeps it.

The prayer for rain in Sukkoth is of special interest. This is the dry season in Palestine and this prayer has always been a part of their harvest festival, in which Jews of old not only thanked God for the crops of the past season but also asked for weather that would be favorable for the next. Now, with many Jews again in Israel and a program of agricultural development going on, the weather is a matter of immediate importance and the ancient prayer has a renewed significance.

Legend tells that back in temple times in Jerusalem this was the day on which the weather for the coming year could be predicted by watching the smoke from the evening sacrifice. If the smoke blew to the north, the poor people were happy and the rich were disappointed, for the rain would be plentiful, crops would be good and food cheap. The wealthy people, who were mostly of the merchant class, would find their profits small. If the smoke moved southward, the rich would expect a dry year that would send prices up. The poor would suffer; it would be a seller's market. If the smoke blew east, everyone was pleased, for this was the best of all possible omens. But if it blew west, that meant a year of famine and all were sad.

The seventh day of Sukkoth is known as *Hoshana Rabba*—literally "great salvation." The main feature is the traditional procession held in the synagogue. Old and young march about, carrying willow branches with which, at the end of the marching, they beat the ground until the branches are bare of leaves. Although the season of judgment (the High Holidays) officially ends on Yom Kippur, there are some who believe that even up until Sukkoth's seventh day God mercifully extends man's opportunity to repent. To some, therefore, this day retains something of the character of Yom Kippur, the Day of Atonement.

The eighth day of Sukkoth is called *Shemini Atsereth*, which means "eighth day of solemn assembly." On this, as on the first day of Sukkoth, no work is permitted. The special events of this eighth day are a memorial service for the dead and the recital of an ancient prayer for rain. This prayer in former times, when the Jews were farmers in Palestine, was simply part of the ritual of the harvest festival. One agricultural season had ended; now they asked God for rain to prepare the soil for the one that would soon begin. In these times the prayer provides a link between the Jews who have returned to Palestine and those who are still scattered throughout the world. Today's Jew is not praying for rain in New York or London or wherever he may live; he is praying for rain on the farms of the new settlers in Palestine.

The final day of Sukkoth is *Simhath Torah—*"the rejoicing of the law." The name comes from the fact that the annual cycle of the reading of the Law in synagogue services comes to an end on this day and will start over on the next Sabbath. It is simultaneously a closing and a reopening, an end and a beginning, of the Jews' most cherished possession, the Torah, and on this day the Jew rejoices in this never-ending gift. Processions are held on this day in which the sacred scrolls, both of the Law and the Prophets, will be carried about the synagogue.

A Worldwide Service

Worldwide Communion Sunday, sponsored by the World Council of Churches, is a fairly new one in the calendar of Christianity, having been started in the 1940's. In every country on earth, Christians join together in spirit at the Lord's table, each in his own church and following his own ritual, but by intention becoming part of a congregation of many millions. The thought behind this universal Protestant act is that the barriers existing between the nations are most effectively brought down as all men everywhere come into communion with one Lord. As they unite in spirit in this great corporate act of worship, Christians are demonstrating to themselves and to the world the oneness of mankind under God. In the United States the observance is sponsored by the National Council of Churches, but it is common practice for many denominations that are not Council members to participate.

Christian Education Week

Attention is focused on a vital part of American religious life during the first week in October each year, when the National Council of Churches sponsors Christian Education Week. The purposes of the week are to give an inspirational send-off to the new Sunday School term that is beginning, to get the new year's program underway as rapidly as possible, and to provide the setting for a concerted nation-wide drive for new enrollments. Practically all Protestant denominations observe Christian Education Week.

Men and Missions Sunday

Men and Missions Sunday is the beginning of Churchmen's Week—a full week of concentrated activity among laymen of the denominations that comprise the National Council of Churches. Sermons, discussions, and printed materials treat the Christian missionary program as the biggest and most important of all business enterprises because it is the Lord's business. They point out that American laymen have the opportunity to use their business ability for the extension of Christianity. Many of the church's problems, particularly those of analysis and organization, are similar to the business problems in which American men have already proved their extraordinary skill. The men's talents should be put to work in the service of the church.

Church leaders suggest also that the laymen has frequent chances to be a missionary himself. Our country is still one of the world's most urgent mission fields, with forty-one percent of the nation not even having nominal religious affiliations. Our high divorce rate, our constantly shifting population, our slums and juvenile delinquency are problems on which the laymen's Christian action can be directly focused. Men can also be effective missionaries simply by being committed Christians in their daily relationships with family, business associates, and the community generally.

Men and Missions Sunday was established in the 1930's by the Laymen's Missionary Movement. When United Church Men, the laymen's organization of the National Council of Churches, was set up in 1950, this new group joined in the sponsorship and made the day the beginning of Laymen's Week.

Laymen's Sunday

Laymen's Sunday is the climax of Churchmen's Week, the eight-day period of special laymen's activities that began with Men and Missions Sunday. The war years and those since have been marked by a tremendous upsurge of interest and activity among laymen, who in former years were inclined to pay the bills and leave church matters to clergy and women. For reasons still unclear, American men began during World War II to assume a role as participants rather than spectators in church work. The result has been a vigorous and aggressive masculine attitude formerly lacking in the Church's approach to its mission.

National Bible Week

National Bible Week is promoted each year during the third week in October by the National Laymen's Committee, an independent, non-denominational group of prominent businessmen devoted to the application of the Golden Rule to the daily affairs of life. Founded in 1940, the committee stated its purpose as "the reawakening of religious thinking in every way possible."

This week of emphasis on the importance of Bible reading is only one of many activities carried on by the

Committee. Perhaps the most familiar of their projects has been the placing of "grace before meals" cards on restaurant and dining car tables. Every traveler has probably seen these little "tent cards" on which are printed three suggested prayers: one for Protestants, one for Catholics, and one for Jews. In the official message proclaiming National Bible Week the committee affirms its conviction that Bible reading "will arouse a new spiritual force for good throughout this troubled world." National Bible Week is publicized each year by proclamations from the President, from governors, mayors, and other civic leaders, as well as through the usual media of printed materials and radio and TV announcements.

World Order Sunday

October 24th is the anniversary of the establishment of the United Nations. Each year on October 24th, or the nearest Sunday, the National Council of Churches observes World Order Sunday, a day on which the morning service emphasizes the Christian hope for a peaceable world community of nations. World Order Sunday was connected with the churches' observance of Armistice Day, but when the great international organization was formed in 1945, its birthday seemed an even more appropriate occasion for the annual statement of the age-old religious goal.

The Feast of Christ the King

The last Sunday in October is the Feast of Christ the King in the Roman Catholic Church, and has been so since 1925, when the day was established by Pope Pius XI. The purpose of the feast is to place special emphasis on one aspect of the Lord's many-sided relationship with His world. That one aspect is His earthly kingship. On this day His authority over all of mankind's political structures is asserted and homage is paid to Him as the ruler of all nations. Protestants have a day of the same name and for the same purpose on the last Sunday in August.

Reformation Sunday

The Sunday nearest October 31st is becoming one of the great Protestant festivals. Known as "Reformation Sunday," the day commemorates Martin Luther's daring challenge on October 31, 1517, when the German monk posted his "ninety-five theses" on a church door at Wittenberg and unexpectedly touched off a reform movement that swept like wildfire over Europe. Luther's intention was merely to find someone who would engage in a public debate with him. The ninety-five theses, or propositions, that he put up on the church door were all about church practices and customs he wanted to change. At the end of October, the town, like all towns, would be filling up with pilgrims arriving for All Saints' Day (November 1st) and Luther expected to get both a worthy opponent and a good sized audience out of the visiting crowd.

The result was far beyond what Luther had counted on. Nobody in Wittenberg argued with Luther. Instead, so many people agreed that the ideas spread immediately over all of northern Europe and half the continent was soon involved in violent controversy. Other leaders arose —John Calvin in France, Ulrich Zwingli in Switzerland, John Knox in Scotland—and in many cases Christians broke their centuries-old connection with the Roman Catholic Church and established new independent churches of their own. This was not the first split in the unity of Christianity. Five centuries earlier, in 1054, the bishops of Rome and Constantinople had come to a parting of ways, and when Antioch, Alexandria, and Jerusalem sided with Constantinople the result was a complete separation between East and West. But the Protestant Reformation started by Luther was no high-level disagreement among bishops. It was a groundswell, a shaking of the foundations, and its participants were the little people who sat in the church pews.

Today, in the western world, there are more than 250 million Christians who are not in communion with the bishop of Rome, and most of them are in churches that owe either their existence or their independence to the action of the fiery German monk who, on October 31, 1517, was merely looking for an argument.

CHAPTER XI

November

America's First Constitution

NOVEMBER 1ST

On this day in 1620 the Pilgrims, while their small ship was still anchored off the New England shore, signed the simple document that has become famous as the May-flower Compact. They were not even thinking about the fact that they were establishing the first constitutional government on this continent. The purpose of the Compact was to get the signed promises of several restless members of the group who were unhappy about the location chosen for the new colony. The original plan had been to land in Virginia, and when the course was changed and the landing was to be made on what is now Cape Cod, some of the brethren threatened to strike out for themselves. Because of this the leaders drew up the Compact and made everyone sign it before landing.

The significance of this document, however, is not that it solved an immediate problem for the Pilgrims. Rather, the Mayflower Compact is of value to all Americans because of its religious nature. What the Pilgrims did was simply to take a typical "church covenant" of the times—the kind of agreement people customarily made when they established a congregation—and in it they included the civil government. Therefore, the very first constitutional government in this country was from start to finish a religious covenant. That gives religion a pretty basic place in American history.

All Saints' Day

NOVEMBER 1ST

A saint is a person who has attained to the presence of God in Heaven. The Christian calendar is full of saints' days, honoring those departed souls who have been officially judged to have reached this blissful state. But there must be many thousands more who have been overlooked or unknown. All Saints' Day commemorates the holy ones of all ages and stations whose names are known only to God. (From one point of view this might be said to be the most meaningful of all Christian festivals because it is in the lives of His saints that Christ's work is fulfilled. A saint is the ultimate example of the presence of Christ in human lives.) The day was established early in the seventh century by Pope Boniface IV. Originally it was set for May 1st, but in 834 it was changed to November 1st. This change in dates brings up some interesting speculation.

The best known feature of All Saints' Day is not the day itself but the evening that precedes it: Halloween. People who have no idea of what All Saints' Day is about are probably the most active of the Halloween revelers. The strange fact is that all the typical Halloween pranks were happening on October 31st long before there was an All Saints' Day, even before Christianity. Scholars say that back in the time of the Druids, November 1st was the feast of Saman, Lord of death. It was on the day on which Saman called up the souls of all the departed. Naturally, the idea got about that the dead would begin to appear at midnight, when the day actually began, and since no one likes the prospect of facing a ghost alone, people soon developed the custom of gathering together in groups on this fearful night. And once they were in one another's reassuring company there was no reason why they should not enjoy themselves.

The new crop of apples and nuts was readily available. Perhaps a little cider had been brought to just the right condition for the occasion. And there was the long night ahead, for certainly no one dared relax and go to sleep. The setup was, of course, perfect for the village pranksters. With most of the population huddled behind locked doors, convinced that ghosts and goblins were running wild outside, what practical joker could miss such a chance to create a chaos which, when discovered the next day, would be blamed on the spirits?

But to come back to the question. All this started a long, long time before All Saints' Day. When All Saints' Day was put into the Christian calendar on May 1st, six months away from the night of ghosts and goblins, why wasn't it left there? Was it moved to November 1st in one of the Church's typical efforts to Christianize a pagan revel? Probably that is the reason, but history is not clear about it.

Incidentally, there is an old Scottish belief that anyone who is born on All Saints' Eve will have "double sight." That is, he will be able to see the spirit world about him and have command over the spirits he sees.

All Souls' Day
NOVEMBER 2ND

The Church is believed by many Christians to be divided into three parts: The Church Triumphant (those already in Heaven), the Church Militant (Christians here on earth), and the Church Expectant (those who have died but have not yet attained to the presence of God). November 1st is devoted to the Church Triumphant; on November 2nd Roman Catholics and some other groups commemorate with special prayers the faithful departed who are in the intermediate stage known as the Church Expectant.

Almost all ancient civilizations had a custom of setting aside a day or more, usually at this time of the year, in honor of the dead. Long before Christianity the pagans had their Festival of the Dead. By the ninth century, the day after All Saints' Day was called All Souls' Day and was dedicated to our faithful friends and neighbors in the state between us and the holy ones who are with God. On this day prayers and masses are offered for the departed who are still on their pilgrimage. Many Protestant denominations still observe All Saints' Day, but having rejected belief in purgatory, they have also rejected All Souls' Day.

Jewish Political Holiday
NOVEMBER 2ND

Jews, particularly those in the new country of Israel, observe Balfour Declaration Day in memory of a turning point in modern Jewish history. On November 2, 1917, Arthur J. Balfour, who was at that time British Secretary of State for Foreign Affairs, wrote in a letter to Lord Rothschild that the British government "views with favor the establishment in Palestine of a national home for the Jewish people." This definite commitment of the British government to the age old hope of Jewish nationalists was of such great importance that the day on which it was made has been kept as a semi-holiday ever since.

Patron Saint of Hunters

NOVEMBER 3RD

You never know who will turn out to be a saint. Young Hubert, a seventh century French duke's son whose chief object in life was to hunt in the forest with his rich young friends, was an unlikely candidate for sainthood. The friends were a wild lot, and Hubert was as wild as any of them. One Good Friday, when all respectable people were in church where they belonged, Hubert and his crowd went hunting, in the forest of Ardennes. What happened in the depth of the forest is unknown, but whatever it was it change Hubert's whole life. He went into the forest a playboy; he came out a mature, serious man. Legend says he met a huge stag with a crucifix between its horns and heard a voice telling him to turn to the Lord. He went at once to the bishop, a man named Lambert, who became his advisor. He entered the priesthood, and when Lambert died Hubert succeeded him as bishop. For obvious reasons, St. Hubert is the patron saint of hunters. For reasons not at all obvious, he has also been invoked as a healer of madmen.

What is a 'Guy'?

NOVEMBER 5TH

If you saw how the British empire celebrates Guy Fawkes Day—with fireworks, bonfires, and burning effigies—you would never suppose that this was a day with a religious background. In 1603, when James I came to the English throne, Roman Catholics in England hoped he would restore to them the religious freedom that his predecessor, Queen Elizabeth I, had denied them. But he did not. By 1605 their resentment had risen to a point where a man named Guy Fawkes and some of his friends were ready to do something violent about it. They conspired to blow up both king and Parliament with a few barrels of gunpowder. The plot was discovered on November 5th, and Fawkes was executed, together with those of his accomplices who had not been killed in trying to escape capture. Within two years the whole country had begun to celebrate the anniversary. The effigies carried and burned on Guy Fawkes Day were, of course, intended to be images of Fawkes. They were called "guys." It is possible that our custom of calling a man a "guy" is traceable to them.

England's Unnamed Saints

NOVEMBER 8TH

Since its separation in 1534 from the Roman Catholic Church, the Church of England has been uncertain of its official procedure for adding saints to its calendar. This question has been a matter of concern to many Anglicans (Episcopalians in this country) for certainly there have been many candidates for sainthood in the Anglican communion during the last 400 years. There have been martyrs who have given their lives for Christianity in foreign missionary fields, and there have been devoted people at home whose goodness has been the subject of song and story—but the Church of England, with one exception, has not canonized them. To overcome this deficiency in its machinery (or its confidence) the English Church has, since 1928, set aside the eighth day after All Saints' Day in commemoration for all who should be but have not been canonized. The day is called Saints, Doctors, Missionaries, and Martyrs Day, in honor of this large body of "unnamed saints of our nation."

Rome's Greatest Church

NOVEMBER 9TH

On this day Roman Catholics commemorate the dedication of their most important church, the Archbasilica of the Most Holy Savior, commonly known as St. John's Lateran, In Rome. This is the church where the Pope's throne is kept. It is to Roman Catholics the cathedral of the world, senior in dignity even to St. Peter's. Carved on the facade of this church are the words, "The mother and head of all the churches of the city and of the world." It is not surprising there should be special rejoicing on the dedication day of such an edifice.

A basilica is simply a church. Originally the word applied to a certain type of secular building—an oblong hall, rounded at one end or both, where public assemblies were held. It is hard to imagine now, but for the first two centuries of the Christian era there was no such thing as a church building. Services were held in people's homes. By the beginning of the third century, however, they began to set special buildings apart for use as places of worship. In the early part of the fourth century the mansion of a wealthy Roman family named Laterani came into the hands of the Emperor Constantine, and he passed it on to the Christians. For a thousand years this palace served as the residence of popes. But the important thing about the home of the Laterani family is that the great hall around which it was built became a church and that church, with a baptistry added and dedicated to St. John the Baptist, became the now famous St. John's Lateran, number one church of Roman Catholicism.

Martinmas
NOVEMBER 11TH

St. Martin's Day or Martinmas is a day rich in traditions in the old country. It is very strange that the many European peoples who have come to America have not brought along the legends and customs in which this day abounds back in their native lands. St. Martin, Bishop of Tours (in France) in the fourth century, is the patron saint of France, of tavern keepers, of beggars, of winegrowers, and of drunkards, both practising and reformed. With such a clientele to celebrate his memory, it is no wonder that St. Martin is honored with one of the most convivial days in the calendar.

St. Martin's Day comes, of course, at a happy time of year for rural people. The crops are in, the animals are slaughtered, the new wine is ready, the hard work of summer and autumn is over. Any saint's day that fell at this particular season would probably have been a cheerful one in medieval times.

One essential to the proper observance of St. Martin's Day is roast goose for dinner. Actually this is probably because geese are fat and plentiful at this time, but legend gives a more colorful reason. The story is that when Martin heard, in 374, he had been elected Bishop of

Tours, the thought of being a bishop so horrified him he ran and hid in a barn. But a stupid, meddlesome goose found him there and set up a racket that led the searchers to the hiding place. Descendants of this goose are still paying for his disservice to the good man.

There is usually a spell of mild weather at this time of year. We call it Indian summer, but in Europe it is St. Martin's summer. Thereby hangs the most famous tale about this saint. It is said that on a cold November day Martin cut his cloak in two and gave half of it to a shivering beggar, whereupon the Lord sent a few days of warm weather to keep Martin comfortable until he could get another cloak.

On this day in Ireland no fisherman will go fishing: if he did he would meet a horseman riding over the sea towards him, followed by a destroying storm. Nor will anyone in Ireland turn a wheel—cart, mill, or spinning— on this day. If he does he will risk great misfortune.

St. George in World War I
NOVEMBER 11TH

Armistice Day (now called Veteran's Day) is, of course, the anniversary of the end of the first World War. It is in no sense a church holiday, but it does bring to mind one of the few religious stories connected with that first world-wide conflict. According to many eyewitness accounts, a miracle happened during the disastrous retreat at Mons, France, in 1914. The Allied strength at one point in their line had dwindled to a small force of only 1,000 English soldiers. The Germans opposing them were many times that number. Fighting against enormous odds, and without adequate ammunition, the defenders were finally reduced to a mere 500.

When all seemed lost the men in the trenches heard a shout of "St. George! St. George for England," and saw before their astounded eyes a line of medieval bowmen, with an angel in command, firing a rain of arrows on the advancing Germans. Ten thousand Germans fell before the ghostly warriors, and the German army is said to have complained that the English had used some secret new poison, for no marks could be found on the fallen German soldiers. The British knew, of course, that this was just one more timely appearance of their country's patron, St. George. From the time of the Crusades, he had come to their rescue when the situation was so desperate that only his help could save England.

"Problem Child" Saint

NOVEMBER 13TH

Two days after St. Martin's Day comes the festival of a saint who gave poor old Martin a tremendous amount of trouble. His name was Britius; he was sometimes called Brice. From all that is left of the records, it is hard to see how Britius ever got to be a saint at all. Only the worst things about him are known. When Britius was a baby his parents set him outdoors and abandoned him, leaving him there to die. This was a fairly common practise in those days—it often happened to unwanted babies. The custom was called "exposure."

But before the baby suffered any ill effects, St. Martin came along and found him, and there must have been many times thereafter when the good man wished he had taken a different route that day. Britius grew up to be one of the most unpleasant little boys in history, completely scornful of the kind old man to whom he was indebted for food, shelter, education, and for his life itself.

The problem child grew into a resentful, arrogant adolescent. He openly referred to St. Martin as "the old fool." But for some reason Martin loved him anyway. He even prayed that Britius might be his successor as Bishop of Tours.

Martin was, nevertheless, realistic about the boy's faults. Once when the clergy begged the Bishop to get rid of Britius he said "If Christ endured Judas, why shouldn't I endure Britius." Hardship must have chastened Britius, for in his later years he gained a great reputation for both brilliance and sanctity; and his people loved him and forgot his youthful failings. It is too bad that only the stories of his early life remain and the record of his saintly old age has been lost.

St. Paul of the Cross

NOVEMBER 16TH

On November 16th members of the Passionist order in the Roman Catholic Church honor their founder, St. Paul of the Cross, who lived in the eighteenth century. Born Paolo Francesco Danei, this Italian priest devoted his life to the development of a congregation of clergy, seminarists, and laymen who would take not only the usual vows of poverty, chastity and obedience, but would add as a fourth vow their promise to promote devotion to the passion and death of Jesus. The full name of the order is "The Congregation of Discalced (barefoot) Clerks of the Most Holy Cross and Passion of our Lord Jesus Christ." For some reason, Paolo Danei had a special concern about England, which was not a notably pious nation in the eighteenth century. He prayed for England at his mass every day for forty years.

St. Clare's Little Sister

NOVEMBER 16TH

"How hardly," said Jesus, "shall they that have riches enter the kingdom of Heaven," meaning, of course, that man's preoccupation with his possessions is almost impossible to break through. And certainly that is the way it usually is. But there was a time at the beginning of the thirteenth century when almost the whole Italian town of Assisi was a shining exception to the rule. First St. Francis, then St. Clare, and her sister St. Agnes—all of them born wealthy—blithely turned their backs on money and position, and soon half the socialites of the community were with them in barefoot poverty. And what is more they were all happier than they had ever been before. If anyone ever found the kingdom here on earth it was this band of voluntary paupers who gave up riches for the joy of the Lord.

St. Agnes of Assisi, honored on this day in the Christian calendar, left home in 1212 to follow St. Francis. Only sixteen days earlier her older sister, Clare, had left for the same purpose. When Agnes went it was more than their father, Count Faverone, could stand. He sent his brother, with a company of soldiers, to bring her back. When his best attempts at persuasion failed, Agnes' uncle flew into a rage and drew his sword to strike her down. Legend says that his arm withered and the sword clattered to the floor. Next the soldiers grabbed the girl by the hair and started to drag her home, but according to the story, her body became so heavy they were unable to move her. Whatever the facts about this skirmish, the point is Agnes did successfully resist all attempts to bring her back to her father's home.

St. Francis soon established the two sisters and a group of other noblewomen as the Order of Poor Ladies of St. Damian's. Later they were known as the Poor Clares. The original name came from the fact that they were housed at St. Damian's Church in Assisi. St. Agnes spent the next forty years working for the order, establishing new houses of it, and leading the happy life that was the chief characteristic of the followers of St. Francis. Her own spiritual life reached such heights that others said she had discovered a new road to perfection known only to herself. Just as she had followed her sister Clare in life, so she followed her in death. Clare died in August, 1253, and Agnes on November 16th of the same year.

Big Business Woman
NOVEMBER 17TH

St. Hilda was a seventh century Northumbrian princess who gave up her royal position and concentrated on the Church. St. Hilda is especially popular in the Episcopal Church, where there are many women's guilds named for her. Usually these St. Hilda's Guilds are made up of business and professional women, and there is excellent reason why such women should take St. Hilda as their patron. Thirteen centuries ago in England, Hilda was a top flight executive. Her talent for organization and supervision brought her to such a lofty place in the affairs of the church that she was the head not only of several convents but of a group of monasteries as well. Her power was so great that even bishops took orders from Hilda.

The Patron Saint of Queens
NOVEMBER 19TH

The patron saint of queens is St. Elizabeth of Hungary, herself a queen. The number of royal ladies who come under her protection has so greatly diminished since Elizabeth's time (thirteenth century) that one wonders what a patron saint will do when his category finally becomes extinct. Perhaps if monarchs through the ages had always been as dedicated as Elizabeth to the welfare of their subjects, there would be more of them on thrones today. Her benefactions to her people were so great they sometimes brought criticism upon her. Once in a time of famine she gave away so much food the royal household itself was in danger of starvation. There were periods when she fed as many as nine hundred people daily at the castle gate.

Elizabeth was concerned, too, about the sick. She founded two hospitals, in which she often tended the patients herself, making their beds and feeding them with her own hands. She was particularly drawn to those whose condition was so repulsive no one else could bear to look after them. It is because of her devotion to extreme cases of illness that many hospitals today are named St. Elizabeth's.

The story of Elizabeth's love and marriage is a story of childhood romance, one of the most beautiful in history or literature. Betrothed to Ludwig, son of the king of Thuringia, when she was four and Ludwig was eleven, she was brought at once to her future husband's home where the two grew up together. Instead of the brother-sister attitude that might have been expected to develop in such a relationship, these two were sweethearts from the time they met. As soon as Ludwig reached the age of twenty-one they were married. The marriage lasted, however, only six years. Ludwig, like nearly all kings and noblemen in those times, went on one of the Crusades to liberate Palestine from the Mohammedans, but he never reached the Holy Land. One of the plagues so common in medieval Europe struck him down en route. When Elizabeth heard of Ludwig's death, she made provision for their three children and then, on Good Friday, 1228, took the vows of the Order of St. Francis.

Musician's Patron
NOVEMBER 22ND

November 22nd is dedicated to St. Cecilia, a Roman lady of the third century, who, for reasons no longer clear, is the patron of music and musicians. Legend says that she played the harp so beautifully that an angel left heaven to come down and listen to her. "She drew an angel down," says Dryden in his Ode to St. Cecilia. Christian paintings, however, always show the angel doing the playing and St. Cecilia doing the listening. Whatever the true details may have been, the Academy of Music at Rome accepted her as its patron when it was established in 1584, and that should give her enough credentials to satisfy anyone. For a large part of the seventeenth century it was fashionable in England to hold special concerts on November 22nd in St. Cecilia's honor. Although that particular wave of extreme popularity has passed, there are still many choirs and music societies named for St. Cecilia in both America and Europe.

He Invented Felt
NOVEMBER 23RD

St. Clement, who was one of the earliest (100 A.D.) of the popes, is credited with having discovered the cloth which is now known as felt. The story is that Clement, before he was pope, was forced to flee from certain persecutors, and that as he trudged along the hot, dusty road, his feet began to blister. To ease the discomfort he put some wool inside his sandals. That night when he stopped he found that by the motion and pressure of walking he had pounded the wool into a uniform and compact sheet. Later when life became a little more leisurely, Clement took time to develop the crude substance into a workable cloth. This legend made Clement the patron saint of hatters, who, in medieval guild times, always held their big annual festival on St. Clement's day.

St. John of the Cross

NOVEMBER 24TH

According to the dictionary a mystic is a person who believes that *direct* knowledge of God is attainable, which means that a man may bypass the usual approaches of intellectual or sensory perception and achieve a direct personal union with God. One of the great believers and teachers of this doctrine was St. John of the Cross, a sixteenth century Spanish priest who is commemorated on November 24th in the Roman Catholic Church. In support of John's teaching Pope Pius XI elevated him to the rank of Doctor of the Church in 1926. There are only twenty-nine men of this title in Roman Catholic history. To be proclaimed Doctor of the Church one must have fulfilled the conditions of "eminent learning" and a "high degree of sanctity," and must have formulated or expounded "doctrine from which the whole church has received great advantage."

John's doctrine in itself was nothing new. He simply believed and taught that the way of the Cross is the way of life. One must lose his life in order to find it. That had been said long ago by the Lord Himself. The important thing about John was not that he had anything to add to it, but that he himself followed the way of the Cross and showed that way to others who would never have found it without his help.

In his book, *The Dark Night*, John put forth the principle that union with God comes only to those who have passed through their own dark night of suffering and have achieved complete loss of self. One can never possess everything until he has gone through the ego-shattering experience of learning to desire nothing. This death and resurrection is the meaning of the Cross for every man. John's own dark night was a long season of persecution and imprisonment during which he was beaten and nearly starved by enemies he had made through his efforts to bring about certain reforms in the Carmelite Order. At the end of it all he thanked his captors for the favor they had done him, for it was in these sufferings, he said, he learned to lose himself and find God.

The Catherine Wheel

NOVEMBER 25TH

A man can't stand a woman who is smarter than he is. That fact was at the bottom of St. Catherine's trouble. She was smarter than the Emperor Maximinus, fourth century head of the Roman empire. Once when he won a great military victory he ordered everyone to sacrifice something to the Roman gods in celebration and thanksgiving. Catherine of Alexandria, a woman of unusual intelligence and cleverness, came to talk to him about it and to show him the falseness of paganism. When Maximinus could not handle her arguments himself he called in his wise men, philosophers, and professors, and, so the story goes, the brilliant lady converted every one of them to Christianity.

This was too much for the emperor. He sentenced Catherine to be executed, and in his rage he invented a new instrument of death to be used upon her. She was put into a machine that consisted of four wheels, turning in opposite directions and having spikes and sawblades inside. One legend says angels carried her, broken and mutilated, from the wheel to heaven. Another says the wheel refused to work and the executioner finally beheaded her. At any rate, it is from this saint's unhappy experience that the flaming piece of fireworks known as the "Catherine wheel" gets its name.

St. Catherine is the patron of two very different categories of people and in both cases the reason is plain. Scholars and philosophers look to her because of her great learning, which she demonstrated in her debate before the emperor. She is also the patron of those whose work has to do with wheels: millers, grinders, wheelwrights, spinners, etc.

He Brought His Brother

NOVEMBER 30TH

St. Andrew, patron saint of Scotland, Russia, and golfers, was neither Scottish nor Russian, nor, so far as anyone knows, did he ever play golf. He was a simple fisherman and one of the Twelve Apostles. He was also the brother of an Apostle, St. Peter—in fact, it was through Andrew's insistence that Peter went to meet the Lord in the first place. Andrew had been a disciple of John the Baptist when John pointed to Jesus and said "Behold the lamb of God" (St. John, chapter I, verses 35 to 40). When he heard this, Andrew went at once to get his brother and bring him to the Lord.

This is the one special act for which St. Andrew is held

up today as an example to all Christians: he went and brought this brother. It is almost impossible now to imagine the New Testament or the early Church with that brother left out, but it might well have happened if Andrew had not been eager—as all Christians must be—to share his Lord with those he loved. Apparently the two brothers spent a day or so with Jesus, in a sort of investigation of this new young prophet whose reputation was beginning to spread. But then they went back to their fishing and nothing happened until some time later when Jesus found them at work and invited them to come along with Him and be "fishers of men." (Matthew, chapter 4, verses 18 to 20).

The New Testament makes no mention of Andrew after the Ascension, but tradition says his special territory was in and around Greece. The story is that in the town of Patrae Andrew converted a woman named Maximilla, who was the wife of the Roman consul there. This so angered the consul that he had the Apostle flogged and then crucified. (The cross was an X-shaped one—that is why the X is called the St. Andrew's cross.) Maximilla saw to it that the body was decently buried and there was a legend in that country for many years which said that manna and a fragrant oil came from Andrew's tomb. People could make predictions about the crops by observing the quantity of these two miraculous products. When they were abundant, crops would be good; when they were scanty, a bad year was in prospect. The Emperor Constantine removed Andrew's body to Constantinople in the early part of the fourth century, but it did not stay there long. In 368 a monk named Regalus took it to Scotland, buried it on the eastern coast and built a church there. It is at this spot that the city and cathedral of St. Andrew's arose and now stands.

Separation of Waters

NOVEMBER 30TH

At Avignon, in France, a celebration is held each November 30th in commemoration of a miracle known as the Separation of the Waters, which occurred there November 30, 1433. The story is that there was a great flood caused by the overflowing of three rivers—the Rhone, the Durance, and the Sorgue—and that the water rose around the Church of the Gray Penitents and finally inside it to a point where the brothers of that order began to fear it might reach the altar and come into contact with the Sacrament. Some of the brothers hastily found a boat and rowed their way into the church. There they found the water separated in front of the altar as if by two glass walls. The altar itself was perfectly dry. The miracle is said to have been witnessed by twelve of the Gray Penitents, three doctors of theology, and a large number of devout laymen.

VARIABLE HOLIDAYS AND OBSERVANCES

Religion in American Life

Each November the National Committee on Religion in American Life sponsors a full month of concentrated promotion aimed at the increase of church attendance in America. Under the leadership of the Committee, American businessmen will make available without charge more than six million dollars worth of national advertising facilities. Throughout the month every modern medium of communication—TV, radio, newspapers, magazines, and billboards—holds before American families the committee's slogan

> "Build a stronger, richer life,
> Worship together every week."

R.I.A.L., as the program is now called, is entirely a lay-men's activity not officially connected with any church or religious body. Its purpose is "to strengthen the place of religion in personal, community and national life," which the Committee believes can best be accomplished "by urging every American to attend regularly the church or synagogue of his choice."

World Temperance Sunday

The Sunday nearest November 1st is World Temperance Sunday in many Protestant churches. The purpose of the day is "to confront the people of the churches with the values of temperance." It is sponsored by several Prot-estant denominations and by various temperance organiza-tions. Congregations and Sunday School children hear preachers and special speakers deal with the prevalence of alcoholism and the evils of strong drink generally.

World Peace Sunday

The Sunday nearest Armistice Day (November 11th) is known as "World Peace Sunday" for Protestants of the National Council of Churches. In line with the Protestant policy of relating religion to current issues, this day in the churches is devoted to prayer for mankind's fondest hope: a world without wars. The theme of world peace is expressed in music, Scripture readings, and prayers in the church services on this day, but beyond that, members are urged in sermons and in study materials to join forces in support of all means of achieving peace. The National Council of Churches believes that concerted Christian opinion and effort is the greatest single influence for peace on earth today.

Man as God's Steward

Every year the second Sunday in November is the day on which many churches in the United States and Canada begin their campaign for financial support in the coming year. Known as Stewardship Sunday, the day is sponsored in the United States by the National Council of Churches' Joint Department of Stewardship and Benevolence. The term stewardship refers to the Christian and Jewish teaching that all creation belongs to God Who made it and each man is God's agent or steward, handling a portion of God's property. The material things a man ordinarily calls his possessions are not really his at all. They belong to God—man only takes care of them for a while.

On this Sunday each year the churches appeal for next year's support to their members' sense of responsibility as faithful stewards of the *money* God has entrusted to them. The annual financial campaign is one great opportunity for the Christian to acknowledge God's sovereignty over "the earth and all that therein is."

First Thanksgiving

Probably one of the most commonly held errors about American history is the popular idea that our Thanksgiving began in the Plymouth Colony in 1621. The colonists did indeed hold a service of Thanksgiving in that year, but it was not the first one in North America and it was not the first one within the boundaries of the present United States. Away back in 1578 English settlers in Newfoundland proclaimed a Thanksgiving Day. And in

1607 another was observed by the Popham Colony, on what is now the coast of Maine. Furthermore, it was not until 1863 that the whole country was invited by presidential proclamation to observe the same day in all states, and even then, because of the Civil War, the response was only partial. And the day was not established as a national holiday by congressional action until 1941.

In spite of these historical facts and statistics it is, of course, the Pilgrims' Thanksgiving Day that set the pattern for our present one. It was then, for example, that the unfortunate turkey became the traditional Thanksgiving bird. This happened quite by chance. Having set the day aside, Governor Bradford sent out four men to bring in some game for the community feast. They happened to find wild turkeys—but it could as easily have been venison, bear meat, or even rabbit. Thus accidentally do customs begin.

Even among the stern Pilgrims the day had its festive side. When the pleasant aroma of the roasting turkeys was wafted into the nearby woods ninety friendly Indians showed up, carrying a vast amount of venison to add to the feast. As the party developed, the men began to engage in such masculine sports as shooting matches and tests of strength, and what had started out to be one day of solemn thanksgiving finally lengthened out into three days of games and feasting. It is recorded, however, that they did stop occasionally for Psalm singing.

World-Wide Bible Reading

Back in the days of World War II, a marine on Guadalcanal wrote to his parents in the United States suggesting that they join him every day in reading a chapter of the New Testament. The parents readily agreed, a list was made for the daily readings, and the family custom began. There the matter might have rested forever but for the mother telling this simple story to the Philadelphia office of the American Bible Society. The alert Society saw in the incident an idea that would link not just one family but millions around the world in the unity the Holy Spirit gives when people read the Scripture together. And so, under the sponsorship of the Society an annual period of World-wide Bible Reading from Thanksgiving Day until Christmas was begun.

Each year the Society selects a theme or slogan, stating concisely the place of the Bible in modern life. Then, featuring the slogan in its publicity, the Society promotes this intensive month of Bible reading in more than forty countries. A list of daily selections is printed on a bookmark, of which fifteen million are circulated through the co-operating churches. The list is also printed in many newspapers.

The Season of Advent

In the Roman, Eastern, Anglican, and Lutheran Churches, the season of Advent is the beginning of the Church Year. Advent is a four-Sunday season ending on December 24th. Therefore, it always begins on the Sunday nearest November 30th, which is always the fourth Sunday before Christmas. Until the sixth century, Christians considered Easter as the beginning of their year, but because the Jewish year also began at approximately the same time, certain anti-Semitic Christian leaders felt that the Christian calendar should be moved as far as possible from the Jewish. Such things seem trivial in these days and in this country, where Jews and Christians are on friendly terms, but in earlier times it was very important to Christians to make every possible denial of any kind of association with anything Jewish. It was this attitude, for example, that brought about the custom among Christians of eating ham at Easter—it emphasized one more difference between the Christians and the Jews, to whom pork was forbidden.

The word *advent* means "coming." The Advent season is primarily a time of preparation for the coming of the Lord at Christmas. It is one of the two penitential seasons in the Christian year, the other, of course, being Lent, which is the season of preparation for Easter. Advent has sometimes been called the "Winter Lent." In former times the disciplines of Advent were just as austere as those of Lent. The rules are greatly relaxed now, but it is still traditional in some churches that there be no weddings during this season.

Although the main emphasis of Advent is the preparation for the coming of the Christmas Babe, the season also reminds Christians of the two other "advents" for which they must constantly prepare: the Lord's constant, continual coming in the hearts of men, and His second coming, in glory, to judge the world. There is nowadays an ever-increasing observance of the Advent season by many of the Protestant denominations.

CHAPTER XII

December

He Carried the Lord's Cross

DECEMBER 1ST

St. Simon of Cyrene was what we would call today an "innocent bystander" on the day when the sad procession, with the Lord carrying His Cross, moved toward Calvary for the Crucifixion. According to Matthew, chapter 27, verse 32, Simon was pressed into service to carry the cross for its intended Victim. Mark, chapter 15, verse 21, adds that Simon was the father of Alexander and Rufus—whoever they were. This, and the fact that he came from the Greek city called Cyrene, is all anyone knows today about this obscure Simon.

At one time, however, there was an amazing story about his place in the events of that tremendous day. In the second century there was a group of strange Christians called Gnostics, who did not believe at all in the humanity of Jesus but thought of Him as a divine spirit which at times used a human body. The Gnostics worked out the appalling theory that when Simon was forced to shoulder the cross, Jesus had changed bodies with him and that it was really Simon who had been crucified. Needless, to say, the Church violently rejected any such fantastic notion, and the story soon died.

The Protector of the Dying

DECEMBER 4TH

St. Barbara, who lived and died at Nicomedia in the third century, is the protector of artillerymen and miners, of hills, mountains, and forts. She is invoked against storms, fire, lightning, explosions, and against death striking so suddenly that the dying person has no time to receive the Sacraments. All these functions have been assigned to Barbara as the result of stories and legends about her which are not accepted as historically true. No mention is made of this versatile saint in any of the authoritative writings of her time, but by the seventh century she was firmly established in the hearts of many Christians.

Legend tells that her father, a wealthy pagan, kept her shut up in a tower in order that she would not fall in love with some man and leave him. In art she is often shown imprisoned in a fort-like structure; a mistaken interpretation of these pictures led to her being called the patron saint of forts, and by derivation, of the artillerymen who manned the forts.

Although no suitors could get into Barbara's tower, Christianity did get in. She was converted and secretly baptized by a priest named Valentinian, who had access to her quarters. Her father was so furious over her conversion that he took her before the judge (Christianity was a criminal offense at that time) and she was tortured and sentenced to be beheaded. Her father offered to carry out the sentence himself, and here the story has two versions. One says he was struck by lightning as he was about to behead his daughter; the other says he did behead her and was killed by lightning on his way home. Both versions agree that the blast from the sky not only killed him but completely consumed his body so that no trace of him was left. This part of the story explains why Barbara is invoked against lightning, storms, and sudden death.

Barbara and another Christian woman, Juliana, who had been put to death at the same time, were buried together. Soon it was said that many sick people were healed at these two graves. An event in the year 1448 gave new support to the belief that St. Barbara looks after those who are stricken suddenly. A man named Henry Kock, in the town of Gorkum, was trapped in his burning house and burned beyond all hope. He prayed to St. Barbara and through her intercessions was kept alive long enough to receive the Sacraments. The report of Kock's experience was circulated widely and Barbara's popularity as the protector of the dying was greatly increased. St. Barbara's Day is considered the real beginning of the Christmas Season in Syria and in parts of France and Germany.

St. Nicholas—Patron of Many Peoples and Places

DECEMBER 6TH

St. Nicholas, the fourth century Archbishop of Myra who has become Santa Claus to millions of Americans, is the patron saint of many peoples and places. He is the patron of Russia, and particularly of Russian peasants, because of his reputation as protector of the weak and poor against the strong and rich. The seaport city of Venice adopted him as patron because of a legend that he had shown power over the sea by quieting a storm when he was on a voyage to the Holy Land. Thieves look to him for help because he once forced a gang of thieves to restore their plunder, thus bringing them back into the right ways.

Boys may depend upon him, as he once demonstrated by reassembling and reviving three boys who had been dismembered and salted in brine by a wicked innkeeper. And young girls have a special place in his heart, as was shown when he anonymously tossed three bags of gold into the window of three sisters who for lack of dowry could find no husbands and were about to be sold into white slavery. He is just about everybody's saint. Even pawnbrokers are under his patronage. Some say that the three gold balls which are the sign of a pawnshop are an adaptation of the three bags of gold provided by St. Nicholas for the three unhappy sisters.

In the old country St. Nicholas does not come on Christmas Eve as he does here, but on his own eve—the night before December 6th. And he does not come down the chimney after everyone has gone to bed; he rings the front door bell and walks in after supper, right before the whole family. He is fat and jovial, and he carries the customary bag on his back, but the bag does not hold the variety of things American children are used to—only cookies and fruits. St. Nick questions the youngsters, amiably but firmly, about their past behavior and their future intentions, and if he is pleased he gives them some sweetmeat and the promise of something more on Christmas. But when Christmas Day comes it is the

Christ Child, not the saint, who brings the promised gifts.

Because Nicholas was little more than a boy himself when he became a bishop, a custom arose in cathedral towns of medieval England of celebrating St. Nicholas' Day by selecting a boy out of the cathedral choir to be a mock-bishop for a term of office extending from December 6th to the 28th (Holy Innocents' Day). In full episcopal regalia, and followed by a magnificent entourage, the boy-bishop put on for three weeks a hilarious burlesque of the pomp and dignity of the cathedral's real bishop, and he not only got away with it but he was actually encouraged by the very prelate whom he was lampooning. The boy-bishop custom, with some modern restraints, has been revived in several English cathedral towns in recent years.

The Conception of Mary
DECEMBER 8TH

On December 8th the Roman Catholic Church and some parts of the Anglican Church commemorate the Immaculate Conception of Mary, the Lord's mother. The Eastern Church observes the same festival on the following day. Great debate centered around this observance for centuries in the Western part of the Church. It was not, of course, that anyone objected to giving special attention to the day on which Mary's life might be said to have begun. The controversial point was in the word "Immaculate."

Christian doctrine teaches that every human being is conceived and born "in sin." This does not mean, as some people suppose, that there is something sinful about the reproductive process. It means that deep in every person there is the tendency to do wrong. It is "born in us." The meaning of the term "Immaculate Conception" is that in the case of the Virgin Mary—the only case in all human history—this basic inclination toward sin was never present. She was without it from the time she was conceived. This was held as a pious belief very early in the Christian Church, and was the occasion of a festival first in England, at Winchester, and then in France. From France the festival spread to all Christendom. Dates are uncertain, but it is sure that the Feast of the Immaculate Conception was in the general calendar by the middle of the fourteenth century. But many leading theologians, including St. Thomas Aquinas, opposed the doctrine, and although various popes approved and even encouraged the commemoration, it was not until 1854, under Pius IX, that the Immaculate Conception was proclaimed a dogma of the Roman Church.

The Holy House of Loreto
DECEMBER 10TH

December 10th is a great day in the little Italian town of Loreto, for it is the anniversary of the day when, in 1291, the angels brought the "Holy House" there. The Holy House of Loreto is believed by the villagers, and by many others, to be the house in which Jesus, Mary, and Joseph lived in Nazareth, and to have been transported through the skies from Nazareth to its present locality. Books have been written to prove that the little cottage that is now set in the midst of Loreto's gorgeous church, and encased in richly carved marble, is actually the home of the Holy Family. And other books have been written to prove that it is not. The Roman Catholic Church has taken no official position in the matter.

On the negative side it is stated that there is no record

of any cottage having vanished from Nazareth in 1291. Nor, indeed, did pilgrims to the Holy Land prior to 1291 ever bring back reports of seeing the Lord's home there. But, on the other hand, there is in Loreto, a tiny cottage, 13x31, of a construction quite unfamiliar to that part of the world, and made of materials that have been chemically tested and found to be exactly the same as the materials used in Nazareth. Whatever may be the real origin of this famous cottage, many popes have given their approval to the popular tradition, and many people have found miraculous cures at the humble shrine within its walls.

Second Greatest Stylite

DECEMBER 11TH

Back in the early days of Christianity there were men called "stylites" who spent all their time at the tops of pillars (*stulos* is the Greek word for pillar). Many of these strange pillar saints spent years on their lofty perches without ever coming down for any purpose. Most famous of them all was St. Simon, who lived for sixty-eight years on his column, moving occasionally to a new and higher one—his last was sixty-six feet high. The second most renowned was St. Daniel, who is honored on this day. He died at eighty-four atop his pillar just outside Constantinople, after occupying it for thirty-three years.

Such eccentric behavior in the name of religion seems bizarre to us today. We joke about these "ecclesiastical flagpole sitters" and tend to think of them as show-offs. But we miss the point. They were only following the mood of their time. Spiritual perfection was thought to come through withdrawal from the ordinary stream of life and through endurance of inconvenience, discomfort, or even pain. And so the most devoted men of that age deliberately sought the lonely discipline—some in caves, some in the desert, some at the tops of pillars—that would set their hearts on the joys that are not of this world.

We make a great mistake if the unfamiliar pattern causes us to assume these men were not men of real and deep piety. Exhibitionists may attract curious people for a while, but in the end the world never calls them saints. Crowds flocked to Daniel, gathering at the foot of his pillar to be healed of illnesses or to listen as he spoke to them quietly about the love of God. Kings and princes came to him for advice on matters that dealt with the world he had renounced. Perhaps one sees the "world" most clearly from a pillar apart from it. Disciples organized themselves around St. Daniel, who neither encouraged nor rejected them. They built a monastery nearby and profited by living in the great man's shadow.

Daniel's life had been dedicated to the Lord even before his birth. At twelve he was put into a monastery and soon afterward he was taken by his abbot to see the great Simon Stylites, who permitted the boy to climb up to him, gave him his blessing, and foretold that he would suffer much for Christ. From that time on Daniel knew what he would do. Simon was his model. When Simon died, Daniel inherited his mantle, and finally his position as the world's number one pillar saint. Daniel died in 493, and was buried at the foot of his pillar.

The Lady of Guadalupe

December 12th

December 12th is Mexico's greatest religious festival: the Fiesta of Our Lady of Guadalupe. It commemorates the appearance of the Blessed Virgin Mary to an Indian convert named Juan Diego, on this day in the year 1531. In those times the Spanish conquerors had just taken that part of North America over from the Aztecs, and of course, a part of that taking over consisted of destroying all the ancient Aztec gods and goddesses. Among the dieties whose idols were smashed was Tonantzin, the goddess of the earth and the growing corn. She had been important in the lives of the people and dear to their hearts and though her shrine and her image were gone, the memory of her was strong.

Into this vacancy, the legend says, stepped the Blessed Virgin Mary herself. At the very spot where Tonantzin's shrine had stood, Mary appeared to the simple Juan Diego, who happened to be passing by. She spoke to him and told him to go to the bishop and say that she wanted a church built on this same site and dedicated to her. Poor Juan, to whom the bishop was much more awesome than Mary, tried to deliver the message, but got nowhere with it. The bishop wanted proof, and Juan had none. So Juan went back to the scene and there the Virgin met him again. This time she filled his homespun blanket with roses—Castillian roses, which the bishop would recognize as foreign to Mexico—and sent him back. But the roses were not miraculous enough. When Juan opened the blanket and spilled out the roses, there, to everyone's amazement, was a portrait of Mary painted on the blanket.

No further persuasion was needed. A church was immediately erected in honor of Our Lady of Guadalupe. The miraculous portrait was hung there, and there it still hangs after four hundred years. It is an amazing story, certainly, but skeptics are faced with the problem of explaining the portrait, which has hung completely exposed

and without any kind of preservative for four centuries
in a climate where other paintings, carefully protected,
will begin to deteriorate within a few years. To the faithful, childlike Mexicans there is no problem to be explained. They come in such numbers to the shrine of their
Lady of Guadalupe that only the French shrine at Lourdes attracts an equal number of pilgrims.

The Saint With the Beautiful Eyes
DECEMBER 13TH

Nearly everyone has sung about Santa Lucia, but not
many people know her as the gentle St. Lucy, who suffered and died for her faith more than 1,500 years ago.
Lucy was a wealthy girl in the ancient city of Syracuse,
late in the third century. There was nothing very remarkable about her, except her goodness. Since childhood she
had been engaged (parents arranged these matters) to a
rich and noble young pagan. Lucy had nothing against
the young man, but she did not want to marry anyone,
and she kept putting off the wedding on one excuse and
then another.

Lucy's mother had some incurable disease—incurable,
that is, as far as the local doctors were concerned. The
records do not tell what the disease was. But stories began to circulate in Syracuse about the miraculous cures
that had been effected at the tomb of St. Agatha, not far
away. The girl took her mother to the tomb and a complete cure was brought about. The mother's joy gave
Lucy her chance and she quickly asked to be released
from the dreaded engagement. Her request was granted.
The jilted young man went in anger to a judge and reported that Lucy was a Christian. The judge called her
in and when she refused to offer sacrifices to the pagan

gods, commanded the soldiers to take her away and execute her. Legend says that the soldiers were unable to
remove the frail girl, even with oxen. They built a fire
around her, but she was unharmed. Finally she was put
to death with a sword.

In pictures St. Lucy is often shown carrying her eyes
in a dish. There is a story about this. It is said that a man
fell in love with her because of the beauty of her eyes,
and Lucy, in order that he might be able to turn his attention to the salvation of his soul, plucked out the lovely
eyes that were distracting him.

The Day of the Four Freedoms
DECEMBER 15TH

On December 15th in 1791, three quarters of the United
States had ratified the Bill of Rights—the first ten amendments to the Constitution. In one sweeping action, all
ten amendments became law. December 15th has been
called Bill of Rights Day ever since. It is not a day of
formal church observance—probably there will not even
be much civil recognition of it—but certainly it belongs
in every American's religious calendar, for it is the day
on which the now famous "Four Freedoms," of which our
religious freedom is one, were guaranteed to us.

Eight Days Until Christmas
DECEMBER 16TH

Here's a day you probably never heard of. It is called
O Sapienta, which means "O Wisdom." Back in the
Middle Ages they didn't talk, as we do, about how many
shopping days were left until Christmas, but when they
came to the 16th of December, they began to sing in all

the churches a series of eight anthems of which the first was *O Sapienta*. All of these eight anthems began with "O." There was "O Key of David," "O Rod of Jesse," "O Emmanuel," and so on through the eight days leading up to Christmas eve. But the one that came first, and therefore the important one, was *O Sapienta*. Before long the day itself came to be called by the name of its anthem.

The Festival Behind Christmas

DECEMBER 17TH

Everyone always looks back to "the good old days." The Romans, whose chief god was Jupiter, believed the time of Saturn, the father of the gods, had really been the greatest time of all, the Golden Age. Once a year, beginning December 17th, they held a great festival, the Saturnalia, in memory of that happy bygone era.

It was a wild sort of festival, one of unrestrained disorder. At first it was three days long, then a whole week. It started in an innocent pagan way with some quite pleasant customs. During the Saturnalia grudges and quarrels were forgotten; business, courts, and schools were suspended; wars were interrupted or postponed; no prisoners were punished. Slaves sat at their master's tables and were served by them in memory of the happy days of Saturn when all men were equal. But this genial reversal of order and suspension of discipline inevitably deteriorated into a week-long revel of vice and crime. Man has never been able to behave very long when the teacher goes out of the room.

To us a Roman festival seems ancient, but behind the Saturnalia lie even more remote celebrations at this time of year. Man's most primitive calendar was based on a simple awareness of the changing seasons, the equinoxes, and the solstices. And always the winter solstice was the time of the greatest festival, partly because agricultural people (as all people were in those days) had little to do at this time of year, and partly because the changing sun now brought the promise of new life in a new growing season. One special feature of the Saturnalia—the giving of gifts—shows that the festival reached back into an antiquity the Romans themselves had forgotten. Traditional gifts were candles, imitation waxfruits, and dolls. Scholars say the dolls were actually symbols of the human sacrifices of an earlier day, and the waxfruits were connected with ancient fertility rites.

The candles meant what they still mean: now in the darkest time of the year mankind has always had, and probably always will have, his festival of light. In the religion of Mithra (Persian) the birthday of the sun was celebrated now. The Jews had, and still have, their Hanukkah whose candles must have been burning in Jewish homes when Mary had her Baby in Bethlehem. The time of year when nature promises new creation and new light, this was the logical time for a festival of lights —and for Christmas, the Nativity of Christ the Light of the World. That December 25th was established as the date of Christmas was due to a mistake in the Julian calendar, in which the 25th rather than the 21st was shown as the date of the winter solstice.

The First Man
DECEMBER 19TH

Adam, the first man, is remembered on December 19th as St. Adam in certain local Roman Catholic calendars. The Hebrew word "adam" means simply "man" or "mankind," and it is sometimes difficult to know whether the account in Genesis is talking about an individual named Adam or about the entire human race. But the names of Adam and Eve are a part of Jewish-Christian tradition as the actual names of the first man and the first woman. There is a legend, however, that says Eve was Adam's second wife—the first having been a most unpleasant person named Lilith.

Adam has put many expressions into our language. When we speak of "the old Adam" in us, we mean that part of us that tends to yield to temptation. When St. Paul says "the last Adam," he means Christ. "Adams's ale" which in Scotland is called "Adam's wine," is water, because in Adam's time there was nothing else available to drink. In Genesis, chapter 3, verse 7, it is stated that Adam and his wife sewed fig leaves together and made themselves aprons. Since presumably there were no needles in the Garden of Eden, one wonders what implement they used. The solution offered is that they used the spines that grow on many cactus-like plants, as, for example, the yucca, and such spines have long been known as "Adam's needles." Gardening is, for obvious reasons, often called "Adam's profession." And the prominent cartilege in the human throat, especially the male throat, is called "Adam's apple" on the legendary theory that one piece of the forbidden apple stuck in Adam's throat and we have all inherited the mark of his sin.

St. Thomas, The Doubter
DECEMBER 21ST

December 21st is set apart in honor of the famous "Doubting Thomas," the Apostle who bluntly declined to believe in the Resurrection until he had seen and touched the risen Lord—see St. John's Gospel, chapter 20, verses

24 to 28. The name Thomas comes from the Greek *didy-mus*, which means "twin," and from this it is assumed that St. Thomas had a twin brother (or perhaps a sister). But nothing at all is known about the other twin.

Legend tells that when the Apostles were ready to start out on their missionary work they drew lots to see what part of the world each would take as his responsibility. St. Thomas, so the story goes, drew India. There are no records to prove this legend, but it is certain that some Christian missionary was in India very early, and it may well have been Thomas.

When St. Francis Xavier went among the Indian people in the sixteenth century, he found many Christian colonies there that showed evidence of having been long established, and their members told him that St. Thomas had converted their ancestors many centuries before. So strong is this tradition that 1952 was celebrated in many parts of India as the 1900th anniversary of St. Thomas' death in that country. Another tradition says that the Apostle supported himself in India by working as a carpenter. For this reason he is still the patron saint of architects, carpenters, and masons, and is usually shown in Christian art with a square rule in his hand.

The Christmas Saint

DECEMBER 25TH

The child whose birthday falls on Christmas usually feels very much out of luck, but the saint who shares December 25th with the Lord is honored indeed. Such a saint is Anastasia, a fourth century martyr. For reasons that are hard to understand today, Anastasia's name appears in the Christmas mass in the Roman Catholic Church. Stories about her are completely unreliable. All we really know is that there was a martyr by this name. But in Constantinople during the sixth century, there grew up a sort of cult—a "fan club," to use a modern term—of St. Anastasia in the church in which she was buried. This cult was named after her. It soon spread to Rome, where there was another St. Anastasia's Church. With so many people devoted to her, St. Anastasia rose for a time to such a peak of popularity that her name achieved just about the highest prominence possible—it was put into the mass for Christmas Day.

The Birth of Jesus
DECEMBER 25TH

Although the exact date of the Lord's birth was not, and still is not, known, and although every month in the year was suggested by various scholars and astronomers, the date was finally set as December 25th. This meant Christmas immediately began to take over many of the good customs—and to drive out the bad ones—that had been associated with the heathen winter solstice festivities. For example, pagans of many lands exchanged presents at this time of year. And there was a widespread custom of calling a truce on all personal feuds and enmities. The Romans even called off wars. Even before Christianity, this was in its own way a time of peace and goodwill toward men.

Everyone takes for granted that Jesus was born in a stable, and yet this is not specifically stated anywhere in the New Testament. St. Luke mentions a manger three times, but never says the manger was in a stable, and it is a fact that many of them were not. They were often placed outside the house, by the front door.

St. Matthew (chapter 2, verse 11) uses the word

"house" to describe the Holy Family's accommodations at Bethlehem, but local tradition, going as far back as the second century, says the birth took place in a grotto or cave on the outskirts of the village. There is really no Scriptural foundation for all our pictures of the Holy Family in a stable.

"Put Christ Back Into Christmas"

Many people these days are concerned, and rightly so, about the lack of real religious tone in much of our Christmas observance. There is, for example, a movement called "Put Christ back into Christmas" which deplores the pagan elements in modern Christmas festivities, such as the office party, the irreligious greeting cards, the over-commercialization, and the excessive drinking. One very interesting fact about this movement is that it has not been prompted by church leaders but has been a spontaneous rebellion of the laity. No one can deny that our modern Christmas celebrations often have little or nothing to do with the fact that we are supposed to be rejoicing over the Saviour's birth. But in fairness it must be added that this situation is no worse than it was centuries ago, and certainly not as bad as it has been at times.

The first Christmases must have been much worse than those of today. A man named Gerson, a theologian living in those early times, wrote, "If all the devils in hell had put their heads together to devise a feast that should utterly scandalize Christianity, they could not have improved this one." There are still some scandalous elements today, but there can be no doubt that progress in the right direction has been made.

A Season, Not a Day

In the Middle Ages Christmas was—as it really is—
a season, twelve days long, in commemoration of the birth
of the Lord Jesus. It isn't all over by the middle of the
morning on December 25th—it goes on until January 5th,
which in olden times was known as Twelfth Night. The
revived folksong, *The Twelve Days of Christmas,* must
be bewildering to people who are not aware that Christmas is a season.

It is too bad most Christians have come to think of
Christmas as a month-long shopping spree followed by an
hour or two of watching the children enjoy their presents
from Santa Claus, and then a big let-down. For them
Christmas is over when it should just be beginning. Modern people miss the wonderful times their medieval ancestors used to have.

It would, of course, be ridiculous to expect people to
pretend they did not know a great and happy time was
approaching. The preparation for Christmas is supposed
to be a solemn, penitential time, but there is no way in
the world to keep the joy of anticipation from coloring
the weeks leading up to Christmas, and indeed it would
not be desirable to do so. But it is a shame that we build
up to such an abrupt letdown, instead of getting the most
out of the full twelve-day period. Something fine and
valuable has been lost in our time.

Christianity's First Martyr
DECEMBER 26TH

December 26th is St. Stephen's Day, in honor of the first
person ever put to death for being a Christian. Stephen
was also one of the first deacons ever appointed in the

Christian Church. And he is the patron saint of stone-cutters.

The story of the first deacons is in the sixth chapter of the Acts of the Apostles. The early Christians, believing that the second coming of Christ was about to happen at any moment, had sold their possessions and pooled their resources, and were living as a community under the leadership of the Apostles. The account tells that the community had grown to such size that the Apostles were not able to look after certain practical details of community life and they asked the people to select seven men "whom we may appoint over this business." Stephen was one of the seven. Because of this setup in the early church, there have been many people who have tried to say that Christianity was communistic in its beginnings. These people miss the point entirely. The only reason the Christians in Jerusalem lived as they did was because they thought the world was about to end. That is a very different thing from Marxian communism as a theory of political organization.

Stephen's death was by "stoning," which explains his position as the patron of stonecutters. It also explains the origin of a cruel custom of throwing stones at wrens on St. Stephen's Day, a custom that was practiced in Ireland, the Isle of Man, and some parts of England for many years until the Society for the Prevention of Cruelty to Animals managed to stop it. According to an Irish legend, St. Stephen was about to escape when the chirping of a wren awakened his guards. Therefore, all wrens were to be stoned as Stephen was stoned, and every year on St. Stephen's Day many of these innocent birds were killed. It was called "Hunting the Wren."

Another name for St. Stephen's Day in England is "Boxing Day," which has nothing to do with prize fight-

ing (or for that matter, with Stephen), but comes from
the fact that servants and minor employees used to
carry little boxes on this day each year and make the
rounds of all the people who might owe them any tips
or year-end bonuses. Over the years "boxing" came to
mean the giving of holiday gifts by superiors to inferiors.
The boxes are no longer carried, but the custom still goes
on and this is the day on which annual gratuities are
handed out.

The Beloved Disciple
DECEMBER 27TH

St. John, "the beloved disciple," was the only one of the
Twelve Apostles who died a natural death. According to
tradition he died at the age of 100 in the city of Ephesus,
where he was the Bishop. All the other Apostles met violent death at the hands of persecutors. It was St. John to
whom the Lord committed His mother at the time of the
Crucifixion, and it probably was this responsibility that
kept John at home while his colleagues were meeting
persecution and death in foreign lands. Not that John
didn't have his share of hardships. One legend tells that
in Ephesus a priest of the pagan goddess Diana gave him
a cup of poison, but he drank it without ill effect. Another story about his encounters with the opposition is
that he was boiled in oil. When the boiling liquid failed
to harm him he was released and exiled. This event took
place outside one of the gates to the city of Rome and is
commemorated on May 6th in the feast of St. John Before
the Lateran Gate.

It is easy to understand from these two legends why
St. John is invoked by the faithful against poisons and
burns. He is also invoked for friendships, which is al-

most like saying that he is the patron saint of friendship. The reason here is obvious, too, for John, of all the Twelve, was the Lord's special friend. He is continually referred to as "that disciple whom Jesus loved," (see John, chapter 21, verse 7) which does not, of course, mean that Jesus did not love the others, but rather that there was a special affection between Him and John.

St. John is sometimes called St. John the Evangelist. An *evangelist*, in this technical sense, is a writer of one of the four Gospels—Matthew, Mark, and Luke were the other evangelists. In spite of ancient and persistent tradition that John did write the Gospel that bears his name, scholars are not at all sure that he really was the author.

Holy Innocents' Day
DECEMBER 28TH

Don't promise anything on this day. Don't scrub the kitchen. Don't trim your fingernails. Above all, don't get married. For December 28th is Holy Innocents' Day, or Childermas, the unluckiest day of the year, and ancient wisdom says all these activities must be strenuously avoided. The day set aside in honor of the children who were slaughtered by King Herod in his attempt to destroy the infant Jesus (see St. Matthew, chapter 2, verse 16) has always been considered an ill-omened day. Legend says that when Edward IV of England found that the Sunday set for his coronation was also Holy Innocents' Day, he moved the ceremony to Monday in order not to start his official reign on that unhappy day. Traditionally, this is the day to carry out what is left of your Yule log; remembering of course, to save a piece of it with which to light next year's log.

St. Sylvester's Day

DECEMBER 31ST

The last day of the year honors, appropriately enough, St. Sylvester, the man who was Pope when one great era of Christian history ended and a greater one began. In the year 325, by decree of the Emperor Constantine, the pagan religion of Rome was abolished and Christianity became the official religion of the Empire. This did not mean that everyone became a Christian, for Christians cannot be made-to-order, but it did mean that the days of persecution were ended and Christianity was now free to come out in the open. It was a very important event in the life of the Christian Church. It is not on record that this happy development was brought about by Sylvester's influence or effort, but he was Pope at the time it happened, and certainly he must have had something to do with it. At any rate, tradition has always given him some of the credit, and in Christian art he is pictured trampling to death the dragon of paganism.

The First American Watch-night

DECEMBER 31ST

The New Year's Eve "Watch-night" service was started in America by a Methodist Church: St. George's in Philadelphia back in 1770. The custom has since been adopted by a number of denominations and throughout the country. Methodists, Baptists, Presbyterians, and many other gather in their churches for special services while waiting for the New Year.

Feast of Lights

Twenty-one centuries ago a little band of Jewish soldiers fought and won the first recorded battle for religious liberty. They resisted and overcame the mighty Syrian hordes, who if victorious would have wiped out Judaism both as a faith and as a way of life. But this war, which is called the Maccabean War because the Jews were led by Judas Maccabeus, did far more than rescue one religion from extinction. The English historian, Cecil Roth, said, "The Maccabean War determined the future of civilization. It decided that modern civilization should have a Jewish-Christian ethic."

It is, therefore, a victory of world-wide importance that the Jews celebrate with their eight-day Feast of Lights, called *Hanukkah*. At first there was considerable hesitation among the rabbis about allowing Hanukkah to become a religious festival, for it is not permissible for Jews to associate human bloodshed and worship. For this reason there are no military references in the symbolism of this festival.

For eight days each year, beginning on the twenty-fifth day of the month of Kislev, Jews give thanks for and draw inspiration from the great event which meant the survival of Judaism. They do not emphasize the fighting or the bloodshed that event involved. On each of the eight days they light candles, one the first day, two the second, and so on. A special nine-branch candelabrum, called a Menorah, is used, the ninth place being provided for an extra candle from which the others are lighted. The special significance of the candle ceremony is that it recalls the rekindling of the lights in the Temple when the holy place was rededicated after the Maccabean warriors had recaptured it from the Syrians.

On a deeper level the meaning of Hanukkah relates not only to the historic incident but rather to the ever-recurring story of the survival of Judaism. Time after time the faith of the Jews has been in jeopardy, but always it has met and overcome the hostile forces. Through all their wanderings over the earth and through all the persecutions inflicted on them, Jews have had to fight against the danger of actual physical destruction. Today the threat is more subtle, but no less real, for now they must be on the alert against an easy, gradual assimilation of their faith into a more friendly, but non-Jewish culture. So Hanukkah has a modern as well as an ancient application as a festival of survival, a symbol of the way the Jews maintain the integrity of their faith in the face of both physical force and alien influence.

American Jews, especially, make much of this winter festival, perhaps because American Christians at the same time of year are making so much of Christmas. In fact, the customs of Hanukkah are not unlike the customs of Christmas. The giving of gifts, the lighting of candles, the decorating of the home—all these fit in well with the general atmosphere of the country at this season, but they also preserve their distinctly Jewish flavor. Traditional Hanukkah decorations are the six-pointed "Star of David" —and blue and white crepe paper. Blue and white are the Jewish colors. Hanukkah gifts are wrapped in these colors. A special symbol of the festival is the elephant, because of the trained elephants used by the Syrian armies and the hammer, in commemoration of the Jewish leader Judas Maccabeus, who was called "Judas the Hammerer."

PART TWO

Customs

CHAPTER XIII

Some Jewish Terms and Traditions

The Jewish Calendar

The Jewish calendar is a "lunar" calendar, which means that it is based on the moon's revolutions around the earth and not, as is the Christian calendar, on the earth's revolutions around the sun. Each Jewish month begins with the new moon. In ancient times before people knew how to figure planetary movements mathematically, the time of the new moon's appearance had to be determined by direct observations. Official witnesses were sent out to watch. They reported to a special court, which examined them carefully, and when the court was satisfied that at least two of the witnesses had actually seen a new moon, the beginning of the new month was proclaimed. Lines of bonfires were lighted on hilltops to signal the procla-

mation to every part of the country. The next day was
celebrated as *Rosh Hodesh*, "new month." In modern
times, of course, it is possible to calculate Rosh Hodesh
exactly. On the preceding Sabbath the congregation is
informed of the precise time when the new moon will appear, and a prayer is said expressing the hope that the
coming month will bring blessing to all Israel.

The Jews actually have two calendars; a civil one and
a religious one. The civil year begins with the month of
Tishri, the first day of which is Rosh Hashonoh, or New
Year's. (Tishri coincides with late August or September
in our Gregorian calendar.) According to ancient Jewish
belief, the world was created on this day more than fifty-
seven centuries ago. All creation began on the first day
of Tishri. The Jewish months are: Tishri, Chesvan, Kislev,
Teveth, Shevat, Adar, Nisan, Ivar, Sivan, Tamuz, Ab and
Elul. The religious calendar begins on the first day of
Nisan, which comes in the spring of the year. This is by
divine order. In Exodus, chapter 12, verse 2, Yahweh tells
the Israelites: "This month will be unto you the beginning
of months; it shall be the first month of the year to you."
It was in this month of Nisan that the exodus from Egypt
and bondage took place, and the Jews became an organized people. Therefore, whereas the month of Tishri
marks the beginning of everything, Nisan commemorates
the beginning of Israel as an organized nation under God.

Synagogues

Just as the early Christians did not have churches, it is
also true that the early Jews did not have synagogues.
The development of places specifically set apart for public worship is apparently an evolutionary process in all
religions. In the primitive times when the Jews were wan-

dering for forty years in the wilderness, they carried with them a large tent, which they set up wherever they camped. In it there was an altar and the sacred Ark, in which were kept the two tablets of stone on which the Ten Commandments were written. It was a place of worship, but there was no permanence about it. In this tent, too, the people used to meet for instructions, asking questions of Moses, their leader, and listening to his teachings about the Law.

When they reached the Promised Land and settled down as farmers, it was no longer possible for them to come together in one place for worship. They were spread out over too much territory. Wherever the Ark was, there was the chief sanctuary of the land, but it was not long before every rural neighborhood had its "high place." These high places, however, were not synagogues. They were more like the pagan shrines of the people whose country the Jews had taken over. Religious authorities did not like them and did all they could to abolish them.

The synagogue as we know it today is said to have started during the seventy years when the Jews were in exile in Babylon, in the sixth century B.C. There the unhappy captives, homesick and grieving, began to gather in the homes of their leaders on the Sabbath and on their special festival days. Nothing could have been more natural. And it was also natural that in these informal meetings the people should read the Scriptures and pray together, and that the more learned among them should comment on the Bible readings, or preach informally. And since no ritual sacrifice was permitted anywhere except in Jerusalem, these home services did not require any priestly officiant. The laymen were in charge.

Here then was the ancestor of the synagogue—a local

meeting, conducted by laymen, serving local needs for fellowship, study, and prayer. When the Jews returned to their own land, they rebuilt the Temple in Jerusalem and resumed the sacrifices offered there by the priests, but they did not discontinue the weekly meetings in their towns and villages. Instead, they built special buildings for these meetings and called them synagogues. Also the synagogues became weekday education centers, with rabbis (teachers) devoting full time to them. The word *synagogue* literally means "school." When the second Temple was destroyed and the Jews scattered over the world in A.D. 70, the synagogues became the only centers of Jewish worship, and they have continued so ever since.

The Ark of the Covenant

The Ark of the Covenant was a beautiful and carefully built wooden box in which the Jews kept the stone tablets on which the Ten Commandments had been given to Moses on Mt. Sinai. Together with its contents, the Ark was, of course, Israel's holiest and most prized possession. It began as a movable sanctuary, carried about during the forty years in the wilderness between the escape from Egypt and the entry into the "Promised Land."

When Solomon built the Temple in Jerusalem, the Ark was given a special place in the innermost room, called the Holy of Holies. But when the Romans destroyed Jerusalem in 70 A.D., the Temple suffered the same fate as the rest of the city. It was leveled to the ground. And the Ark has never been seen since.

There is one small clue as to what happened to the sacred box. The general who destroyed Jerusalem was Titus (later he was an emperor) and in Rome an arch of triumph was erected in his honor. On this arch, reproduced in the carving, was a picture of the Ark of the Covenant. This one meager historical fact has for centuries supported a strong suspicion that Titus carried off the holy object along with the other spoils of war. No one knows what became of it after that.

The Mezuzah Box

On the right of the door of every Jewish home there is a small metal or wooden container, often beautifully decorated, which Jews touch as they go in and out of the house. It is called a Mezuzah box. *Mezuzah* means "doorpost."

Inside the box is a little parchment scroll on which are written two Biblical passages: Deuteronomy, chapter 6, verses 4 to 9, which deals with love and devotion for one God; and Deuteronomy, chapter 11, verses 13 to 21, which tells of the rewards man receives for obeying God's commandments. The scroll is so arranged inside the box that the word "almighty" is seen through an opening. In many cases the Mezuzah is not only on the outside doors but also on the door of every inhabited room in the house. Among the Orthodox, it is the custom to kiss the fingers after touching the Mezuzah.

The Star of David

People frequently ask the meaning, or the origin of the Star of David, the six-pointed star used as a symbol of the Jewish faith. This is a very old symbol whose meaning has long been lost. The star is simply two triangles placed together in such a way as to make six points. This figure was found on a Hebrew seal dating back to the seventh century, B.C., and also was a familiar device in other ancient cultures, such as the Egyptian, the Chinese, and the Peruvian.

It is hard to say when this star became the symbol of Judaism in the popular mind. It began to appear on synagogues in the sixteenth century, but most people probably became aware of it when the United States Government during World War I first used it to mark the graves of Jewish soldiers. Immediately after the war the International Council of Zionists adopted a flag that featured the Star of David. It is also used by some modern Jews in much the same way that Christians use the Cross, as a mark or design on church buildings, sacred vessels, etc. But still nobody knows where it came from or what it means.

The Shewbread

An interesting question about a Jewish sacred article arises from St. Luke, chapter 10, verses 1 to 5. When the Pharisees tried to rebuke Jesus for allowing His disciples to pick grain to satisfy their hunger on the Sabbath, He answered them by pointing out that David in the Old Testament had similarly broken the ceremonial law by eating the shewbread and giving it to his hungry soldiers. What was this shewbread? The passage refers to the time when the Lord made it plain to His hecklers that a man's hunger is more important than a church regulation. The shewbread—or showbread, as we would spell it now—was sacred bread that was placed on a gold-topped table in the tabernacle where the holy Ark was kept. It started very early in Jewish history, while the Israelites were wandering in the desert after their escape from Egypt. When Solomon built the Temple at Jerusalem, the gold table, with the bread, was placed in a part of the building called the outer court of the Levites.

Although Exodus, chapter 25, verse 30, states that the bread is to be kept always on the table by divine command, nothing is said anywhere in the Bible about how much bread was to be used, or how the people, who had only manna to eat in the wilderness, were to make the bread. All that is known about the shewbread, or the customs surrounding it, comes from Jewish writing outside the Bible.

Traditionally there were twelve loaves of shewbread, which were exposed on the table for one week. They were replaced every Sabbath, and only the priests were allowed to eat the old ones. When David and his men were hungry they ignored these regulations and ate the bread themselves. (See I Samuel, chapter 21, verses 1 to 6.)

The Shofar

The shofar is a horn. Normally it is a ram's horn, but it may be from any animal except a cow or an ox. When the shofar is blown it is a signal that something big is about to happen. The Jews use it for important national occasions, for festivals, for the new moon, and for (but not on) the Sabbath. And it is blown every day except the Sabbath in the month of Elul.

The shofar may not be decorated in colors, but it is usually engraved with texts and sacred designs. The man who blows this ceremonial horn in the synagogue is carefully selected. The honor ordinarily goes to a person of known piety and uprightness.

The Torah

The word *Torah* is used in two senses. First, *Torah* means the first five books of the Bible: Genesis, Exodus, Leviti-

cus, Numbers, and Deuteronomy. These books are called
the books of Moses, and according to Jewish belief they
contain all the laws that God revealed to Moses. Secondly, the word *Torah* is also the name of the scroll on
which these five books are written, and which is kept in
the Ark, the place of honor and prominence in every synagogue. The writing on this scroll is always carefully done
by hand. Selections from the Torah are read at all regular
services.

The "Double Bread"

When the Jews escaped from Egypt and began their forty
years of wandering in the wilderness, it was not long until
they began to worry about where their food was to come
from. The answer was soon given by Yahweh Himself,
who "rained bread upon the ground" for them every
morning. The bread from Heaven was called "manna,"
which comes from the Hebrew *man hu,* meaning "what
is it?" This is what the people said when they first saw the
food. (Read the 16th chapter of Exodus.) No manna fell,
however, on Saturdays (the Sabbath) and the story tells
that every Friday the Jews gathered a double supply to
tide them over the two days.

This tradition is the basis of a Jewish custom that is
still carried on. On Friday mornings in Orthodox house-
holds, the wife bakes two loaves of bread and puts them
at the husband's place for the evening meal. The two
loaves, called "double bread," stand for the double portion that was gathered in the wilderness every Friday.
The loaves are covered with a cloth which symbolizes the
dew that covered the manna every morning.

Jewish Home Ceremony

Out of the prohibition against kindling any fire on the Sabbath day (see Exodus, chapter 5, verse 3) has come one of the most beautiful of Jewish home customs: the lighting of the Sabbath candles by the housewife. Originally it was probably just a matter of seeing that some light was provided before the rule went into effect at sundown, but over the years this simple and practical act has acquired a ritual and a symbolism that keep it alive even though the light from the candles is no longer a household necessity. In modern times the wife, because she and not the husband attends to household affairs, places two—in special instances, more—candles on the family table and lights them a half-hour before the Sabbath begins, saying a prescribed blessing as she does so. These candles are left burning for light through the family dinner and through the evening. Once in place on the table, they may not be moved.

The Jewish Priesthood

An interesting thing about the Jewish religion is that in it priesthood comes to a man not by ordination but by inheritance. In the 40th chapter of Exodus the account is given of how God established Moses' brother Aaron as the first priest and provided that the sacred office should be inherited by Aaron's descendants forever. Orthodox and Conservative Jews still think of Aaron's line as occupying a special position. Men named Cohen, Kohn, Kahn, Katz, or Kaplan are probably in the priestly family, and although they are not considered clergymen they are given certain ritual tasks, such as the blessing of the congregation at the synagogue services.

A Jewish Rabbi

A Jewish rabbi is not a clergyman in the same way that a Christian priest or minister is a clergyman. The word *rabbi* means "teacher," and a rabbi is literally an instructor rather than a pastor. Among Orthodox Jews the rabbi most of the time does not even lead the religious services. The cantor conducts the worship, and a layman may rise from the congregation to lead the prayers.

In America, however, much modern Jewish practise has been influenced by the general church patterns of the country, and rabbis usually have pastoral duties much like those of Protestant ministers. They preach at the weekly services, preside over the worship, supervise religious education, counsel their people, and perform the ministerial ceremonies surrounding birth, marriage, and death. But originally the rabbi's function had to do only with instruction.

The Perpetual Light in the Synagogue

In every temple and synagogue hangs a silver or bronze lamp in which a light is kept burning. This tradition goes back to the earliest times when the Jews were a wandering desert tribe, and the lamp burned in a tent before the Ark of the Covenant. (See Leviticus, chapter 24, verses 2 and 3.) The lamp, called *Ner Tamid*, is usually in the form of a kettle, and pure olive oil is the customary fuel. The ever-burning light symbolizes the continuous presence of God and the permanence of the Law.

Bar Mitzvah

Any Jewish boy who has reached his thirteenth birthday is a *bar mitzvah*, that is, a "man, or son, of duty." It is considered in Jewish tradition that a boy of thirteen is old enough to accept responsibility for his own actions and to fulfill the religious duties of a man. On the Sabbath preceding his thirteenth birthday the boy is called to the altar of the synagogue and there reads the Torah (the scroll on which the Law is written) to the people, thus symbolizing the beginning of his full participation in the life of the congregation.

It marks the point at which the boy becomes an adult in the synagogue, much as his first vote at the polls marks his coming of age in civil life. This achievement of religious adulthood is almost always the occasion of a party, at which the new bar mitzvah's family and friends gather to rejoice with him. Some people mistakenly apply the name bar mitzvah to the party instead of the lad in whose honor the party is given.

Burnt Offerings

The rules about sacrifices and burnt offerings as God gave them to Moses are recorded in the Book of Leviticus. The system was elaborate, with a different kind of animal to be sacrificed and a different ritual to be followed for almost every request a man might make of God. The Jews gave it up in 70 A.D. when the Temple was destroyed, because it was only in the Temple that such sacrifices could be made. Even before that, its strength was declining. Leaders were beginning to say, along with the writer of the 51st Psalm, that "the sacrifices of God are a troubled spirit, a broken and a contrite heart . . ." rather than burnt offerings.

The Chosen People

There is an ancient Jewish legend which says that when the Torah (the Law) was given, God offered it first to several other nations, but all of them turned it down because they did not wish to assume its difficult responsibilities. Last of all it was offered to the Jews, who took it without reservation. Israel might therefore be more accurately called the "choosing people." They have accepted "the burden of the Torah"; that is, the responsibility of handing down through the centuries God's basic moral and spiritual truths. But there is in this sense of appointed duty no suggestion of Jewish superiority. Rabbi Mordecai M. Kaplan sums up the Jewish attitude when he says, "In a sense, every great people that has contributed to enlightenment and progress is chosen of God."

The Wanderings of the Jews

When the Israelites escaped from Egypt under the leadership of Moses, they were on their way to the "Promised Land," a fertile strip of country known in those days as Canaan. God had told Moses that this land would belong to the Jews. Moses at once picked out a prominent and reliable man from each of the twelve Jewish tribes and sent them ahead as a reconnoitering party, with orders to look over the land and come back with a report on just what kind of place this future home was. They were gone forty days, at the end of which period they returned, carrying great armloads of luscious fruits and saying that the country was indeed as predicted, "a land flowing with milk and honey."

But, they also said, the people were too strong and too fierce, and the cities were too big and well-defended—the Jews would never be able to take it. The mood of pessimism spread and everyone began to clamor for Moses to take them back to Egypt. For this lack of faith Yahweh meted out a terrible punishment, see Numbers, chapter 14, verses 33 and 34. No person then in adult life could expect to enter the Promised Land. The nation would wander for forty years—one year for each of the forty days the searching party had been away—until all this faithless generation had died. Then their children would be permitted to claim the land.

Where Does 'Jew' Come From?

When King Solomon died, the Hebrew nation was split into two kingdoms. The one in the northern part of the original country was called Israel; the one in the south was called Judea or Judah. Ten of the original Hebrew tribes lived in Israel; the other two in Judea. The northern kingdom was destroyed and its ten tribes lost when Assyria conquered the people and carried them into captivity.

This left only the Judeans, and when Jerusalem fell nineteen centuries ago, the Judeans scattered to all parts of the world. Each country in which some of them settled adapted the word "Judean" to its own language. In German, it became *Jude;* in French, *Juif;* in English, "Jew."

Smoking on the Sabbath

Orthodox Jews, and many others less strict than the Orthodox, refrain from smoking from sundown on Friday to sundown on Saturday—the duration of the Jewish Sabbath. This custom has nothing to do with moral notions about smoking nor with theories of sacrifice or self-discipline. The laws dealing with the Sabbath include a prohibition against the making of a fire. (Exodus, chapter 35, verse 3.) Among the most conscientious observers of the laws, this regulation is interpreted as preventing even the turning on of an electric light.

Jewish Dietary Laws

Many Gentiles are curious but uninformed about Jewish laws concerning what may and may not be eaten. The Book of Leviticus lays down three main rules:

1. Certain meats, such as that of pigs and horses; and certain sea foods, such as shrimp, lobster, crab, and oysters are forbidden.
2. Meats must be slaughtered according to ritual and must conform to specific health standards.
3. Meat and dairy products must not be eaten together.

Approved foods are called *kosher*, which means "clean." Forbidden foods are *treyfah*—"unfit." No restrictions are placed on fruit and vegetables, except that the fruit must not come from a tree less than three years old. Obviously, some of these regulations arose out of such purely practical considerations as the avoidance of food-poisoning: meat and seafood deteriorated rapidly in the semi-tropical Palestine climate—and conservation: a fruit tree needed at least three years to develop.

But there is much more to it than that. Moral values are involved, too. The slaughter of animals must be painless and compassionate. It is done, therefore, by a specifically trained man, properly certified as to his piety and learning. Meat killed for sport is not acceptable. And religious values are involved. The self-discipline of the diet is a powerful one. If a man can learn self-control in the matter of resisting temptation in this basic area of his life, that control will be likely to extend to other more subtle areas.

Adam and Eve

Folklore says that Adam had a wife before Eve, and that her name was Lilith. The story is that she refused to submit to the authority of her husband, and that she nagged and berated him so much he finally expelled her from the Garden of Eden. Her next step was a natural enough one: the shrewish wife became the mother of demons.

Part of the old superstition about Lilith was that she used her demonic powers especially against little children. She must have been a most unpleasant character, and no one can blame Adam for getting rid of her.

Some authorities think our word "lullaby" is connected with Lilith and her destructive interest in children. They say that the word was originally two words "Lilith abi," that is, "Lilith, begone!" and that mothers sang it to drive away the evil mother of demons.

Do the Jews Still Expect the Messiah?

Some Jews still expect the Messiah, and some do not. The Old Testament refers in many prophecies to a "deliverer" (Messiah means "anointed one") who would come from God and lead the world into a wonderful new age in which God would rule. Orthodox Jews still hold to the belief that these prophecies are to be fulfilled by a person. Reformed Jews, however, have abandoned the expectation of a personal Messiah. They believe that mankind by applying religious ideals to daily life will bring in an era of peace, brotherhood, and righteousness which will be the Messianic Age, but they do not expect that any one person will be divinely appointed leader of this wonderful development. Because this ideal was first revealed to

Israel, Jews consider that it is their special mission and duty to work for its fulfillment.

The Bible's Unusual Book

In the Book of Esther, which Martin Luther said he wished did not exist, there is no reference to God, nor to prayer, worship, or the Law. This is not true of any other book, in either Old or New Testament. Fasting is mentioned, but the book is patriotic, not spiritual, in character. The story in this book tells how the Jewish Esther, married to the Persian king, saved her people from the massacre plotted for them by the villainous Prime Minister Haman. This great deliverance is celebrated in the joyous Purim holiday. Scholars believe that the popularity of the Purim festival accounts for the inclusion of such a book in the Old Testament.

Kol Nidre

Here is an amazing and little-known story. In 1492, in the reign of Ferdinand and Isabella, the Jews were expelled from Spain. As with any national upheaval, there were many acts of violence and force connected with the expulsion. In one area—the Ebro river valley (remember that name)—there were many Jews who were compelled by fanatical Christians to accept Christianity and be baptized, forced to profess a faith they did not believe. In Jewish congregations everywhere there is a ritual known as Kol Nidre. The words *Kol Nidre* means "all vows," and the idea behind the ceremony is that before the beginning of Yom Kippur, the great Day of Atonement, when the burden of every Jew's sins is so great, men should not have to worry about vows they have made under pressure during the past year. And so the Kol Nidre prayer is chanted, releasing the people from promises made hastily under emotional stress, or fearfully under pressure.

Now here is the part of the story that fascinates historians. Very shortly after 1492 a new formula came into the Kol Nidre service. Just before the chanting of the prayer, the rabbi and the leaders of the congregation, carrying the scrolls of the Law in their arms, repeat three times a statement, the gist of which is "tonight we are permitted to worship with sinners." But by a change of only two letters, which would not be taking too great a liberty with the Hebrew language, the word for sinners would become "the people of the Ebro." The fact that this particular piece of ritual was added to the service at the time when these people were compelled to swear an allegiance they did not mean makes it seem quite possible that it was added entirely out of consideration for them.

Ages of Men

The arrival in New York a while ago of a 167-year old man from South America, together with the news that many people in this man's native Colombia live at least as long, reminded some of us of the ages recorded in the Old Testament. In earliest times, according to the book of Genesis, this South American would have been a mere adolescent, hardly even of voting age at 167. Adam was 930 when he died, Noah, 950, and Methuselah, 969. Later on he could have qualified a little better. Abraham died at 175, Moses at 120. This matter of how long the ancients really lived is one of the mysteries of the Bible. Those who believe the Scriptures literally and word-for-word have no problem, but others have long looked for some explanation. By the time the Psalms were written, the Psalmist was saying, "the days of our years are three score and ten"—just about par for the present.

What happened? Are the figures wrong, or has man so greatly deteriorated? There have been many theories. Some have said a year in Genesis was equal really only to a moon or a month, but this won't quite work. It would be all right for Methuselah—969 moons would have been about 80 years, but Moses by this reckoning would have been less than ten years old at his death. The most plausible idea is the Hebrews, like all ancient peoples, had a tradition that their ancestors were somehow special beings, something more than flesh and blood.

A Quorum for a Service

The number ten apparently had a great fascination for ancient Israel. There were ten commandments, ten plagues on the Egyptians, ten days of penitence at the beginning of each year, ten generations from Adam to Noah, and so on. When it came to the question of how many men were needed to hold a public religious service it is not surprising that the rabbis said there had to be ten. This quorum is known as a *minyan*. A minyan is ten male persons over thirteen years of age. In modern times only Orthodox Jews apply this rule of the minyan.

CHAPTER XIV

>>>>>>>>>>>>>>>>>>>>>>>>> · ·<<<<<<<<<<<<<<<<<<<<<<<<<

Some Holiday Customs

>>>>>>>>>>>>>>>>>>>>>>>>> · ·<<<<<<<<<<<<<<<<<<<<<<<<<

Assumption and Fireworks

In American cities where there is a large Latin population
there is always a great dazzling display of fireworks each
year in connection with the Feast of the Assumption.
This brings up the question—what do fireworks have to
do with religious festivals? Most Americans, accustomed
to thinking of Independence day as the proper time for
pyrotechnics, are puzzled by the Assumption displays,
just as they are by the shooting of fire-crackers at Christmas time in the southern part of the United States.

The answer, once discovered, is simple and logical
enough. Light has always been a feature of the festive
celebrations of all religions, not only Christianity. From
earliest pagan times people have carried torches and
built bonfires on their big religious occasions. What could
have been more natural than the addition of the spectac-
ularly colored and self-moving light of fireworks to the

festivities when these lights became available. As to the shooting of fire-crackers, the explanation is similar. Noise-makers of all kinds have always been part of humanity's happiest festivals. And when Marco Polo in the thirteenth century came back from China bringing gunpowder, it was only natural that it should be used—in guns, cannons and firecrackers—to add to the joyful uproar.

Christmas Eve and Christmas Day

The eve of any festival is supposed to be a solemn vigil, but two eves have lost nearly all traces of such serious tone. One, of course, is Halloween, the eve of All Saints Day, and the other is Christmas Eve. The joy of Christmas just can't wait. It spills over into the days and even weeks preceding the great day and reaches such a happy peak that Christmas itself is almost an anticlimax. No single twenty-four-hour period in the year is so rich in custom, lore, and tradition as Christmas Eve.

It is on Christmas Eve, for example, that cattle and horses were once considered to have the gift of speech, and sheep went in processions to commemorate the angels' visit to them and to the shepherds on that famous night of long ago. It was this night that the beasts in their stalls and the wild animals of the forest were thought to kneel and adore the Lord of all Creation; while all through the day the bees were said to have hummed the 100th Psalm, "O be joyful in the Lord all ye lands."

No evil spirit is ever out on Christmas Eve. For weeks cocks have headed them off by "crowing for Christmas"—crowing, that is, with special volume and vigor to frighten the spirits away. Nevertheless when your clock strikes midnight on Christmas Eve, it would be a good idea to open all your doors to let out any spirits that have been hardy enough to withstand the cocks' raucous threats. But you needn't worry at all about ghosts. They definitely never appear on Christmas Eve.

Armenians must have spinach for supper on this evening. They do this in honor of the Blessed Virgin, who is said to have eaten spinach on the night before the Christ child was born. In Bohemia (when there was a Bohemia) it was the custom to cut apples in half on Christmas Eve. If anyone in the family found a perfect star in the center of his apple, it meant that person would have health and happiness all during the coming year.

In Romania, husbands and wives go through a ritual out in the orchard on December twenty-fourth. The husband speaks sternly to each one of his trees, threatening to chop it down because he is not satisfied with its production record. And the gentle wife defends the tree, saying, "Spare this tree" and promising it will bear better next season.

French people used to insist that as the midnight mass was ended another mass must begin at once, for the belief was that any child born between the midnight mass and the next service would lose his soul to the devil.

If you will leave a loaf of bread on the table on Christmas Eve, after your evening meal is over, you can be sure of having bread on the table all through the coming year.

Christmas in the New World has been enriched by the customs brought here by people from many lands. Santa Claus, for example, is a Dutch contribution, brought first by the Dutch settlers in New York. The hanging of stockings over the fireplace can also be traced to the Dutch, whose children placed their wooden shoes in a row on the hearth for Santa to fill with gifts. English and American children were astute enough to substitute their stockings—shoes won't stretch, but stockings will.

The yule log goes back to pre-Christian times in Scandinavian history, back to the feast of Juul, which was held at the winter solstice. Fires were lighted then to symbolize the heat, the light, and the life-giving properties of the returning sun. Our Christmas cookies come from, of all places, ancient Rome, where it was the custom at this time of year to present members of the Roman Senate with these small confections baked in human and animal shapes.

If you refuse a piece of mince pie at dinner on Christmas Day, you will have bad luck all year. If you eat an apple at midnight it will keep the doctor away not just for a day but until next Christmas. If you don't have plum pudding on Christmas Day you will lose a good friend sometime during the coming year. If you take down your Christmas decorations before "Old Christmas" (January 6th) you will have bad luck. And the decorations must be burned, not just thrown away. A person born on Christmas Day will never be hanged.

The Mistletoe

One good pagan custom that has carried over to Christmas is that of the mistletoe, which comes from the Druids. They were much more serious about it than we are. They regarded the little plant with great reverence. Priests, using a golden sickle, cut it out of the oak trees where it grew, and burned it on their altars as a sacrifice to their gods. They also distributed small pieces of it to the people, who took it home and hung it in doorways just as we do now. It was considered a symbol of peace. When enemies met under it, they took off their swords, forgot their quarrels, and embraced each other.

Easter Superstitions

Easter is another one of those times when the Church calendar and the world of nature fit together perfectly. The earth itself has been dead all winter. Now its resurrection is an illustration of the Resurrection that Easter celebrates. It is not strange that everyone feels the need to wear new clothes at Easter, or that there was once, in fact, a superstition that it was unlucky not to wear new Easter apparel. Another pleasant old superstition was that even the sun was so happy on Easter morning that it danced in the sky. Even wise old scholars debated the question quite solemnly. They did finally come to the conclusion that the sun did not dance, but there were many who did not accept this verdict. There may be some remote original connection between the popular Easter sunrise services and the desire to get out early to see if the sun would express its joy so playfully.

In old times it was a very lucky omen to see a lamb first thing on Easter morning. Of course, it was always lucky to see a lamb, since the only two forms the devil cannot assume are those of a lamb and a dove. But the lamb was the special Easter omen, because Easter is the feast of the Lamb of God that was slain and rose again.

Easter Foods

In medieval times eggs were especially plentiful at Easter time, because people were not allowed to eat any during the Lenten fast and they accumulated during the six-week period. The custom of eating ham at Easter is English in origin. At first Englishmen ate bacon to show their repudiation of everything Jewish. William the Conqueror liked ham better, and he encouraged the people to substitute it for bacon. A legend about colored Easter eggs says that Simon of Cyrene, who carried the Lord's cross (see St. Luke, chapter 23, verse 26) was an egg-peddler. When he returned to his basket of eggs after his sad journey to Calvary, he found the eggs all miraculously and beautifully decorated.

Pentecost Customs

The observance of Pentecost goes back to the earliest years of the Christian era, and so do some of the customs connected with the day. Centuries ago people used to shoot fire from the church roof to represent the tongues of flames, or let doves (the traditional symbol of the Holy Spirit) loose in the church during services. In old Russia they decorated the church with young birch trees, the idea being that in order to receive the Holy Spirit one must shed as many tears for his sins as there are dewdrops on the birch bough. In England, Pentecost was the day on which people paid their money for the support of the church. They were assessed according to the number of fireplaces in their houses, or sometimes according to the number of chimneys. Whitsunday (Pentecost in England) collections therefore came to be known as "hearthmoney" or "smoke-money."

It was believed that all wishes made at the exact moment of sunrise on Whitsunday were sure to be fulfilled.

The Paschal Candle

In Roman Catholic churches, and in some other churches, an unusually large candle is installed near the altar on the day before Easter, removed on Ascension Day, and brought back for a last appearance on Pentecost. It is

called the "Paschal" candle, because it is used during the
Paschal season—the fifty days following Easter. The term
"paschal" is derived, with some intermediate steps, from
the Jewish word for Passover. (Some form of this word is
used to denote the Easter season in every language except English and German.) The great candle is a very
ancient accessory of the Easter season. It is referred to in
writings as early as the fourth century, and even then it
was not new.

This huge candle, ornamented with five grains of incense representing the five wounds of Jesus, is blessed on
Easter Eve and then lighted with newly blessed fire. In
medieval times parishes competed with one another to
see which could construct the largest candle, and some
of the candles were gigantic. In Salisbury, England, in
1517, there was a candle thirty-six feet high, and the one
created in Westminster Abbey in 1558 required three
hundred pounds of wax. The old custom was to melt
these tremendous candles down after Pentecost and make
them into smaller tapers for the funerals of the poor.

Many New Year's Days

All Christian countries, and many that are not Christian,
now begin the new year on January 1st, but this is a comparatively recent development. All through history men
have used many other dates as the beginning of the year,
and indeed most of them were more logical than January
1st. Nothing in nature really begins on January 1st. The
ancient Egyptians celebrated the new year on September
22nd, the time of the autumn equinox, and the Jews began their civil year (and still do) at about the same time.
The Romans began their year on December 21st—the
time of the winter solstice—and so did the Greeks for

many centuries, until in 432 B.C. they changed to June 21st, the summer solstice.

There is good reason for thinking of any of these days as a time of beginning. Something is happening in the natural cycle at these times. Changes can be seen in the world around us. And there is the best reason of all for thinking of the spring equinox as the new year—it is then that nature herself actually does become new. The Jews, who have two New Year's Days, saw the logic of this. Their religious year begins at this time. So, for many centuries, did the Christian year. March 25th was New Year's Day for Christians all through medieval ages and almost up to modern times in some places. In the sixteenth century most of the Christian world gave up the old calendar, which was called the Julian calendar, and adopted our present one—the Gregorian. When this was done January 1st was generally agreed upon as New Year's Day. Protestant countries, however, continued to use the old calendar, and it was not until 1752 that England (and the American colonies) gave in.

CHAPTER XV

Words and
Expressions

Adam's Apple

That projection in the front of the human neck which is formed by the thyroid cartilage of the larynx has for many centuries and in many languages been called the "Adam's Apple." Of course, there is a legend behind this name for it. The story is that the forbidden fruit that Adam and Eve ate in the Garden of Eden (Genesis, chapter 3, verses 1 to 6) was an apple, and that while Eve seems to have swallowed her bite without any trouble, Adam ran into some difficulty. A piece of fruit lodged in his throat—and in that of his descendants forever. There is an apparent confirmation of the legend in the fact that this cartilage is so prominent in men but usually almost unnoticeable in women.

The Amen Corner

The Amen Corner is not, as many people believe, a corner in the front of the church where the most pious and
vocal of the breathren sit and shout their agreement with
the preacher's pronouncements. It is a street corner in
the city of London.

In the days before the Reformation there was always a
procession in London on Corpus Christi Day, and all
points along the route still bear names that indicate the
progress of the procession. Beginning at Cheapside the
clergy moved down the street chanting the *Lord's
Prayer,* which in Latin is called the *Paternoster* (Our
Father). That street is still named Paternoster Row. Over
the years they learned to time their singing so exactly
that they always finished the prayer and sang "Amen" just
as they reached a certain corner. Naturally that corner
came to be called "Amen Corner." Then, as they began the
Ave Maria, they turned the corner and proceeded down
another street, which to this day is known as Ave Maria
Lane.

Angels

According to a fifth century cataloguing of the heavenly
powers by a man named Dionysius (who was probably
not the real author), there are nine orders of spiritual
beings, of which the lowest are angels. They are the lowest because they minister directly to man, while the
others have no dealings with man at all, although some
of the archangels have made an exception to this rule.
Archangels are one rank above the angels, which makes
them eighth in the hierarchy. The word angel is directly
derived from the Greek word *angelos,* which means

messenger. They are God's messengers. Religions other than Christianity believe in angels. The Mohammedans say that as man was created out of clay, so the angels were created out of pure, bright gems.

Apple Polishing

To a certain extent all of us are literally "apple-polishers." It just seems natural to rub on an apple and make it shine a bit before biting into it. In olden times it was considered bad luck not to perform this ceremony, and today with the spraying of poisons having been added to the usual dangers of dust and insects, it might be worse luck to omit it.

But we all know the deeper meaning of the term, too. To polish the apple is to flatter someone for one's own selfish purposes, "to lay it on a little thicker" in our effort to influence someone to do our will. Legend says the reason such unscrupulous tactics are called apple-polishing is that the serpent in the Garden of Eden shined up one special apple on the tree to make it attractive to Eve and thus make her more susceptible to his persuasion.

Beads

A bead is simply a prayer. In the Anglo-Saxon language, and later on in early English, the word *bede* meant "prayer" and nothing else. People said their bedes. The way the word got its modern meaning is interesting. As a memory help, so that they wouldn't forget any of the bedes they had to say, people tied knots in a piece of string—one knot for each bede. Naturally before long the knots were called bedes, too. And because man always likes to beautify his religious objects, it was only natural that the knots were soon decorated. Over a short period of evolution the knot became a jewel or a little ball of gold, each one still the symbol of a prayer, and still called, therefore, a bead.

"Bible," a New Name

Bible as the name for the collected Jewish-Christian sacred writings is a comparatively new term. Even up to the time of the King James translation (early seventeenth century) these writings were called only "The Holy Scriptures." Back in the Jewish and early Christian days they were thought of as many books, not one.

The word "bible" comes from the Greek *biblos,* which originally meant the bark of the papyrus reed. It was from this that paper was made in ancient times. After a while the word was applied to the books that were written on the papyrus bark. But it was not until many centuries after our sacred books were gathered together that the word was used for this one volume. Literally, "bible" simply means "book"—any book. It is only our tradition—and recent tradition at that—that has made it mean to us the "book of books."

Blood Money

The common expression "blood money" goes back, as might be expected, to the money received by Judas Iscariot as payment for his betrayal of the Lord. When Judas, in his guilty panic, threw the money at the feet of the priests, they said among themselves, "It is not lawful to put it in the treasury, because it is the price of blood." (Matthew, chapter 27, verse 6) Blood money has as a result come to mean any payment to a person who gives evidence leading to the conviction of another.

Book Burnings in the Bible

There is nothing new about book burnings. There is one Old Testament book that we do not have in its original form because an angry king burned the only copy in existence. It was the book of Jeremiah. You can read in chapter 36, verses 22 and 23 of the present Jeremiah, what happened to the first one. While a foreign prince, the famous Nebuchadnezzar, was beseiging the city of Jerusalem, the prophet Jeremiah wrote a book in which he said that the king had better accept the enemy's terms. Jeremiah was immediately labeled an appeaser and put in jail. The king sent for the book (in those days there was only one copy of any book—a handwritten one) and after reading only a little of it, tossed it into the fire.

Verse 32 of the same chapter tells how Jeremiah called in his secretary, a man named Baruch, and dictated the whole thing over again, with a few additions about the bookburning. It is this second edition that we now have in the Old Testament.

There is a bookburning in the New Testament, too, but it is of a very different kind. Acts, chapter 19, verse 19, tells that St. Paul's preaching in the city of Ephesus was so effective that certain practitioners of black arts and sorcery, having been converted to Christianity, made a bonfire of their magic books as a gesture of renunciation of their former practices.

The Caduceus

The traditional emblem of the medical profession is called the Caduceus. It is a serpent coiled around a rod. It is more than likely that this symbol can be traced to a Biblical origin. In the 21st chapter of Numbers it is told that many of the Israelites at one point in their forty year journey through the wilderness, were bitten by serpents, and that among those who were bitten many died. Moses prayed for deliverance, and, according to verse 8, God told him "Make thee a fiery serpent and put it upon a pole: and it shall come to pass that everyone that is bitten when he looketh upon it, shall live." Thus, the serpent on a pole became a symbol of healing.

Cathedral

To many people the term "cathedral" means any large or important or particularly magnificent church. Such people are mistaken. A "cathedra" is a bishop's throne. A "cathedral" is a church in which the "cathedra" is kept.

The geographical area over which a bishop presides is a "diocese," and according to ancient custom one church in the diocese is the bishop's own church, where he maintains his throne and his general headquarters. A cathedral properly does not have any members. In America, a bishop will often designate some parish church to serve as his cathedral, but a real cathedral, as in Europe, belongs equally to all the people of the diocese.

Having no membership, a true cathedral never has pews. Its seats are single chairs, because pews (although this applies only rarely nowadays) were traditionally the property of individuals or families who were members of the parish.

Driving Like Jehu

Frenzied, headlong drivers, from taximen to juvenile hot-rodders, are often said to "drive like Jehu." The expression goes back to the Old Testament, long before the days of automobiles. Apparently, a wild driver in any age can express himself with whatever means of locomotion happens to be in fashion at the time. Jehu drove a chariot, and it is on record that violent activity was his distinguishing mark. He did not spare the horses.

An officer in the army of Israel, Jehu led a rebellion in which he killed the king and took over the throne. As the rebellious forces were moving to battle, but were still too far away for individual recognition, a watchman standing by the king identified one man with certainty. "The driving," he said, "is like the driving of Jehu, the son of Nimshi; for he driveth furiously." (II Kings, chapter 9, verse 20.) It is from the watchman's statement that we get the expression still in use today.

People have been comparing reckless drivers with Jehu for at least three centuries, perhaps longer. *The Oxford Dictionary* of 1682 records the expression, "to drive like Jehu," as common usage at that time.

Fleshpots

"The fleshpots of Egypt," or simply "the fleshpots," is a phrase that has crept into our language as an expression of high living and luxury, but very few people who use the phrase are aware of its Biblical origin. When Moses was leading the children of Israel on their forty-year journey from Egypt to the Promised Land, he received complaints from them about many things—particularly the food. The people lived on "manna," that strange food that fell from Heaven each night and was gathered off the ground each morning. It was only natural that they should tire of eating the same fare day in and day out.

The 16th chapter of Exodus shows that even though the Israelites must have been glad to be free from the Egyptian tyrant, they still looked back with a certain

nostalgia on the good red meat they had had in Egypt.
"They remembered," the story says, "the fleshpots of
Egypt." They wished they could have just one good meal
again. The fleshpots were the utensils in which meat
was cooked. A person can get mighty hungry for meat,
and it would be hard to blame the Israelites for thinking
about it.

It was Cervantes, in his great book, *Don Quixote*,
who first used the term "the fleshpots of Egypt" as a
synonym for love of luxurious and self-indulgent style of
living.

The Forbidden Fruit

Was it an apple that Eve ate in the Garden of Eden?
The Bible doesn't say so. In the account of man's down-
fall, in the 3rd chapter of Genesis, the fruit is neither
named nor described. It is called simply "the fruit of the
tree." And it is not at all certain that apples as we know
them were to be found in that part of the world in those
times.

In eastern countries the ancient tradition was that the
forbidden fruit was the banana, and that the serpent
spoke to Eve from his hiding place within the banana
bunch. Early classifiers of bananas, on the strength of this
belief, gave the name "fruit of paradise" to one variety of
banana, and "fruit of knowledge" to another.

Gentile

The definition of a "gentile" depends on who is using the
term—it has different meanings for different groups. In
fact, it has different meanings within the language of one
group, the Jews. *Gentile* is a Hebrew word which
means literally "nation." Sometimes when the Jews called

people "gentiles" they meant only that they were people of other nations, people outside the covenant that had been made between God and Abraham. At other times, though, when they said "gentile" they meant "heathen, pagan."

Jesus Himself used the word in this latter sense. When He said it isn't enough just to love those who love you and pointed out that even the "gentiles" do that, He meant that even barbarians are capable of that much spiritual development. Other people besides the Jews use the word "gentile," too. In India the Mohammedans call the Hindus, "Gentiles," and in our own country the Mormons apply the word to all non-Mormons, even Jews.

Jew, Hebrew, Israelite

The three terms Jew, Hebrew, and Israelite are used interchangeably by most Americans, but actually each has its own special shade of meaning. The word *Hebrew* is the oldest of the three. It refers especially to a people, rather than to a religion. We speak of the Hebrew race, the unorganized tribe that dwelt in slavery in the land of Egypt. And we speak of Hebrew literature, Hebrew history, and the Hebrew language.

Nor does the word *Israelite* refer to religion. It seems to have more to do with political organization. When we speak of the Israelites we are speaking of a national group. It is, of course, impossible to keep the idea of religion entirely separate from the government of this group, for Israel was a "theocracy," that is, a nation whose ruler was Jehovah. But in a general way when we say a person is an Israelite we are talking about his nationality and not about his religion.

The word *Jew* in its largest sense means both Hebrew

and Israelite, but in modern times it has come to have a special reference to religion. It is preferred by Jews in America, who like to have it understood that they are Americans whose religion is Jewish, just as their neighbors religion is Christian. A gentile could, by accepting the religion, become a Jew. He could not become a Hebrew or an Israelite.

Jeremiad

A "jeremiad" according to Webster is "a lamenting and denunciatory complaint, a dolorous tirade." It comes from the name of the old Hebrew prophet, Jeremiah, who may well be the all time champion at thundering denunciation. Jeremiah, a furious man, appeared in Jewish history at a time (seventh century B.C.) when the people of Israel were falling under pagan influences that threatened to ruin the nation's relationship with Jehovah. He told his people exactly what would happen to them if they did not mend their ways. As all preachers know, this is not the way to make oneself popular. Jeremiah found some satisfaction, and perhaps a ray of hope, in writing his "jeremiads." He was at his best when he was denouncing those nations and cultures that would lure Israel away from the true God.

Layman

In modern speech, the term "layman" usually means anyone, man or woman, who does not have the same professional training as the speaker and therefore does not have the same depth of understanding of the particular subject under discussion. When the doctor talks about the layman, he means one who is not a doctor. Educators use the word to mean those outside the teaching profession. It has become a polite way of saying "this man's opinion does not really have the necessary background of information."

The word has been borrowed directly from the vocabulary of the church. It came originally from the Greek *laikos* which meant, "of, or from, the people," and was used to distinguish the general population from the ordained clergy. In the days when only the clergy were educated and the laymen completely illiterate, it was quite natural that the term should carry an implication of ignorance. This, however, was an additional meaning brought about by conditions that no longer exist. Certainly in America many laymen have more learning than many of the clergy. So only the original meaning remains, at least within the language of the church. A layman is anyone who is not an ordained clergyman.

"Lettuce"

The slang use of the word "lettuce" to mean "money" may go way back to a story that is told about Pope Sixtus V, who once sent a salad to an impoverished friend of his. The tale tells that a certain lawyer, who had been a friend of Sixtus' before he became Pope, fell on evil days and in his desperation decided that the only thing for him to do was to go to the Pope and ask for financial help. But on the way to Rome he fell ill and was not able to complete the trip. Sixtus, however, heard of his old friend's plight and said that he would send him a salad that would cure him. Whereupon he dispatched a messenger with a basket of lettuce. When the lawyer opened the lettuce heads he found them filled with paper money. In Italy they still have a saying about a man who is in need of money. They say "He wants one of Sixtus V's salads."

The Lost Books

In the Bible there are references to, and sometimes even quotations from, books about which nothing is known. For example, in Numbers, chapter 21, verse 14, there is a quotation from the "Book of Wars of the Lord," but nobody knows anything more than that about even the existence of such a book. Elsewhere in the Bible one finds mention of the Book of Jasher, the Book of Nathan, the Prophecy of Abijah, the Visions of Iddo, and the Book of Gad. These books (and perhaps there are many others) that were once part of Jewish religious literature but are no longer available for study, are called the "Lost Books." There are some theories and guesses about what some of them contained. The Book of Jasher is thought to have been a collection of poems about Jewish military heroes. The Book of the Wars of the Lord probably was made up of ballads about the victories of the Hebrew armies in the early years after the escape from Egypt.

Nimrod

In Genesis, chapter 10, verse 9, there is a reference to "Nimrod, the mighty hunter before the Lord." Scholars are not quite sure what this means. The Hebrew word here can be translated "hero" as well as "hunter" and it possibly indicates that Nimrod was a fine soldier. But Nimrod was an Assyrian king, and Assyrian kings had a reputation for being great sportsmen, devoted to the chase. There is therefore a very good chance that this ancient monarch got his name into the Bible only because he excelled at killing game.

At any rate, his name has come into our language as a term applied to hunters, especially skilled ones. Nimrod occupies the same position in Mohammedan legendry. The Moslems claim to have his tomb, and show it to tourists in the city of Damascus. There is a tradition that no dew ever falls on Nimrod's tomb. Perhaps some hunter can explain what the advantage of this would be.

Pharisees

The Pharisees have come to be a much-misunderstood and much-maligned group, probably because at the time Jesus lived on earth they were in a position to be of considerable trouble to Him. Christians, because of many uncomplimentary New Testament references, think of them as stiff-necked reactionaries, but they were in fact the liberal party of their time.

The real reactionaries were the Sadducees, but not much is heard of them because they were in the minority at the time. They represented the upper classes and they looked down their noses at the middle- and lower-class Pharisees, who were willing to modernize Jewish customs to fit the times.

It is too bad that the word "Pharisee" in most Christians' minds means ultraconservatism. In fact, some of the Lord's best friends were Pharisees: Nicodemus, who came to Him by night (St. John, chapter 3, verse 1-21); Joseph of Arimathea, who provided His tomb, and may indeed have been His uncle; and even St. Paul, who was Christianity's greatest champion of all time.

Puritan and Pilgrim

What was the difference between Puritans and Pilgrims, or were they the same? The answer, which needs a little explaining, is that all Pilgrims were Puritans but not all Puritans were Pilgrims.

The Puritans were extreme reformers in England in the time of Queen Elizabeth I and later. Although the Church of England had broken its ties with Rome and had introduced many changes, there were still a large number of Englishmen who were far from satisfied. They wanted a "radical purification" of the church. They rejected all human tradition and said that the Bible, which "was the *pure* Word of God," was the sole authority in Christianity. By their constant use of the word "pure" in one form or another, they earned the name Puritans.

The Mayflower brought to America one hundred and two of these Puritans, who because of their journey to the new land were called Pilgrims. The term was later extended to include all the early Puritan settlers in Massachusetts. The point, then, is that Puritans who came to New England were Pilgrims; those who stayed in the old country were not.

The Quick and the Dead

The expression "the quick and the dead" is familiar to all Protestants who say the Apostles Creed. The word "quick" did not originally mean rapid or nimble as it does today. It came directly from the "Anglo-Saxon *cwic,* and it meant "living" or "alive." It was in general English usage in 1549 when the Latin prayers and other religious material were translated into English and even in the early 1600's when the King James Version of the Bible was translated. This is why "the quick and the dead" appears in the creed as it is said by churches within the English language tradition. The Roman Catholic Church, however, translates directly from the Latin

without the intermediate Anglo-Saxon step. They therefore say "the living and the dead."

"Quick," meaning "alive," appears in Shakespeare as
well as in the King James Bible. When Hamlet, desperate
over the death of Ophelia, says to his friend Laertes, "Be
buried quick with her and so will I," he means he feels
like committing suicide by being buried alive with her.
This old use of the word has not quite dropped out of
our everyday speech even now. For example we still call
mercury "quick-silver," just as the English did four hundred years ago, because it moves about as if it were alive.

Red Letter Days

Nowadays when we speak of red-letter days we mean
any gala or memorable occasion. "This" a man will say
"will be a red letter day in my life"—and he may be
speaking of almost anything from falling in love to holding a lucky sweepstakes ticket. Originally, however, like
so many of our expressions, the term was specifically a
part of the church vocabulary. It simply goes back to the
time when the biggest and most important festivals and
saints days appeared in red print in calendars and prayer
books, while minor days appeared in black.

Reverend

Perhaps the most widespread grammatical error in the
English language is in the use of the term "Reverend" in
connection with a clergyman's name. The word is an adjective, but millions use it as a noun, making a title of it,
like "Captain" or "Doctor" or "Professor." People who say
"Good Morning, Reverend" to a minister are guilty of
this mistake. The best parallel by which to show that it

is wrong is the term "Honorable" as applied to office holders. For example, if a judge were "the Honorable John Jones" no one would address him as "Honorable Jones," or say to him "Good morning, Honorable." But Reverend has not fared so well and it is probably too late now to correct an error that has become so firmly established in the language.

Silver Spoon

Strangely enough, the expression "born with a silver spoon in his mouth" was, in its origin connected with the sacrament of baptism. In the Middle Ages it became the custom for godparents at baptism to give spoons to their godchildren. Both rich and poor gave them—the rich folk gave silver spoons, the poor gave spoons of baser metals. Everyone, of course, gave of as costly material as he could afford, and in many cases the baptismal spoon was an important addition to the child's worldly goods. When the expression came into use it was a way of indicating that to certain children the gift was of no importance. Children of wealthy parents already had all the silver they needed. They were born with silver spoons—in their mouths, naturally, because that is where spoons go. Incidentally, the usual baptismal spoon was the "apostle spoon" of which antique collectors are now so fond— a spoon with the figure of one of the Twelve Apostles carved on the handle. Some lavish godparents gave the child the complete set of twelve.

XXX (Kiss)

Lovers who put XXX's on their letters are not usually aware that the custom goes back to a time when a cross-mark had all the force of a sworn oath. The cross was of course a religious symbol. Not only did it refer to the Cross of Calvary; it was also the first letter of the Greek word *Christos* or Christ.

In the days when few people could write, they made their mark—a cross—as they do today, and it was accepted as a signature. But in those times, they always kissed the cross after they made it, as a sign of their complete sincerity. It was this practice of kissing the X that led to its becoming a symbol of a kiss. During World War II both the British and American governments forbade people in the armed forces to put XXX's on their letters. It was feared that spies might use such marks for code messages.

CHAPTER XVI

A Few Interesting Facts

The Ananias Club

It is said that President Theodore Roosevelt once called an untruthful man a member of the Ananias Club. For many years now in the United States a particularly gifted group of yarn-spinners has held an annual meeting in some selected city and competed in the brazen manufacture of tall tales. This group also calls itself the Ananias Club. A prize is given for the most imaginative falsehood, and the tale itself is usually printed in the newspapers, along with several of the runners-up.

It all comes from the sad account in Acts, chapter 5, of a man named Ananias and his wife Sapphira. These two belonged to the early Christian church in Jerusalem, whose members sold all their possessions and lived together on the pooled proceeds. The man and his wife sold their land, but they held back part of the price they had received. St. Peter, with quick intuition, saw through the deception and pointed out to them that they were really lying not to men but to God. When they realized the enormity of their fraud they both fell dead. The name Ananias has come into our language as a synonym for "liar."

Christianity and the Fish

During the past few years men of several Protestant denominations have begun to wear in their coat lapels a small metal representation of a fish. This is one of the earliest of all Christian symbols. There was a time when Christians dared not publicly admit their faith, but could recognize one another's homes by this mark placed on their doors. It was their secret symbol. The way this came about was that in very early times somebody saw that the Greek word *ichthus*, which means "fish," can easily be broken down into an acrostic, which spells out the sentence "Jesus Christ, Son of God, and Savior." If you write the Greek word in a perpendicular line you can make each letter stand for one of the words of this sentence. (It is from this word *ichthus* that we get our word ichthyology, the study of fish.) Those who wear the fish nowadays need have no worries about being detected and brought to trial, but they are wearing a symbol which if understood by the wrong people 1900 years ago would have meant certain death.

Do All Churches Have the Same Bible?

All churches start out with the same Bible, basically, but some end up with more than others. The Jews, of course, have only the Old Testament, which consists of the same thirty-nine books that are found in the Protestants' Old

Testament. But there are fourteen other pre-Christian books, which are known as the "Apochrypha" and are treated variously by the different groups. Apochrypha means "hidden." The Roman Catholics, for example, include these fourteen books as part of their Old Testament, and give them the same status as the other thirty-nine. They do not refer to them as the Apochrypha.

The Episcopalians include the fourteen books as a third section of their Bible, placing them in a separate position between the Old and New Testaments. The Protestant denominations in general do not include them at all. All Christians are in agreement about the twenty-seven books of the New Testament. The Mormons, however, have a twenty-eighth one: the Book of Mormon, which in their tradition was revealed to their founder Joseph Smith by the angel Moroni.

A Bible Verse That Saved Men from Hanging

Back in the Middle Ages no clergyman had to stand trial before a secular court, except for high treason. If he were accused of any other crime he was tried before a court of the Church. This special privilege was known as "benefit of clergy." In those days, when monks and priests were always wandering over the countryside and there were almost no communication lines between one part of the world and another, it was inevitable that many imposters would try to avoid secular court trial by claiming to be clergymen, because the justice of the church courts was much gentler. In the regular courts many crimes that today would be considered trivial were punishable by death.

When a man claimed benefit of clergy the authorities had no way of looking him up in a directory or telephoning his bishop's office as they could today. They had to have some way of determining right then and there whether or not he was telling the truth. There was one infallible test that they could apply very easily. Only the clergy could read. If the prisoner could read, then there just wasn't any doubt about it—he definitely was entitled to benefit of clergy, which usually meant that he went free.

For some reason, the first verse of the 51st Psalm came to be the passage most often used in the test. A Psalter—in Latin, of course—would be brought to the accused, and if he were able to read "Have mercy upon me O God, according to thy loving kindness, etc.," he could save himself from the severity of the magistrate, which usually meant that he was saving his neck from the gallows. For this reason Psalm 51, verse 1, came to be known in the slang of the times as the "neck verse." Some historians say that a million necks were saved in this way during the six hundred years in which benefit of clergy was part of the law. It was legal to plead benefit of clergy here in America during colonial times, but the first United States Congress, in 1790, passed an act forbidding such pleas in the federal courts.

Why We "Touch Wood"

When we make some statement about our good health or good fortune why do we feel that we have to say "touch wood" or "knock wood" and put a hand on some nearby piece of wood? It is because we feel we are challenging fate, which doesn't approve of boasting, and so we appeal to holy forces to protect us against the anger of fate.

Some say the appeal is to the protection of the Cross of

Christ which is, of course, the holiest of all wood. But actually, the superstition goes back much farther than that. It goes back, in fact, to the days of tree worship. The oak tree, observed by primitive people to be the tree most often struck by lightning, was thought to be the favorite tree of the sky-god, who, incidentally, hated braggarts. It, therefore, behooved even the least boastful to be in touch with the sky-god's tree, for everything in contact with it was beneficially affected. In its original form, the expression was probably "touch oak."

No Meat on Friday

Why is Friday meatless? This is really a double question; why is Friday a fast day, and why does the fasting in this case mean abstinence from meat? The reason for fasting on Friday is that every Friday is a memorial of Good Friday, just as every Sunday is a little Easter. Since the earliest times, many Christians have fasted on Fridays in memory of the day of Holy Week on which Jesus suffered and died. The reason for going without meat is that the eating of meat was thought in old times to stimulate the passions. Therefore anyone who was trying to develop his spiritual nature and to conquer his fleshly lusts would be greatly helped by going without meat. In the Roman Catholic Church, if Christmas falls on Friday, that Friday is not a fast day. The Episcopal church excepts all Fridays between Christmas and Epiphany.

Year of Our Lord

It is surprising to note that the Christian era went along for a thousand years before people began to number the years from the time of the Lord's birth, and to talk about

B.C. and A.D. In the Roman empire, which at one time was most of the known world, years were counted from the time when the city of Rome was founded. A date would be given, for example, as Jan. 1, 850 A.U.C. The A.U.C. stood for *Ano Urbis Conditae*, Latin words meaning "the year of the founded city."

More than five hundred years after the birth of Jesus a learned monk in Rome, named Dionysius Exigues, thought it would be interesting to try to fix the date of the holy birth. At that particular time the Church would be counting the Nativity as having happened on Dec. 25th, 753 A.U.C. Since the year in which Dionysius was making his calculation was 1285 A.U.C., he simply subtracted 753 from 1285 and declared that the current year was the Year of Our Lord 532. The new numbering took hold very slowly. It was about the year 1000 A.D. before Dionysius' system was officially adopted. Many scholars now believe that the old monk was four or five years off in his reckoning.

Is Sunday the Sabbath?

Although many Christians call Sunday the Sabbath, the two terms do not mean the same thing. *Sabbath* is a Hebrew word, meaning "to rest." The Sabbath falls on Saturday, the seventh day of the week, because, according to the Bible story of Creation, God made the world and its inhabitants in six days and rested on the seventh day. This was one reason why man was ordered to rest on the seventh day. There was another reason; since the Sabbath is consecrated to God, man must not use it for any enterprise of his own.

Among early Christians, most of whom were Jews, a movement soon began to make Sunday, the first day of the week, the weekly holy day, because this was the day on which the Resurrection had occurred. Every Sunday became a commemoration of Easter. Sunday is therefore a festival day, and indeed an abandonment of the Sabbath. The change was unofficial and gradual during the first three centuries. By the fourth century it had evolved into universal custom throughout the Christian Church.

CHAPTER XVII

Wedding Customs

A Few Pointers for Brides

June is the month of marriages mainly because May has always been considered an unlucky month in which to marry. June gets not only its own normal quota but also all the weddings postponed from May by the superstitious. Why May is unlucky is not especially clear at this late date, but for centuries there has been the couplet:

"Marry in May
And rue the day."

May, in Roman folklore, was for some reason the month of old men, while June, dedicated to Juno, was the month of the young, for Juno was the goddess of young people.

Most of our present marriage customs go all the way back to Rome, so it is not surprising that their origins are forgotten. The custom of carrying the bride over the

threshold of the couple's new home may well be connected with the Roman legend about how Rome's soldiers stole the Sabine women. The story is that Romulus,
whose men needed wives, lured the Sabine men away
and told his soldiers to take the women while the husbands were absent. Carrying the bride into the house
may be reminiscent of the forcible carrying off of these
women.

The wedding ring, too, may be associated with a time
when wooing was less gentle than it is today. It is possible that the ring symbolizes the fetters with which the
bride was bound when she was captured by her husband.
If this is true, the presently popular double ring ceremony indicates that the girls have come a long way toward equality. The reason usually given for putting the
ring on the third finger of the left hand is that there is a
vein (or a nerve) from that finger directly to the heart.
Actually there is no such nerve or vein.

The shoes that are often thrown at a newlywed couple
have a most surprising meaning. People ordinarily assume
that shoes are thrown "for luck," but this is not the reason at all. The throwing of a shoe in ancient times was
somehow a renunciation gesture. When Yahweh said in
the Bible, "Over Edom I cast out my shoe," the meaning
was that He was through with Edom. At weddings the
shoe should be thrown at the bride by her parents as a
renunciation, not of their daughter herself, but of their
authority over her.

There is an endless list of superstitions having to do
with what must or must not be worn by the bride. She
will run into the worst possible trouble, perhaps death,
if she wears green. This is because green belongs to the

fairies, and they will actively resent the wearing of their color. Irish girls are an exception—the fairies don't mind if they wear green, and it is good luck for an Irish bride. To all others, though the old rule applies:

> "Married in white
> You've chosen right."

The bride must never wear pearls—they symbolize tears. But she had better wear a veil, for the veil will ward off the evil eye, and at nearly every wedding there are a few people around who would put the evil eye on her if they could. She must not wear her ring before the ceremony. She must not make or help to make the wedding cake. She and the groom must not meet on the wedding day until they meet at the ceremony. The couple must never pose for their wedding picture before the wedding—this cannot be a very old tabu, since photography itself is only a century old.

What the bride *should* wear is outlined in the old jingle:

> "Something old, something new,
> Something borrowed, something blue.
> And some money in her shoe."

Nobody knows where the rhyme came from originally. The last line seems to refer to the old Welsh custom of putting a silver sixpence in the shoe to insure a prosperous married life. The other two lines, however, are impossible to interpret. One can guess at the reason for: "something blue," for blue is the color of constancy, but the reasons behind the "old," "new," and "borrowed" things are lost.

One old saying seems to exaggerate the importance of the weather: "Blest be the bride the sun shines on; curst be the bride the rain falls on." It can't really make that much difference.

Most weddings nowadays are held on Saturdays but according to superstition Wednesday is by far the most favorable of all days.

Index